Emory Hol

For my good friend
Gay Allen

Oct. 31, 1965

Young Emerson Speaks

Young Emerson Speaks

Unpublished Discourses on Many Subjects
By RALPH WALDO EMERSON

Edited by
Arthur Cushman McGiffert, Jr.

HOUGHTON MIFFLIN COMPANY · BOSTON
The Riverside Press Cambridge
1938

COPYRIGHT, 1938, BY THE RALPH WALDO EMERSON MEMORIAL ASSOCIATION

ALL RIGHTS RESERVED INCLUDING THE RIGHT TO REPRODUCE
THIS BOOK OR PARTS THEREOF IN ANY FORM

The Riverside Press
CAMBRIDGE · MASSACHUSETTS
PRINTED IN THE U.S.A.

Preface

BIOGRAPHICAL, religious, and literary interests control the selection of these twenty-five sermons from the total number of approximately one hundred and seventy unpublished manuscripts. Emerson's first sermon, the one he preached the most times, the three at the time of his ordination and its anniversary, one delivered immediately after the death of his wife, and another on his return from his European trip, — throw a vivid light upon the life and thought of the young preacher, preparing and delivering his weekly sermons during the most critical and formative years of his life. His views on themes which elsewhere in his writings receive scant attention are exhibited in a wide range of 'curiosities' such as the discourses on Astronomy, Conversation, the Choice of a Vocation, Miracles, and Religious Liberalism and Society. His first full-length treatments of the central principles of his thinking also appear. Editorial attention is given to the character of his literary craftsmanship and his methods of preaching.

The old religion and the new find juxtaposed expression in the sermons. The young preacher belonged to both the first and the second stages in the development of religious liberalism, associated with the names of William Ellery Channing and Theodore Parker; and in his own thinking he bridges the gap between them. His place in the on-going movement of American religious thought and culture assumes new significance in the light of the sermons.

The sermons have been printed in chronological order, that

PREFACE

the growth of Emerson's powers and interests as a preacher and a thinker may be observed. Most of the Essays were originally delivered as lectures but before publication they were worked over by Mr. Emerson. The sermons, however, retain the informality and freshness of their original delivery and illuminate more than do the Essays Emerson's manner of speaking. Two of the sermons, which have already been printed ('The Lord's Supper,' *Miscellanies*, p. 3 ff., and 'Right Hand of Fellowship,' *Uncollected Writings*, p. 11 ff.) are not included.

In addition to the sermons themselves, other materials have been drawn upon, particularly the Journals, in order to complete the picture of the young preacher. The publication of the letters will add a few further graphic details. In the meantime I am indebted to Professor R. L. Rusk of Columbia University, who is editing *The Letters of Ralph Waldo Emerson*, for allowing me to refer to the contents of two or three of these unpublished letters. (See pp. 218, 220.) But my primary indebtedness is to The Ralph Waldo Emerson Memorial Association and to Mr. Edward W. Forbes in particular, not only for permission to edit the sermons and to make use of subsidiary unpublished material like the Preaching Record and early lectures and portions of unpublished Journals, but for many delightful courtesies that have facilitated the preparation of this volume, in which members of his staff have had a much appreciated share. The University of Chicago, through the kind offices of Professor William Warren Sweet has enabled me to make photostatic use of a number of the manuscripts. The Widener Library has been generous in its assistance. Miss Frances A. Plimpton and the staff of the Massachusetts Historical Society have given me access to the records of the Second Church of Boston; Dr. E. Stanton Hodgin has sent me a copy of records of the Church in New Bedford. A number of people also have done gallant work at the typewriter, and their help in transcribing manuscripts and preparing copy is not forgotten.

For counsel in matters relating to the introduction and notes

PREFACE

and for other assistance, I am under primary obligation to the learning and interest of Samuel A. Eliot, Francis Greenwood Peabody, and Gertrude Huntington McGiffert. Members of my Seminars in American Religious Thought at the Chicago Theological Seminary will recognize the share they have had in this book. Finally, without the constant help and encouragement of the members of my immediate family the work could not have been brought to a conclusion.

Unless otherwise indicated the references to Emerson's writings are taken from the Centenary Edition (12 vols.) or the *Journals* (10 vols.) published by Houghton Mifflin Company.

ARTHUR CUSHMAN MCGIFFERT, JR.

December, 1937

Contents

Introduction	xi
Pray Without Ceasing	1
On Showing Piety at Home	13
The Christian Minister: Part I	22
The Christian Minister: Part II	31
Summer	39
Trifles	46
A Feast of Remembrance	54
Conversation	60
The Ministry: A Year's Retrospect	67
The Individual and the State	75
Religious Liberalism and Rigidity	82
The Authority of Jesus	90
Self-Culture	99
Trust Yourself	105
How Old Art Thou?	112
Miracles	120
Self and Others	127
✶ Consolation for the Mourner	138
Hymn Books	145
The Choice of Theisms	151
Find Your Calling	163
Astronomy	170
The Genuine Man	180
Religion and Society	191
The Miracle of Our Being	203
Notes	213
The Preaching Record	261
A List of the Sermons	263
Index	273

Introduction

THE mature Emerson ranks as one of the most familiar and influential figures in American culture. Emerson, the young preacher, on the other hand, is almost unknown. But it was in the pulpit that he first tried his wings. There he made his initial efforts to set free his own imprisoned thoughts, to find the proper vehicles for their expression, to practice the art of communication, and to deal at full length with the themes that were to 'character his brain' throughout his life.

I

Emerson began his career as a preacher. For years his ambition had been directed toward the ministry. When he reached the age of twenty he deliberately dedicated his time, his talents, and his hopes to the Church. He 'burns to speak.' The Journals contain a wealth of 'hints for a peculiar pursuit at the distance of the years.' Even in the intervals of illness which punctuated his youth he was 'moulding sermons for an hour which may never arrive.'

After being graduated from Harvard College in the class of 1821 Emerson turned to school-teaching to earn money to help his family and to pay for further education for himself. But he found time enough for private professional study, in part with the help of his pastor, William Ellery Channing, so that he was admitted in 1825 to the middle (second year) class of the recently established Harvard Divinity School. At this time

INTRODUCTION

many men still prepared for the ministry, as well as for medicine and law, by private study and apprenticeship with individual ministers.

Religious liberalism and religious orthodoxy both had a share in forming Emerson's mind. His father was one of the ministers who, before the break occurred within Congregationalism, had already shown a lack of sympathy for Calvinism. After his death in 1811 the family attended the church of William Ellery Channing, whose 'Baltimore Sermon' in 1819 was the wedge that split the denomination apart. Channing probably had a good deal to do with Emerson's decision to enter the ministry. Channing's tolerant, non-partisan temper was congenial to his young admirer. His preaching was 'sublime.' His thought had an emphatic influence on Emerson's mind. The latter was, in fact, a 'Channing Unitarian,' as those religious liberals have been called who broke away from Calvinism because of its degrading views of human nature, but who remained impervious to the subsequent currents of fresh religious thought that came in with the Romantic movement and its representatives — men like Coleridge and Wordsworth in England, Goethe and Schleiermacher in Germany. The formative and transitional years of Emerson's ministry corresponded with the transitional and reformative period of the age in which he lived. Emerson, the young preacher, belongs to the first stage of the liberal reform of traditional Christian orthodoxy. Emerson, the lecturer and essayist, belongs to the second stage of that movement. His three years as a minister enabled him to come to grips with the new religious mind of his century. Ultimately he determined to devote himself to its exploration and expression, even though to do so meant the abandonment of the institutional traditions of his ancestors. His decision to break with the religious liberalism he inherited found reinforcement in his temperamental disability to work effectively in an organization in constant and responsible connection with a group of people.

To Emerson's personal and intellectual good fortune he had

INTRODUCTION

in his Aunt Mary Moody Emerson a person of rare capacities for drawing out the best in him and for interpreting to him the tradition of Calvinism with a sympathy all the more effective because of its tinge of irony and skepticism. She it was who wrote the prayers which first his brother, and, when William went to college, he himself read aloud morning and evening at the family devotions, and years afterwards they still sounded in his ear with their prophetic and apocalyptic ejaculations. When he came to write sermons for his own church, he could find no examples or treasuries of piety so high-toned, so profound, or promising such rich influence, as his remembrances of his aunt's conversations and letters. (Paraphrased from *Journals*, Vol. IV, p. 231 f.) From her, too, he learned that religion is not inextricably associated with the particular forms it assumes in a given cultural era; and from her he seems to have received the Promethean ambition to purify not only the old faith but the liberal faith as well of 'what narrowness and error adhered to it and import all its fire into the new age.' (*Journals*, Vol. V, p. 548.) From the perspective of added years he came to appreciate how much happier was his star, which rained on him influences of ancestral religion, than that of the young men whose theological instruction was exclusively owed to Cambridge and to public institution. (*Ibid.*, Vol. IV, p. 230.)

Emerson's stay in the Divinity School was cut short after a month's residence, by ill health, and he spent the winter on a trip south. In June, 1827, after his return from Florida he again took up residence in the newly erected Divinity Hall, though not as a matriculated student, and remained there for a little over a year, picking up what he could from the lectures, writing sermons, 'living cautiously' and preaching in vacant pulpits, but still too frail to be able to accept any of the three or more calls he received from churches to become their minister.

In 1828 Henry Ware, jr., minister of the Second Church of Boston, resigned his pulpit on account of ill health. Paul Revere had been one of the committee that called him in 1816.

INTRODUCTION

Ware's resignation was not accepted. Instead the church gave him an extended leave of absence and voted to call a Colleague-pastor to carry on his work and on his return to relieve him of some of the burden of his office. Their choice fell upon Emerson, who had already supplied the pulpit twenty-one times, at a fee of fifteen dollars a Sunday for two services. The church called Emerson, on January 11, 1829, by a vote of seventy-four out of eighty-three, at a salary of twelve hundred dollars, which was to be increased to eighteen hundred when the connection of the Senior Pastor should cease. The budget of the church was approximately thirty-five hundred dollars. The church contained one hundred and forty pews, of which eleven were free. For the remainder their proprietors paid a quarterly tax ranging from two dollars and eighty-six cents to seven dollars and fifteen cents.

The Second Church of Boston (the 'Old North') was founded in 1649. It numbered among its ministers such giants as Increase Mather and Cotton Mather. Emerson was the ninth minister. Henry Ware, jr. had been installed as minister in 1817, the church being at the time in point of numbers the smallest of the Unitarian congregations in Boston, and composed of people 'in the middling class,' both financially and culturally.

In the invitation to become the pastor of 'an ancient and respectable church,' Emerson 'recognized with acute sensibility the hand of his heavenly Father.' (*Journals*, Vol. II, p. 261.) His only hesitancy in accepting the call was due to the precarious state of health of his fiancée, Ellen Tucker. Eventually he accepted the call. In a sermon preached immediately after his ordination he spoke of it as 'the occasion to which all the years of my education have looked forward.'

In a letter written the end of March, Mr. Ware writes thus of the young minister: 'My colleague has begun his work in the best possible spirit and with just the promise I like. The few who talked of leaving the Society are won to remain and it is as flourishing as ever.'

xiv

INTRODUCTION

Shortly after his return from Europe where he had spent his leave of absence Mr. Ware resigned from the church in order to become Professor of Pulpit Eloquence and Pastoral Care at the Divinity School of Harvard College. In a brief farewell address on September 5, 1830, he said to the congregation: 'I leave you to the guidance of able hands and to the instruction of faithful lips.' Emerson now became officially what in fact he had been from the beginning, the only minister of the church. He served for over three years, from March 15, 1829, to October 21, 1832.

Looking back upon these years of experience in the pastorate Emerson referred to 'those earlier days — many anxious, many pleasant, all thoughtful days.' During them he passed through four major crises. First he entered upon his long chosen vocation at the age of twenty-five, and was ordained to the Christian ministry. Second, he married. Third, his young wife, Ellen Tucker, after a year and a half of married life died. And finally, having concluded that, from his own point of view at least, he was a vocational failure, he abandoned the profession of the ministry.

II

Save for the intermittent light thrown by the Journals the career of the young minister during these critical years has hitherto remained largely in the shadow. But the sermons, supplemented by the records of the church, and other material, give a graphic picture of his inner and outer life during this period.

Incongruous at first glimpse, to one familiar only with the famous Sage of Concord, is the activity of the young preacher of the Second Church. He is to be observed addressing his congregation as 'My Christian friends.' He visits the sick. He delivers discourses in order to raise money for local philanthropies carried on by a group of liberal churches in the city. He makes Baccalaureate addresses at girls' schools and talks at

INTRODUCTION

the Orphan Asylum and the House of Correction. He delivers the Great and Thursday Lecture. He attends ordination councils and to the accompaniment of decorous remarks, extends the right hand of fellowship to the new minister. He administers the rite of baptism thirty-two times in one year, eighteen being private. His weddings average eleven a year. He receives into membership in the church in successive years, eleven, two, nine — a lower average than that of his predecessor. He conducts funerals and makes parish calls. He organizes special monthly week-day meetings to attract religious persons who are not church members. He reads a lecture, that is, preaches at the monthly precommunion services on Friday evenings. He participates in all probability in discussion as to ways to prevent the noise of carriages passing and repassing on the cobblestone pavement during services on Sunday. He delivers courses of expository lectures on the Bible, to raise money for the building of a new vestry. The old vestry was situated inconveniently on the third story of the meeting house and was altogether too small for the educational activities of the parish. He raises questions with the Standing Committee of the church as to the correct disposition of the income of trust funds for the poor. He places people on the poor-fund list and has at his disposal a yearly sum of money to distribute to the poor at his discretion. When two gold rings are put into the communion collection box one Sunday morning he buys them from the treasurer for $1.00. He acts as chaplain of the state senate.

All these activities are of course subsidiary to his main and most welcome responsibility, the preparation and delivery of a new sermon each Sunday. Preaching was no novelty to him. During the two and one-half years that lay between the writing of his first sermon in October, 1826, and his ordination at the Second Church in March, 1829 he had preached nearly two hundred times. Yet, even so, born as he was with a pen in his hand, he looked forward with the dismay of any other young minister to the thought of preparing a fresh sermon each

INTRODUCTION

week, as one of his unpublished letters of the time reveals. As in the case of other ministers, however, the habit of thinking in terms of next Sunday's sermon became so fixed that he continued to make note of sermon topics long after he had any need for them. The young preacher wrote his sermons out in full and read them, as he later did his lectures, for he never trusted himself to extempore speech, nor did he ever master the art.

How long he took to read one of his sermons cannot be ascertained. Certainly the two hour sermons of the previous century were no longer fashionable. Emerson appears to have taken to heart the anecdote about a Mr. Willis who was famed for long sermons. 'Dr. Allyne put his head into his window one morning and asked him what he was doing. "Writing a sermon," said Mr. W. "What are you writing about?" asked the doctor. "The Golden Calf." "Well," said the Doctor, "I should be glad if you would come down Sunday afternoon and bring my people a hind quarter."' (Blotting Book II, pp. 16, 17.) Pencilled on some of the sermon manuscripts are the phrases, '27 minutes,' '30 minutes,' 'with the omissions, 26′,' which refer probably to the length of time taken for the reading of the discourse. His later lectures took about fifty minutes to deliver.

The task of preparing a fresh discourse each Sunday was lightened in several ways for the young minister. Once a month ordinarily he was absent from his pulpit both morning and afternoon. On these Sundays and at other times, too, following the custom of the time, he exchanged pulpits with fellow-ministers in Boston and indeed further afield. Another common ministerial device for decreasing the burden of writing a new sermon weekly was the practice of using the same sermon more than once. Emerson brought with him to the Second Church the manuscripts of twenty-six sermons, all but four of which he repeated one or more times after his ordination, as he did a large number of those written later.

INTRODUCTION

III

These sermons have a profound biographical interest. Take, for example, the very first sermon Emerson ever wrote. It is at the same time one of the first things of any kind he wrote with a specific audience in view, although of course he had from an early age been writing and experimenting with words, filling his notebooks and journals and preparing themes and prize essays. For the text of his first sermon he took First Thessalonians, chapter five, verse seventeen: Pray without ceasing. How strange a title that Biblical quotation would make for one of his later essays! This first sermon is notable for the large number of ideas it contains which are characteristic of Emerson, both as preacher and essayist.

It was in connection with the writing of this sermon also that Emerson cautioned himself: 'Take care, take care, that your sermon is not a recitation; that it is a sermon to Mr. A. and Mr. B. and Mr. C.' (Blotting Book, No. II, p. 42) — a rhetorical principle which he restates many years later as a lecturer: 'One must think with his audience in mind, so as to keep the perspective and symmetry of the oration.' (*Journals*, Vol. VI, p. 492.) In one sermon he jots down the names of two men (John Orpiment, Edward Ground) when he is writing about the beneficence of that provision that has made everyone 'acquainted with some men who are possessed of some virtues in a high degree.' (No. 140.) Again and again individuals in Emerson's congregations must have recognized themselves in his anonymous references to varieties of human condition and experience. 'I see the disappointed man in whose hands every prospect fails; I see lonely and unhappy women, I see age left childless and the invalid of many years. I see the oppressed debtor, the suspected, the friendless and the mourner.' (No. 153.) They heard themselves thinking out loud, too, for the young preacher frequently introduces brief bits of fabricated dialogue or interrogation into his sermons — thus dramatizing his hearers to themselves.

INTRODUCTION

If there is any particular group in the congregation to which Emerson addresses himself it is the young people. He appeals to every young person who is forming resolutions of leading a good life. 'If any young person desires to raise himself in his own esteem, to feel himself arrived at the dignity of a rational being, to be the master of his hours and his fancies,' the young preacher believes he has something to say to him. One of the methods of cultivating the mind, he informs his young people in a sermon on the theme, is to keep a journal. As the years went on Emerson was to find the greatest responsiveness among young men and women who were in the process of asserting their independence of all inherited traditions and of forming and testing a philosophy of life of their own.

The young preacher never attempts to win his way to his hearers' attention, young or old, by sensational preaching. 'Brethren,' he declares, 'I deal in solemn truths. I have no ambition to startle you with sounding paradoxes.' (No. 32.) This does not mean that he will not use all the arts of an increasingly skillful literary craftsmanship to hold the minds of his people to the thought he is trying to express. Nor does the young preacher ever try to overwhelm his congregation by a flood of oratory or of vehement emotion. His delivery was quiet and strained, but his flexible and melodious voice had great carrying power and it is reported that he could startle his hearers by its sudden strength and fire. His determination is to speak with 'fervor and authority,' of course, 'for he has a passionate love for the strains of eloquence'; but he will respect the minds of his people. He is not so much interested in converting them to his point of view as in exhibiting to them his views for them to adopt if they see fit. 'I wish your credit and consideration to this doctrine no whit farther than it forces itself on your own conviction,' he declares in one sermon (No. 32); in another he italicizes words as if to emphasize the fact that, '*It is only so far as you find Christianity within your own soul that I recommend it.*' (No. 88.)

xix

INTRODUCTION

Yet he is quite aware that at times he is saying things that his congregation will not agree with. After making a statement about the Holy Spirit for instance that might be misinterpreted, he endeavors to reassure them by the ejaculation: 'O yes, I believe in spiritual influences.' (No. 110.) Another indication that he knows he is treading on delicate ground from the point of view of the traditionally minded members of his congregation is the occasional introduction of a statement by the words, 'I say it in all reverence.'

For the most part his homiletical strategy seems to be to state the positive principles of his thought rather than to attack or criticize the views he has abandoned. He practices what he later preached to the preachers and 'Speaks the affirmative.' Occasionally he seems to be thinking out loud in the pulpit, as though he were endeavoring to share with his congregation the process by which he has reached his conclusions, instead of presenting to them the conclusions alone with no clues as to how he reached them. In a sermon on 'God's Wrath and Man's Sin,' for example, in which he asserts that all men desire to appear happy, he continues, 'As this view seems to me an important one I proceed to notice an objection that may be urged against it.'

Even before he is fully embarked on his career, Emerson decides not to talk down to people. (See *Journals*, Vol. II, p. 243.) Some accommodation, however, he does employ. Professor Bliss Perry, in commenting on the Journals points out that 'There is a certain freshness and charm in these original jottings that is sometimes lost in the smoothly finished paragraphs of the published Essays.' What the young preacher does in his sermons is to substitute general terms for the more specific names he has put down in the Journals. Thus, he changes Hercules to 'the man'; Chesterfield becomes 'a man of great worldly wisdom'; Hume becomes 'the skeptic'; George Fox becomes 'many a martyr.'

xx

INTRODUCTION

Of further biographical interest are two sermons Emerson preached on the Sunday morning and afternoon after his ordination as Junior Colleague of Henry Ware, jr. (Nos. 28 and 29.) In them Emerson sets forth for the first time his views of the function of the Christian ministry. They serve as the earnest inaugural statement of a young man looking at the ministry not in retrospect but in prospect, and at his own ministry, to boot; trying to tell himself and his people what he hopes to do and what standards of success and failure he thinks they should apply to this great calling. With homiletical conventionality he enumerates the duties under several heads. There are first the public ministrations, which include prayer and preaching. No hint is given in this sermon, nor in any other sermons of distaste on his part for public prayer. He takes for granted its reasonableness. (See p. 24.) In his preaching he will strive to be direct and concrete.

Always his aim is practical. 'I direct your attention to such views as involve conclusions of great practical value. We preach the worth of the individual soul, its infinitude, its capacity and virtue... for the practical effect which such contemplation can hardly fail to produce.' (No. 155.) In the first draft of a sermon on the Authority of Jesus (No. 76) he indicates reminiscently the kind of effect preaching ought to have, referring apparently to his great ministerial hero, William Ellery Channing: 'When I heard Dr. C. I felt that a development had been given to the best parts of my being as I listened. When I heard *Walker* (James Walker, later President of Harvard University) he exercised my reason, my indignation and so on but did not stretch all the muscles. The very best part of me was not touched. True of Walker, however, only on that narrowing topic Sectarianism.'

Emerson criticizes contemporary preaching on the score of its narrowness. He proposes in his own preaching 'to use a freedom befitting the greatness of the Gospel and its universal application to all human concerns.' He will not be 'so much

INTRODUCTION

afraid of innovation as to scruple about introducing new forms of address, new modes of illustration, and varied allusions into the pulpit when I believe they can be introduced with advantage. I shall not certainly reject them simply because they are new. I must not be crippled in the exercise of my profession.' This is a refreshing declaration of homiletical independence. In several sermons he apologizes for the unconventionality of his choice of theme and his matter of treatment. Some years after his resignation his friend and former parishioner, George Sampson, told him that after he preached his sermon on Habit, another parishioner said that he wished he was in the habit of hearing such sermons as that, 'which speech' adds Emerson 'I found to be good praise and good blame.' (Unpublished Journals A, p. 89, October 1834.) So far as his preaching is concerned he has 'put an end to all that is technical, allegorical, parabolical in it.' (No. 165.)

On the anniversary of his ordination Emerson preached a sermon (No. 69) in retrospect that sheds further light upon his life and career. It contains more than one hint that he has not had an altogether happy time as minister. The tone is apologetic; the attitude defensive. He has failed to resolve a dilemma of the minister who tries to be both a preacher and a pastor. (See p. 71.)

A considerable body of legend has grown up respecting Emerson's skill as a pastor, most of it far from complimentary to him. It is difficult to sift the truth from out these rumors. Certainly Emerson knew how to make and retain intimate friends; but his diffidence of temper made him uneasy in casual personal contacts. His very shyness, however, may have occasioned his turning his attention inward upon himself and served as a kind of protective device to guard his rich spiritual nature against the insistent demands of an importunate world.

Emerson seems also to have heard some criticism of a lack of variety in the subject-matter of his preaching. His answer is: 'I count it the great object of my life to explore the nature of

INTRODUCTION

God.' He is never guilty of triviality in the pulpit. He hews to the line of fundamental principles and supreme values, concentrating on major issues of life.

Emerson recognizes that no matter how pure the mind may be, its idea of God is most inadequate and elementary. 'We feel that our highest theology, i.e. our description of God must be the gropings of infant weakness, when compared to God himself.' (No. 51.) Yet, he continues, it can never be impertinent to strive to give steadiness and distinctness and elevation to our idea of God; to get rid of superstition and uncertainty. This is the great business and design of each human soul in the world. His own thought of God appears with considerable clarity.

IV

God, according to Emerson, is the eternal, extempore, creative power, sustaining and superintending the universe, which he has designed, not for his own glory but for the benefit of mankind. On him men are dependent not only for their origin but for their present existence, since without his omnipresent activity the world would cease to exist and the human soul would lack both intelligence and conscience. Though dependent upon God for their being men are free to obey his laws or not; his grace will not overrule their own choices. The personality of God the young preacher assumes without question. It was only later that serious doubts arose on that score, as the idea of Omnipresence came to an almost exclusive dominance over his thinking.

Emerson arrives at his conception of the character of God by 'stripping the human soul of all inferiority' (No. 86), — a use of the historic theological method known as the *via eminentiae*, that is characteristic of the religious liberalism of which he is an exponent. 'That there is a justice in the mind of God that differs from justice in the mind of man,' seems to

INTRODUCTION

him nonsense. Twice he refers to the grandeur of the enthusiastic expression of an ancient philosopher, giving both the Latin and the English: Bonus vir tempore tantum a Deo differt; the good man differs from God only in his duration. As Parent of the mind, God is both intimate and friendly. Certain traditional attributes of God, which appear to contradict the thought of God as good, Emerson interprets in subjective terms. It is unreasonable to speak of the wrath of God; yet the words are not just language, for they describe in objective terms a common human experience. Perhaps he is recalling the religious terrors of his own childhood. 'The guilt of man paints the clouds with angry faces as the murderer reads an accusation in every countenance.' (No. 89.) Emerson avoids, however, the subjectivism that such a principle of projection often leads to.

The perception of God, according to Emerson, marks the whole difference between religion and irreligion. Among the several ways of knowing God which he discusses, is, first, the way of reason. Emerson champions the speculative method in theology, 'as the dearest privilege of every active and virtuous mind.' (No. 109.) But already as a young preacher he has noticed what seem to him to be limitations in this method — it gives an 'external religion' — and he proposes a more reliable epistemology.

The second way of religious knowledge he calls the 'heart,' the 'moral faculty,' the 'moral sense,' the 'oracle within.' 'The reason why so few men have found the Father' is, he thinks, due to the fact that 'so few men watch their own mind.' (No. 109.) The validity of this intuitional method of knowing God arises from the structure of the mind itself: 'The human mind is so framed that when it is in healthful action, the thought of God appears in it as inevitably as a music-box plays the tune for which it was constructed.' (No. 108a.) The young preacher has not yet invented the term 'Over-soul' for this theory of the immanence of God in human personality. Biblical words like the Holy Spirit, or Emmanuel, or God within us still satisfy

xxiv

INTRODUCTION

him. But the idea is there. How God is thus present in the mind Emerson makes no pretense of understanding, but that God is present he is confident. By virtue of this 'spark of God' in us, we not only know that God exists but we are able to know what his will is and to think truthfully. Conscience, 'the domestic God,' is both the proof and the voice of God. But the young preacher is careful not to say that the soul is God. That is to come later. 'It is not our soul that is God but God is *in* our soul.' (No. 109.)

Emerson occasionally uses the word Reason to refer to this mystic way of religious knowledge: 'This pure and holy inmate of every human breast, this conscience, this Reason, — by whatever name it is honored is the Presence of God to man.' (No. 109.) Not until the publication of *Nature* did he adopt this as the regular meaning of the term, and like Coleridge employ the word Understanding for the rational processes of thinking.

According to historic Christian theology the relevant and available body of knowledge which can serve as a check upon the mystic's alleged truth is to be found in the Bible or in the Church. So far as the Bible is concerned Emerson rejects it as a final authority over Reason or the moral sense. To be sure he accepts the central contention of Christianity that God has made a special revelation of his mind and will in the Bible. But in line with both the rationalistic and mystical movements of the time he insists that in the case of conflict the Bible must give way. 'Let it be supposed that in any case a man is clearly of the opinion that Saint Peter or Saint Paul is mistaken, and positively lays down a false doctrine, the faith he follows has educated him, I say, to reject that doctrine.' (No. 92.) Emerson, in fact, is much more interested in asserting the ethical prerequisites to the discovery of religious truth than in criticizing the mystic way of knowledge. There is an apparent touch of autobiography in a passage in 'Independence in Faith': 'As a man advances in goodness, as he resists his appetites and overcomes his indolence, these times of refreshment from the

xxv

presence of the Lord, once rare, become more frequent, as they are more sought... The pure in heart shall see God.' (No. 106.) The way to God lies along the path of moral decisions.

The other common historic control over the mystical way of religious knowledge is social, the mind of the church. Emerson in one breath acknowledges and destroys this authority: 'I am aware that the allusion [your body is the temple of the Holy Ghost] is not to individuals but to the whole church, — Ye, as a temple of Christ, are a temple of God and he dwelleth in you. But this is in substance the same assertion, for it is only as made up of spiritual natures that a church can be the temple of God, and it is only as God is present to the individual members that he can be present to the church.' ('The Oracle Within,' No. 88.) His theory that the relation of God to the individual has priority over the relation of God to the institution eliminates the possibility of social control over the individualism of the mystic. On occasion, to be sure, Emerson grants that 'Christianity corrects the distortions of the mind.' But he is not interested in emphasizing that aspect of the relation between the individual and the social institution. He is much more concerned lest the church stifle the individual than that the individual shall endanger the unity of the church. The theory he expounds he soon put into action, with drastic consequences upon his career.

Emerson's critical acceptance of a third source of religious knowledge, Revelation, also reflects the period in which he lived. Like other religious leaders he reacts unfavorably to the claim that the Christian gospel contains truth about the meaning of life that can be learned nowhere else. The assumptions which prompted earlier generations to emphasize revelation at the expense of reason have scant appeal for the young preacher. He holds human nature in high and hopeful regard, and thinks it as unnecessary to commend blind reception of dogmas as it is to hoodwink the mind. (No. 92.) The importance of maintaining the integrity of the church by insistence on its special

INTRODUCTION

and exclusive deposit of truth means little to him, for he is equally suspicious of special privilege and of institutional dictatorship. From the point of view of ethical standards and religious philosophy he sees no great superiority of Christianity over paganism. He is not jealous of the goodness of others, nor does he think it derogatory to Christianity to extol the achievements of other religions. He feels small need of enhancing his sense of security by reference to the authority of the ages; in fact, he is thoroughly iconoclastic with respect to any idolatrous worship of the past. Most of all he thinks of life as all of a piece, and deprecates the suggestion of a difference existing between the nature of God and the nature of man so fundamental as to make God unknowable by the mind.

In his theory of religious knowledge, then, as at so many other points in his philosophy of religion, the young preacher has not yet completely forsaken the views he learned from his elders, nor on the other hand, has he given the full and final consent of his mind to ideas of which he later became the ardent champion. But even during the period of his ministry the tendency of his thinking is unmistakably clear.

v

In addition to the sermons which have a biographical interest, is a second group that may be labelled curiosities. They deal with subjects on which Emerson in his other published writings is silent. It would be difficult to guess the content of a sermon by him on Hymn-books, Astronomy, Miracles, New Year's Eve, Summer, Religious Liberalism and Rigidity, The Progress of Religious Opinion, Faith and Works, The Holy Spirit, Time, or the Living Christ.

Take, for example, the sermon on Miracles. (No. 103.) It has a two-fold interest. For one thing Emerson seems to have had unusual difficulty in organizing his exposition. The first two pages he wrote did not please him and he scratched them

INTRODUCTION

out. Pages five and six fared no better. Few of the manuscripts show as many false starts and rewritten passages. But the content of the sermon furnishes still greater surprise.

Every reader of Emerson's Divinity School Address is familiar with his views on miracles; but an earlier and contradictory phase of his thinking on the subject is almost unknown. His Journals contain hints of it but the sermons, and this sermon in particular, express his younger thinking most fully. At few points in his intellectual development does a more striking change take place than in regard to his views of the significance of miracle.

The later Emerson was the rapt prophet of Omnipresence. 'In the universal miracle petty and particular miracles disappear.' With this doctrine of divine immanence, he ushered in a new era in the history of religious thinking in this country. Emerson, the minister of the Second Church, however, believed in particular miracles. Like his contemporaries he is a supernaturalist. By a miracle, he means, to quote from his sermon, 'a special act of God's power for a moral purpose.' A miracle he holds to be more than a wonderful and mysterious occurrence. It is a sign, a testimony, of the existence and activity of God and of his purpose to advertise something to human beings. Emerson's definition of miracle falls in line with both orthodox and liberal Christian teaching of the day.

His sermon on Miracles exhibits clearly the naturalistic position against which he sets forth his own belief. He has accepted without question the 'permanence of the laws of nature.' He appreciates the powerful impetus given to scientific investigation and control by the discovery of the 'certainty in their operation.' Yet he declines to draw the conclusions of a skeptic like Hume. The sermon is an exposition of his grounds for continuing to believe in the credibility of the New Testament miracles.

Emerson's arguments are those of the supernatural rationalists of his time. William Ellery Channing may be taken as the

INTRODUCTION

most notable representative in this country of their point of view; more particularly as it is wholly probable that Emerson is indebted to him for many of his views on the subject of miracle. A comparison of Emerson's sermon with Channing's notable Dudleian lecture on 'The Evidences of Revealed Religion' shows striking parallelisms of thought. Yet there is a vast difference in attitude and tone between the two men. Channing 'rejoices in miracle.' Emerson's tone is apologetic.

The sermon, however, contains within it the seeds of new life for his thinking. 'All our life is a miracle,' he writes; a statement which he amplifies in a later sermon: 'There is not a minute in the twenty-four hours that is not filled with miracles when once we attempt to detail and explain all.' Furthermore, he ends his sermon with a quotation from 'an eloquent English writer,' Samuel Taylor Coleridge, the poet, literary critic, philosopher and theologian, whose fertile but unsystematic thought was a potent ferment in the development of two great American religious leaders, Emerson and Horace Bushnell.

Emerson's sermon on Miracles, then, looks backward to the eighteenth and forward into the nineteenth century and to our own. Henceforth historians of American religious thought will no longer contrast Channing and Emerson as the representatives respectively of dualistic supernaturalism and monistic idealism; for Emerson holds both philosophies in turn. Within his own mind the transition took place that enabled religion to maintain itself in a new world of thought wholly alien to its inherited philosophy and forms of doctrine.

VI

I have called attention to the fundamental theological likeness between Channing and Emerson the young preacher. At one significant point, however, they diverge sharply. In his social ethics Channing follows the tradition of the early New England Church, a tradition re-established by men like Jona-

INTRODUCTION

than Mayhew, who asserted that the Christian churches have a stake in contemporary civilization and must exercise a leadership of criticism and reform of the social order. Emerson, however, stands rather in the evangelical tradition of such men as Jonathan Edwards. Like Edwards, he is primarily concerned with the salvation of the human soul, though he would not put it quite that way. He, too, is the individualist. To be sure he never undertakes a conventional revival of religion, although in one of his sermons he expresses his sympathy with the aims of such revivals.

In spite of his individualism the young Emerson has done some profound thinking about the nature of society and its influence upon the individuals who compose it. A well-developed philosophy of society controls all his remarks on the subject. It is curious therefore, to observe that Emerson never explicitly applies his sociological theories to the church.

In respect to the part individuals play in the transformation of society Emerson shares one of the common assumptions of the evangelical tradition. Change individuals, he declares, and you will change the social system. The true way to reform states is to reform yourself. 'Let us say to ourselves: We are the men who cause the increase of profligacy. We are the sinners. We are the world.' It is not surprising, then, that Emerson shows little or no interest in social action on the part of the church or of private agencies. To the reform movements which issued from or were vitally reinforced by William Ellery Channing he gives scant attention. He seldom mentions current events in the pulpit, though his Fast Day sermons have a certain timeliness about them. As for politics, that is taboo in church. (See p. 76.)

Emerson on the whole then follows the other-worldly tradition of Christianity. 'The day may come when a palsy shall wither the arm of Art; when the looms, the presses and the forges of New England shall stand still; when this strong population which is marching to the west over mountains and lakes

xxx

INTRODUCTION

shall disappear ... All this may impend and not touch our greatest blessings ... It is really of trifling importance what events await America; for we are citizens of another country.' (No. 12.) Yet he does not carry the principle of non-intercourse between church and state quite as far as did his immediate successor in the pulpit of the Second Church, Chandler Robbins, who boasted during the Civil War that 'neither sermon, prayer, nor hymn had in his church reminded people of the strife.' (See No. 70.)

VII

In the passage just quoted from one of Emerson's Thanksgiving Day sermons, occurs the phrase, 'the looms, the presses and the forges of New England.' The manuscript originally had the word 'printing' before presses and read 'the looms, the printing-presses and the forges of New England.' Emerson struck out the word 'printing' apparently to make the rhythm of the sentence smoother. This correction is characteristic of his writing as a young preacher. The same may be true of his later writing, but the manuscripts are no longer accessible with which to make the comparisons. Many of the sermons are hurriedly written, with words abbreviated and some misspelled or omitted; but again and again they exhibit his careful attention to literary technique in matters of style. Alongside a phrase in another sermon he has written, 'ugly expression'; and again, 'I don't like these chasms in discourse.'

The way in which he hits upon the subjects for many of his sermons he describes in his Journal. 'As there is always a subject for life, so there is always a subject for each hour, if only a man has wit enough to find out what this is. I sit Friday night and note the first thought that arises. Presently, another, presently five or six — of all these I take the *mean*, as the subject for Saturday's sermon.' (See further *Journals*, Vol. II, p. 294.) 'Saturday's sermon'! As the dates on the manuscripts

xxxi

INTRODUCTION

indicate, Emerson ordinarily wrote his sermon on the day before he delivered it, occasionally copying it over again on Sunday in order to have a fair page. In a few cases both the original writing and the later copy exist in manuscript form, labelled respectively 'princeps edit' and 'palimpsest.' Prior to a second delivery, he often appears to have worked on the manuscript again. The changes that he later makes have commonly to do with the shortening of his introductions and his conclusions.

Frequently it appears that the inspiration of Friday night was sufficient to launch his thought on a topic that required more than one discourse to unfold it. Occasionally he works out a series of sermons on the same general theme. More frequently he has pairs, like the two on The Christian Ministry or on Sabbath Observance. His later habit of stating his theme without qualification and presenting the opposite side of it in another essay he probably acquired while he was writing sermons.

One of the striking features of the annotations of the Emerson-Forbes edition of the *Journals of Ralph Waldo Emerson* is the cross-references to the essays. The editors have omitted passages from the *Journals*, which have already been printed in the essays. A similar correlation may be made between the sermons and the journals. The cases of borrowing are more frequent than might be surmised from the sermons which have been selected for publication in this volume. Approximately thirty sermons contain passages borrowed from the journals. Early in his career as a writer — and Emerson whether as preacher or lecturer was essentially a writer — he began to use his journal as a 'savings bank' in which to set down ideas that might some day see public utterance. Sometimes a passage lies unused in the journals for eight months. The entry on Prayer, February 28, 1830, for instance, appears in a sermon on that subject the following August 29. (No. 86.) Sometimes the Journal is drawn upon the next day. Occasionally Emerson groups three or four Journal passages of different dates, in a single sermon; a practice he later describes as 'composition.' (*Journals*, Vol.

INTRODUCTION

III, p. 478.) Seldom is the passage taken from the Journals incorporated verbatim in the sermon, for the preacher was always on the watch to improve his diction and amplify his thought. Once in a while, although the subject of a Journal entry is used almost immediately for a sermon, none of the language of the passage itself is repeated.

In later years Emerson turned not only to his Journals but to his sermons for material for his lectures and essays. But there are relatively few instances of the reappearance in the essays of unaltered excerpts from the sermons. It is the themes and the general ideas of the sermons that are to be found again and again in the essays, rather than the particular phrasings of those themes which the young preacher had penned.

The Journals also served Emerson as a memorandum for possible sermons, as the following entries indicate: 'Write upon the several classes of ignorant men and upon *the wise* man'; 'write upon the coincidence of first and third thoughts and apply it to affairs, and to religion and skepticism'; 'Shall I not write upon Envy?' (Sermon No. 156 is his own answer to this question.) In the margin of the Journals alongside some remarks on the Objects of Prayer (omitted in the published edition) Emerson has written: 'See these thoughts developed in Sermon 86,' a kind of notation that appears not infrequently. One of his Journals is aptly entitled, 'Sermons and Journal.'

VIII

One turns from these sermons of the young Emerson with no single answer to the question why he left the ministry of the church. His decision not only to resign from the pastorate of the Second Church but also to withdraw from the conventional, professional ministry of religion had been a long time maturing. The Journals contain several hints of his increasing restlessness. 'It is the best part of the man, I sometimes think, that revolts most against his being a minister.' (*Journals*, Vol. II,

INTRODUCTION

p. 448.) Most inclusive of all such expressions of doubt about his fitness for the pastorate is the complaint: 'Finney can preach, and so his prayers are short; Parkman can pray, and so his prayers are long; Lowell can visit, and so his church service is the less. But what shall poor I do, who can neither visit nor pray nor preach to my mind?' (*Ibid.*, p. 457.)

The sermons corroborate the occasional doubt and dissatisfaction which Emerson expresses in the privacy of his Journal. On the first page of one of his manuscripts he encloses in parentheses the exclamation: 'I would like to write as a man who writes for his own eye only.' (No. 81.) Twice he pencils at the end of a sermon the enigmatic words: 'Plurima nix.' Do they mean that he was surfeited or discouraged with sermonizing? In still another sermon he states: 'I am not speaking as a preacher of Christianity only.'

Even more revealing of his state of mind is his choice of subjects for his sermons during the closing months of his ministry. If ever a preacher preached to himself, Emerson was doing so when he preached on, 'Do Thyself No Harm' (No. 141), 'Find Your Calling' (No. 143), 'Judging Right for Ourselves' (No. 145), and 'The Genuine Man' (No. 164).

The ostensible reason for his withdrawal was his unwillingness to continue to celebrate the Lord's Supper in the traditional way. He discussed this problem in the now well-known discourse on the Lord's Supper (No. 162; *Miscellanies*, p. 1 ff.). As in the case of several of his other sermons there are two manuscripts of this discourse. The first draft contains passages omitted from the final copy, which throw further light upon Emerson's mind at this crucial time. Despite his cavalier attitude toward the past Emerson knows how and when to use history to his purpose: 'Time, the great Instructor, gradually opened the eyes of the disciples to the meaning of their Master's words. Time modified their too literal interpretation of his words. Time, which enlarged their numbers, taught them the impracticability of a community of goods. Time pacified and

INTRODUCTION

ended one after another the fierce disputes about meats offered to idols, about circumcision and uncircumcision, about gifts of tongues, and the deportment of women, and anti-Christ. Time, which has overtaken the Gnostic and the early controversies about the question of the intent of this rite, the white robe, the consecrated pall, the extreme unction, has yet preserved to us the use of this rite which seems to have no better foundation than those frivolous disputes. Time which has destroyed so many trifles that seemed huge matters once has magnified also what then seemed small. Time has every day unfolded more and more the sublime spiritual sense of the gospel of Christ. The words, the dogmas of apostles and bishops and sects are dropped one after another, but the eternal truths come out like stars and take their place forever in the firmament. This process will go on.'

The sermon on the Lord's Supper could not have come wholly as a surprise to the congregation, for three months earlier he had imparted to a committee of the church his views on the subject. He had done little, however, during his pastorate to indoctrinate his people with his new views. But immediately after his first announcement to the committee he did go so far as to refer in two sermons to the kind of religious philosophy which, if accepted by the church, would have made the issue of the Lord's Supper appear as meaningless to them as it appeared to him. 'Men make their religion a historical religion. They see God in Judea and in Egypt, in Moses and in Jesus, but not around them. We want a living religion. As the faith was alive in the hearts of Abraham and of Paul, so I would have it in mine. I want a religion not recorded in a book but flowing from all things.' (No. 158.)

Sentiments similar to this Emerson had expressed more than once in passing, though not often in so explicit and antithetical a form as this. But his occasional expositions of these novel ideas were insufficient to leaven the mass of his congregation. They failed to rise. And nothing remained for Emerson but

xxxv

INTRODUCTION

to make his concluding remarks in the sermon on the Lord's Supper, remarks which are as straightforward as they are intransigeant.

In his Preaching Record (after enumerating the two sermons of the day) he has added a parenthesis: 'Sent a communication to the Proprietors this day.' And on October 28 he noted: 'This day the Proprietors voted to accept my letter of resignation of office.' Thus 'the checkered space of time which domestic affliction and personal infirmities [had] made yet shorter and more unprofitable' was brought to a sudden close. (See Cabot, *Memoirs*, p. 685 f.) The closeness of the vote — thirty to twenty — indicates that Emerson was not altogether unjustified in his expectation that he might persuade the church to follow his lead in considering the Lord's Supper 'a matter of subordinate importance.' 'I had hoped,' he said many years later to E. A. Horton, one of his successors at the Second Church, 'to carry them with me but I failed.' Undoubtedly the young preacher felt both disappointed and sorrowful at the time but his other self was ready to forsake society for solitude, social obligation for independence. As the Journals indicate he had more than one string to his bow. There was literature. There was even the newly organized movement for adult education, the Lyceum, whose aim was 'improvement not amusement.'

Throughout this episode no rancour was exhibited on either side. After his resignation Emerson was requested by the Proprietors of the Church to arrange for the supply of the pulpit with the help of a committee. He complied and his Preaching Record gives the names of the men who filled his pulpit up to the end of the year, when Mr. Ware consented to make the arrangements.

Emerson himself preached once more during the interval between the presentation of his resignation and its acceptance. Thereafter he hoped to do so again but his health failed him. The tension had been severe and the reaction was too much for

INTRODUCTION

him. His brother reports to their Aunt Mary: 'Waldo is sick. His spirits droop.... I never saw him so disheartened.' He finally decided to accept Dr. Ware's advice and seek to recover his health by a trip to Europe. On December 23 F. W. P. Greenwood read to the Second Church the letter Emerson had written on the eve of his departure. It was voted to print and distribute three hundred copies of this letter to the proprietors and worshippers of the church.

Emerson's people were fond of him and he was fond of them. While he was abroad his letters ask for news of the church. And soon after his return when he preached again in his former pulpit, he said, 'I cannot tell you, my friends of this religious society, with how much pleasure I see you again and learn of your welfare and your virtues.' (No. 165.)

As his Preaching Record and his Journals disclose, he continued to preach on almost every Sunday for a number of years. In fact, he began and ended his preaching career as a supply preacher. He was tempted to accept a call to the New Bedford church but by this time he had acquired another prejudice against the conventions of worship — the obligation to lead in public prayer whether he felt like it or not — and the church was unwilling to make so unheard of an experiment. During this time, although he wrote few new sermons, he could not get out of the habit of putting down in his Journal one 'good suggestion for a sermon' after another. And when Sunday came round, if he was not preaching himself, he attended church, returning home, like Samuel Pepys, to comment in his Journal on what he had heard. Finally he ceased attending church altogether (1838). But that was not until after he had supplied the pulpit of the little meeting-house at East Lexington for three years. On one occasion there he interrupted his delivery to say quietly to the congregation, 'The sentence which I have just read I do not now believe,' and then went on to the next page.

At the East Lexington church, according to the Preaching

INTRODUCTION

Record, Emerson not only used many of his old sermons but often, at the afternoon service gave one of the lectures he had previously delivered in his courses in Boston. Martin Luther, George Fox, Peace, found their way into the pulpit. He also enlarged earlier sermons on Self-Culture (No. 87) and on Duty (No. 154) by portions of his Boston lecture on Religion. On the fifteenth anniversary of his ordination Emerson addressed the Second Church, once again, when they were about to rebuild their meeting-house. 'I do not think,' he said, self-revealingly, 'that violent changes of opinion very often occur in men. As far as I know they do not see new lights and turn sharp corners, but commonly, after twenty or fifty years you shall find the individual true to his early tendencies.' Neither in his ideas nor in his manner of living did Emerson himself turn any sharp corners. The transition from his earlier to his later career in respect both to time and to subject matter took place gradually.

Emerson's dislike of religious forms, — sacramental, institutional and theological alike — partly explains his withdrawal from the Second Church. 'Rites are nothing in themselves' he remarks in 'The Power of the Soul.' (No. 67.) He declares that a religion of forms is not for him. Yet he had the capacity to detect the truth concealed from literal eyes by the theological forms in which it is expressed and to 'translate' it into his own forms of thinking. (See *Journals*, Vol. III, p. 382; Vol. II, p. 478.) He could point out that 'Fénelon and Calvin and Taylor and Priestley kneel and worship side by side and Christianity forgets in her love of these holy men that they were the champions of four arrogant churches.' (No. 43.) He was also able to see the meaning that lies behind religious ceremonies. 'If you bereave religion of the types, leave the things signified,' he counseled in an early Christmas sermon. 'If you take down the green boughs, do not forget the hope. If you dispense with the feast, do not forget the joy. If you do not outwardly keep the Christmas, revere the Christ.' He was not ready for himself or for

INTRODUCTION

others to abandon the forms and organizations and creeds of religion. But he wanted to be their master rather than their servant.

It was not alone Emerson's dislike of forms that caused the break, nor the chasm between his new philosophy of religion and the traditions which his people had so recently acquired and so jealously cherished. It was not that he could not preach as he pleased and about what he pleased. It was not rites and ceremonies and the half-truths of Christian doctrine. It was not the logic of his theory of Omnipresence. It was not his lack of aptitude for pastoral duties, nor his distaste for being a 'party-man.' It was not the irksomeness of administration and routine nor the imposition of a schedule. It was not the example of his brother William who had abandoned the profession some years before. It was not constraint in the free expression of his thought. All these taken together had great weight. But had it not been for the way Emerson interpreted the function of leadership he would probably have stayed on at the Second Church until he had brought his people around to his views and his methods.

There are two types of leaders in every field. One kind of leader sets forth his platform, outlines his goals and proceeds to move in their direction at his own pace, regardless of followers or of their capacity to keep up with him. If they can follow, let them. The other kind of leader is just as sure of his objective and confident in his convictions, but he declines to move ahead so fast that those who follow lose sight of him. He slows down his pace to suit their stumbling feet. He adjusts his message to their understanding. He knows how long and slow is the process of educating a stable group of people.

Now Emerson represents the first kind of leadership. He was no teacher. He was a prophet and a preacher. He did not conceive of his leadership as that of a teacher. In an unpublished fragment of his Journal he states: 'The two conditions of Teaching are: 1. That none can teach more than he knows.

INTRODUCTION

2. That none can teach faster than the scholar can learn. Two conditions more: 1. He must say that they can understand. 2. But he must say that which is given to *him*. It is true undoubtedly that every preacher should strive to pay his debt to his fellowmen by making his communication intelligible to the common capacity. It is no less true that unto every mind is given one word to say and he should sacredly strive to utter that word and not another man's word; his own, without addition or abatement.' Emerson here is voicing the deepest truth of his own temperament. He must and will be free of all restraint, even the restraint of having to adapt himself to those whom he is anxious to enlighten with his truth and to enlist in the cause of truth he holds dear.

He could never quite understand why a truth that is so clear to him should not appear equally crystalline to others. Somewhere in his Journals he remarks that Plato thinks for his thousands and Aristotle for his two thousands. In like manner unconsciously the young preacher assumed that he himself thinks for his hundreds. Fortunately he had the courage to rely on his own inspiration, on the divinity within, and in due time he came to think for thousands upon thousands and still does. His withdrawal from the pulpit enabled him to gather his following from a much wider range of listeners.

No longer limited to a single pulpit for his utterance, he became, first an itinerant lay preacher not only to New England but to the advancing West; and finally minister at large to imprisoned, dormant and inquiring minds everywhere. But it may well be doubted whether he would have become the Emerson the world knows save for the unhurried years of experiment, discipline and growth, as an obscure young preacher.

Young Emerson Speaks

Pray Without Ceasing

Pray without ceasing. First Thessalonians V, 17.

It is the duty of men to judge men only by their actions. Our faculties furnish us with no means of arriving at the motive, the character, the secret self. We call the tree good from its fruits, and the man, from his works. Since we have no power, we have no right, to assign for the actions of our neighbor any other motives than those which ought in similar circumstances to guide our own. But because *we* are not able to discern the processes of thought, to see the soul — it were very ridiculous to doubt or deny that any beings can. It is not incredible that the thoughts of the mind are the subjects of perception to some beings, as properly as the sounds of the voice, or the motion of the hand are to us. Indeed, every man's feeling may be appealed to on this question, whether the idea, that other beings can read his thoughts, has not appeared so natural and probable, that he has checked sometimes a train of thoughts that seemed too daring or indecent, for any unknown beholders to be trusted with.

It ought to be distinctly felt by us that we stand in the midst of two worlds, the world of matter and the world of spirit. Our bodies belong to one; our thoughts to the other. It has been one of the best uses of the Christian religion to teach, that the world of spirits is more certain and stable than the material universe. Every thoughtful man has felt that there was a more awful reality to thought and feeling, than to the infinite panorama of nature around him. The world he has found indeed consistent and uniform enough throughout the mixed sensations of thirty or forty years, but it seems to him at times, when the intellect is invigorated, to ebb from him, like a sea, and to leave nothing permanent but thought. Nevertheless it is a truth not easily nor early acquired, and the prejudice that assigns greater fixture and certainty to the material world is a source of great practical error. I need hardly remind you of the great points of this error. I need not ask you if the objects that every day are the cause of the greatest number of steps taken, of the greatest industry of the hands and the feet, the heart and the head, are the perishable things of sense, or the imperishable things of the soul; whether all this stir from day to day, from hour to hour of all this mighty multitude, is to ascertain some question dear to the understanding concerning the nature of God, the true constitution and destination of the human soul, the proper balance of the faculties and the proper office of each; or (what of immortal thought comes nearer to practical value) whether all men are eagerly intent to study the best systems of education for themselves and their children? Is it not rather the great wonder of all who think enough to wonder that almost all that sits near the heart, all that colours the countenance, and engrosses conversation at the family board are these humble things of mortal date, and in the history of the universe absolutely insignificant? Is it not outside shews, the pleasures of appetite, or at best of pride; is it not bread and wine and dress and our houses and our furniture, that give the law to the great mass of actions and words? This is the great error which the strong feeling of the reality of things unseen must correct. It is time greater force should be given to the statement of this doctrine; it is time men should be instructed that their inward is more valuable than their outward estate; that thoughts and passions, even those to which no language is ever given, are not fugitive undefined shadows, born in a moment, and in a moment blotted from the soul, but are so many integral parts of the imperishable universe of morals; they should be taught that they do not think *alone*; that when they retreat from the public eye and hide themselves to conceal in solitude guilty recollections or guilty wishes, the great congregation of moral natures, the spirits of just men made perfect; angels and archangels; the Son of God, and the Father everlasting, open their eyes upon them and speculate on these clandestine meditations.

I. The necessary inference from these reflections, is the fact which gives them all their importance, and is the doctrine I am chiefly anxious to inculcate. It is not only when we audibly and in form address our petitions to the Deity, that we pray. We pray without ceasing. Every secret wish is a prayer. Every house is a church, the corner of every street is a closet of devotion. There is no rhetoric, let none deceive himself; there is no rhetoric in this. There *is* delusion of the most miserable kind, in that fiction on which the understanding pleads to itself its own excuse, when it knows not God and is thoughtless of him. I mean that outward respect, that is paid to the name and worship of God, whilst the thoughts and the actions are enlisted in the service of sin. 'I will not swear by God's name,' says the wary delinquent; 'I will not ask him to lend his aid to my fraud, to my lewdness, to my revenge; nor will I even give discountenance to the laws I do not myself observe. I will not unmask my villainy to the world, that I should stand in the way of others, more scrupulous, nay, better than I.'

And is it by this paltry counterfeit of ignorance that you would disguise from yourselves the truth? And will you really endeavour to persuade yourself, that God is such an one as you yourself, and will be amused by professions, and may, by fraudulent language, be kept out of the truth? Is it possible, that men of discretion in common affairs, can think so grossly?

Do you not know that the knowledge of God is perfect and immense; that it breaks down the fences of presumption, and the arts of hypocrisy; that right, and artifice, and time, and the grave, are naked before it; that the deep gives up its dead, that the gulfs of chaos are disembowelled before him; that the minds of men are not so much independent existences, as they are ideas present to the mind of God; that he is not so much the observer of your actions, as he is the potent principle by which they are bound together; not so much the reader of your thoughts, as the active Creator by whom they are aided into being; and, casting away the deceptive subterfuges of language, and speaking with strict philosophical truth, that every faculty is but a mode of his action; that your reason is God, your virtue is God, and nothing but your liberty, can you call securely and absolutely your own?

Since, then, we are thus, by the inevitable law of our being, surrendered unreservedly to the unsleeping observation of the Divinity, we cannot shut our eyes to the conclusion, that *every desire of the human mind is a prayer uttered to God and registered in heaven.*

II. The next fact of sovereign importance in this connection is, that *our prayers are granted.* Upon the account I have given of prayer, this ulterior fact is a faithful consequence. What then! if I pray that fire shall fall from heaven to consume mine enemies, will the lightning come down? If I pray that the wealth of India may be piled in my coffers, shall I straightway become rich?[1] If I covet my neighbor's wit, or beauty, or honourable celebrity, — will these desirable advantages be at once transferred from being the sources of his happiness, to become the sources of mine? It is plain there is a sense in which this is not true. But it is equally undeniable that in the sense in which I have explained the nature of prayer, and which seems the only proper sense, the position is universally true. For those are not prayers, which begin with the ordinary appellatives of the Deity and end with his Son's name and a ceremonial word — those are not prayers, if they utter no one wish of our hearts, no one real and earnest affection, but are formal repetitions of sentiments taken at second hand, in words the supple memory has learned of fashion. O my friends, these are not prayers, but mockeries of prayers. But the true prayers are the daily, hourly, momentary desires, that come without impediment, without fear, into the soul, and bear testimony at each instant to its shifting character. And these prayers are granted. For is it not clear that what we strongly and earnestly desire we shall make every effort to obtain; and has not God so furnished us with powers of body and of mind that we can acquire whatsoever we seriously and unceasingly strive after?

For it is the very root and rudiment of the relation of man to this world, that we are in a condition of wants which have their appropriate gratifications *within our reach*; and that we have faculties which can bring us to our ends; that we are full of capacities that are near neighbors to their objects; and our free agency consists in this, that we are able to reach those sources of gratification, on which our election falls. And if this be so, will not he who thinks lightly of all other things in comparison with riches; who thinks little of the poor man's virtue, or the slave's misery as they cross his path in life, because his observant eye is fixed on the rich man's manners and is searching in the lines of his countenance, with a sort of covetousness, the tokens of a pleased contemplation of the goods he has in store, and the consideration that, on this account, is conceded to him in society; will not such an one, if his thoughts daily point towards this single hope, if no exertion is grateful to him which has not this for its aim; if the bread is bitter to him that removes his riches one day farther from his hand, and the friends barren of comfort to him that are not aiding to this dishonourable ambition; — will not such an one arrive at the goal, such as it is, of his expectation and find, sooner or later, a way to the heaven where he has garnered up his heart? Assuredly he will.

And will not the votary of other lusts, the lover of animal delight, who is profuse of the joys of sense, who loveth meats and drinks, soft raiment and the wine when it moveth itself aright and giveth its colour in the cup; or the more offensive libertine who has no relish left for any sweet in moral life, but only waits opportunity to surrender himself over to the last damning debauchery; will not these petitioners who have knocked so loudly at heaven's door, receive what they have so importunately desired? Assuredly they will. There is a commission to nature, there is a charge to the elements made out in the name of the Author of events, whereby they shall help the purposes of man, (a preexistent harmony between thoughts and things) whereby prayers shall become effects, and these warm imaginations settle down into events.

And if there be, in this scene of things, any spirit of a different complexion, who has felt, in the recesses of his soul, 'how awful goodness is, and virtue in her own shape how lovely,' who has admired the excellence of others, and set himself by precepts of the wise, and by imitation, which, a wise man said, is 'a globe of precepts,' to assimilate himself to the model, or to surpass the uncertain limit of human virtue, and found no model in the universe, beneath God, level with his venerated idea of virtue; who looks with scorn at the cheap admiration of crowds, and loves the applause of good men, but values more his own; and has so far outstripped humanity, that he can appreciate the love of the Supreme; if he aspire to do signal service to mankind, by the rich gift of a good example, and by unceasing and sober efforts to instruct and benefit man; will this man wholly fail, and waste his requests on the wind? Assuredly he will not. His prayers, in a certain sense, are like the will of the Supreme Being.

> 'His word leaps forth to its effect at once,
> He calls for things that are not, and they come.'

His prayers are granted; all prayers are granted. Unceasing endeavours always attend true prayers, and, by the law of the universe, unceasing endeavours do not fail of their end.

Let me not be misunderstood as thinking lightly of the positive duty of stated seasons of prayer. That solemn service of man to his maker is a duty of too high authority and too manifest importance to excuse any indifference to its claims. It is because that privilege is abused, because men in making prayers forget the purpose of prayer, forget that praying is to make them leave off sinning, that I urge it in its larger extent where it enters into daily life.

I have attempted to establish two simple positions, that, we are always praying, and that it is the order of Providence in the world, that our prayers should be granted. If exceptions can be quoted to me out of the book of common life, to the universality of either of these doctrines, I shall admit them in their full force, nor shall I now detain you by any inquiry into the abstract metaphysical nature of that happiness human beings are permitted to derive from what are called possessions, and how far it belongs to the imagination. I shall content myself, at present, with having stated the general doctrine and with adverting to its value as a practical principle.

And certainly, my friends, it is not a small thing that we have learned. If we have distinctly apprehended the fact which I have attempted to set in its true light, it cannot fail to elevate very much our conception of our relations and our duties. Weep no more for human frailty, weep no more for what there may be of sorrow in the past or of despondency in the present hour. Spend no more unavailing regrets for the goods of which God in his Providence has deprived you. Cast away this sickly despair that eats into the soul debarred from high events and noble gratification. Beware of easy assent to false opinion, to low employment, to small vices, out of a reptile reverence to men of consideration in society. Beware, (if it teach nothing else let it teach this) beware of indolence, the suicide of the soul, that lets the immortal faculties, each in their orbit of light, wax dim and feeble, and star by star expire.

These considerations let our doctrine enforce. Weep not for man's frailty — for if the might of Omnipotence has made the elements obedient to the fervency of his daily prayers, he is no puny sufferer tottering, ill at ease, in the universe, but a being of giant energies, architect of his fortunes, master of his eternity. Weep not for the past; for this is duration over which the secret virtue of prayer is powerless, over which the Omnipotence of God is powerless; send no voice of unprofitable wailing back into the depths of time; for prayer can reverse in the future the events of the past. Weep not for your wasted possessions, for the immeasurable future is before you, and the wealth of the universe invites your industry. Nor despair that your present daily lot is lowly, nor succumb to the shallow understanding or ill example of men whose worldly lot is higher. Be not deceived; for what is the past? It is nothing worth. Its value, except as means of wisdom, is, in the nature of things actually nothing. And what is the imposing present? What are the great men and great things that surround you? All that they can do for you is dust, and less than dust to what you can do for yourself. They are like you stretching forward to an infinite hope, the citizens in trust of a future world. They think little of the present; though they seem satisfied, they are not satisfied but repine and endeavour after greater good. They, like you, are born to live when the sun has gone down in darkness and the moon is turned to blood.

My friends, in the remarks that I have just made I have already in part anticipated the third great branch of our subject, which is that *our prayers are written in Heaven.*

III. The great moral doctrines we have attempted to teach would be of limited worth if there were no farther consideration in this series of thought. You are pleased with the acquisition of property; you pray without ceasing to become rich. You lay no tax of conscience on the means. You desire to become rich by dint of virtue or of vice, of force or of fraud. And in virtue of the order of things that prevails in the world as I have stated you come to your ends. Is this all? Is the design of Providence complete? Is there no conclusion to this train of events, thus far conducted?

The wicked has flourished up to his hope. He has ground the faces of the poor. He has the tears of the widow and the curse of the fatherless but they lie light on his habitation; for he has builded his house where these cannot come, in the midst of his broad lands, on a pleasant countryside, sheltered by deep ornamental woods, and the voices of the harp and the viol tinkle in his saloons; the gay and the grave, the rich and the fair swarm to him in crowds and though they salute him and smile often upon him they do not utter one syllable of reproach nor repeat one imprecation of the poor. But far away, too far to be any impediment to his enjoyment, the wretches he has cruelly stripped of their last decent comforts, and the well loved means with which sinking poverty yet strives to bear up and make a respectable appearance in society, — are now, in small accommodated tenements, eating a morsel of bread and uttering in unvisited, unremembered solitude, the name of the oppressor. And have we seen all, my friends, and is poor struggling worth to be rewarded only with worth, and be poor and vile beside, and is vice to go triumphing on to the grave? Aye; to the grave. Hitherto, shalt thou go, and no farther, and here shall thy proud waves be staid. My friends, there is another world. After death there is life. After death in another state, revives your capacity of pleasure and of pain, the evil memory of evil actions; revives yourself, the man within the breast, the gratified petitioner in the exact condition to which his fulfilled desires have, by the inevitable force of things, contracted or expanded his character. There is another world; a world of remuneration; a world to which you and I are going and which it deeply behooves us to survey and scrutinize as faithfully as we can, as it lies before us, 'though shadows, clouds and darkness rest upon it.' It is plain that *as* we die in this world, we shall be born into that. It is plain, that, it is, if it be anything, a world of spirit; that body, and the pleasures and pains appertaining to body can have no exercise, no mansion there; that it can be the appropriate home only of high thought and noble virtue. Hence it must happen, that if a soul can have access to that ethereal society, fleshed over with bodily appetites, in which no love has grown up of thought and moral beauty, and no sympathy and worship of virtue, but in their place gnawing lusts have coiled themselves with a serpent's trail into the place of every noble affection that God set up in the recesses of the soul when he balanced the parts and modulated the harmony of the whole; and there pampered appetites that grew in the soil of this world, find no aliment for them in heaven, no gaudy vanities of dress, no riotous excitement of song and dances, no filling gluttony of meats and drinks, no unclean enjoyments, finding none of all this, it must happen, that these appetites will turn upon their master, in the shape of direst tormentors; and if the economy of the universe provide no natural issue, whereby these mortal impurities can be purged with fire out of the texture of the soul, they must continue from hour to hour, from age to age, to arm the principles of his nature against the happiness of man.

Of this mysterious eternity, about to open upon us, of the nature of its employments and our relation to it, we know little. But of one thing be certain, that if the analogies of time can teach aught of eternity, if the moral laws taking place in this world, have relation to those of the next, and even the forecasting sagacity of the pagan philosopher taught him that the Laws below were sisters of the Laws above — then the riches of the future are dealt out on a system of compensations. That great class of human beings who in every age turned aside from temptation to pursue the bent of moral nature shall now have *their* interests consulted. They have cast their bread on the waters (for the choice lay often between virtue and their bread), trusting that after many days a solemn retribution of good should be rendered to them in the face of the world. Insult and sorrow, rags and beggary they have borne; they have kept the faith though they dwelled in the dust, and now, the pledge of God that supported them in the trial must be redeemed, and shall be, to the wonder of themselves, through the furthest periods of their undying existence.

Their joy and triumph is that revelation of the gospel which is most emphatically enforced by images borrowed from whatever was most grand and splendid in the imaginations of men; but crowns and thrones of judgment, and purple robes are but poor shadows of that moral magnificence with which in the company of souls disembodied, virtue asserts its majesty, and becomes the home and fountain of unlimited happiness.[2]

Nothing remains but the obligation there is on each of us to make what use we can of this momentous doctrine. Is it to another condition than yours, to some removed mode of life, to the vices of some other class of society that this preaching, with strict propriety, belongs? No, my friends, if you are of the great household of God; if you are distinguishers of good and evil; if you believe in your own eternity; if you are tempted by what you feel to be evil attractions; if you are mortal, — it belongs to you. If you have ever felt a desire for what conscience, God's vicegerent, enthroned within you, condemned; if impelled by that desire, and wilfully deaf to that condemnation, you swerved towards the gratification, and obtained the object, and stifled the monitor — then it is you, and not another; then you have uttered these unseemly prayers; the prayer is granted and is written in heaven. And at this moment, though men are not privy to all the passages of your life and will salute you respectfully, and though it may be your own violated memory has ceased to treasure heedfully the number of your offences — yet every individual transgression has stamped its impress on your character, and moral beings in all the wide tracts of God's dominion and God over all fasten their undeceived eyes on this spectacle of moral ruin. To you therefore it belongs, to every one who now hears me, to look anxiously to his ways; to look less at his outward demeanour, his general plausible action, but *to cleanse his thoughts*. The heart, the heart is pure or impure, and out of it, are the issues of life and of DEATH.

On Showing Piety at Home

Let them first learn to show piety at home.   First Timothy, V, 4.

It is a very common mistake to regard the eminence of the actors in our estimate of virtue. A king's virtues never suffered in the telling. Those who stand high in society are thought to derive from that circumstance some degree of licence to vice and there is therefore something gratuitous and deserving of more praise in their goodness. Hence it happens that we ourselves desire conspicuous occasions for the exhibition of our own moral principle; wish that we had our neighbor's immense possessions to edify men with our charity or the gifted mind of our friend that we might plead with a most devoted eloquence the cause of the afflicted, oppressed and poor. When therefore we consider our own characters we are very apt to take to ourselves credit for what we think we should do in any case of extraordinary trial. We omit the examination of what we are and what we do and please ourselves with the contemplation of our possible virtues in possible cases.

'But the main part of life is made up of small incidents and petty occurrences.' It is the duty of but very few of us to command armies or rule or counsel nations. If we therefore keep our virtue in store till it find a field which we shall think worthy of its action it will wait long, or rather it will never exist for virtue exists only in action.

In the next place let it be remembered that no virtue can be properly called small. A great end makes the means great. We read with the utmost interest the most insignificant particulars that relate to the life and actions of a genuine hero because we esteem them, however slight themselves, to be all of them steps to some high rational end, which was then uppermost in the actor's soul. The same thing determines our opinion of all action, not the movement itself but its tendency and end. If to pluck a rose or to snap the finger had been made a concerted signal of a man's resolution to die for a particular cause there would be grandeur in that frivolous action. If it were possible for us to go back and see the person and actions of our Lord precisely as they were seen in Nazareth and Galilee eighteen hundred years ago, would any trait of his demeanour, do you imagine, appear to you small and indifferent? Knowing the sublime purpose that glowed within his bosom as he sat in benevolent discourse with his twelve observant friends, would a glance of his eye, would the lifting of his hand escape our notice? Would not his least motion seem to us fraught with extreme and tender interest? Now the case is precisely the same with whatever conduct is prompted by high principle. It dignifies the act, be it ever so minute. You need not endow a hospital to be very good. You may be greatly virtuous even though through the blessing of God, you do not live in times when you must give your body to be burned or to be sawn asunder for your faith. Less imposing duties are great enough and sometimes more than enough for our languid obedience. The narrow confines of home are a field of preparation large enough for all the glories of Heaven. The strict adherence to truth at all risks, the denial of an indulgence at the table, the suppression of a merry or petulant remark likely to wound the feelings of another, even the charity of an encouraging word or smile given to humble worth — the least of these — done out of a solemn sense of duty, done in the Eye of God, is great and venerable.

ON SHOWING PIETY AT HOME

Since it is in our houses that we spend the greatest part of life, since we can never be great if we are not reverenced there and nowhere be good if we are vicious at home, I shall need no apology for asking your attention to the duty of domestic piety. For the main regard of religion must be to make us good at home.

It seems to be thought as has been intimated that our virtue demands for its strenuous exertion a great occasion, an active life, and something removed from the quiet dulness of home. But who made this distinction between times and seasons and occupations? Did God, my friends, limit virtue by rule or line or distinctions? Did he command us to love and fear him only in one place or another, at noon or night, or yield us permission of following our inclinations twice, if we did his bidding once? Do you find any compromise in his word that you may give your winter to sin, if you will give your summer to God? or doth he ask or will he accept anything less than the whole? Provided that you are scrupulously upright in business in the street does he sell you the privilege of vicious indulgence in your own house? Must you not love God with your whole heart and mind and strength? No, nothing of all this. The household hours are hours of life. The household hours carry their accusing or approving testimony on high, and they have a weightier evidence than others because they contain in them the sincere expression of the heart; for no man is a hypocrite at home.

'Let them first learn to show piety at home,'[1] said the affectionate apostle to his friend. For he knew how prone men are to commit fatal mistakes, to deceive themselves by pushing forward any substitutes in the place of vital piety, to shroud an immoral life behind the best professions or the strictest creed; behind a virtuous carriage before the great; behind good humour and a liberal mind before the world. But let them show piety at home. That shall be the test of the character. There is many a man who goes out into the world gaily drest in smiles and kindness, who is full of grace and bounty abroad, of correct views and pleasing conversation. But when he returns home where the doors are shut and the curtains drawn, and the hours pass without event, he says, 'There is no need to shine, these are of necessity my friends, by blood, or by dependance.' He takes off his goodness like a cumbersome garment and grows silent and splenetic. He has got rid of the prepossessing elegance of his address, that buoyant alacrity in the offices of politeness that won your praise. He is intemperate at his table; he is a sluggard in his bed; he is slothful and useless in his chair; he is sour or false in conversation. He breaks the commandments because he is at home. A strange reason surely for licence and vice! Will the curtains of his windows shroud him from the Omniscient Eye? When we need the stimulus of a great occasion and many observers to excite our virtue, what is it in effect but to say that we fear men more than God and respect men more than we respect ourselves?

That virtue must needs be the most acceptable tribute of obedience which is practised before few persons and on humble occasions. If a man is good before a king or a sage it is possible that his goodness springs from a calculating prudence; if he is pure before a child or a beggar, it is manifest he loves virtue for virtue's sake. And hence the high value we set on piety at home.

Let it be remembered that it is not ourselves so much as Providence that appoints our situation in life, that appoints us to great or to humble occasions of usefulness. But our virtue is in all cases determined by ourselves. It is ours to say whether we will rise in our daily life to the dignity of angels or whether we will creep nameless and worthless through infamous years of selfishness and sin to a dishonourable old age of shame and sorrow. One who contemplates the beauty of a life that is nobly led under the unerring guidance of religious principle is sometimes astonished how there should be hesitation upon its advantage; that all men do not run to render the homage of their obedience to the law of God. It is a beautiful but moni-

ON SHOWING PIETY AT HOME

tory thought that not an hour of our waking time after we have learned to distinguish good and evil — that not an hour of the longest life but may be signalised by a virtuous action, by some sacrifice though small and unknown to another's wish or of our own inclination to our duty; and as it is the consequence of all goodness to increase the power of him that has it, that one of us, my brethren, by a rigid study of himself may every hour become a richer and mightier moral agent; may tomorrow be happier than today; may rake together with each flying moment the bright atoms of knowledge and goodness [2] until he ceases to count his days by the wretched marks of passing time, by his returning pleasures of the table, by his periodical augmentations of property, or yet by the furrows of his brow, but numbers them on the golden dial of his own soul by the acquisitions he has made and the good deeds he has done. He sees in the virtues of his children with joy the genuine fruit of his own; he beholds in the beggar at his door the living record of his charitable years.

And let me ask which of all those much magnified goods which others pursue so fondly, of which we are all apt to think so much, delicate food, a gay dress, personal beauty, the regard of people in higher rank and fashion, friends, flattering prospects or whatsoever accidental advantages, ought so much as to be named in comparison with the value of one well spent hour? I beg that this may not be understood as mere declamatory praise of virtue proper enough to this place and of no imperative interest, but that it is true to the letter and every one in this house shall one day feel its force; that a well spent hour in the life of a man is, when he comes to die and see things in their true dimensions, felt to be a solid advantage by the side of which opinions and conditions, earthly pleasures and advantages become extremely contemptible. One well spent hour is the proper seed of heaven and eternity. For he who has opened his heart for an hour to all the influences of religion, who has devoted himself for a time to the service of conscience and fulfilled its dictates to the letter will go back to that hour with pure and justifiable delight. That time will be laid up in his mind and become the pleasant place of the memory. Good will come out of it whenever it is reviewed. It will be like the embalmed body of the mighty. The fragrance of Arabian myrrh and spikenard shall steal from it when it is visited. It will strongly incite in his breast the desire to copy its beauty into the yet unwritten page of this day and the morrow.

Reward

II. Again, let them first learn to show piety at home, for there our piety can do some good. That is the place where we are best known, and where if we are religious some one will have the good of it by benefit from us or at least by our example. Our ways of thinking, talking and acting there will exercise a stronger influence than ever we can hope to create elsewhere. Have you never coveted a more extensive influence than you possess? Did you never wish you were of more importance among your fellow citizens? Did you never covet the influence of a great man? Have you never sighed to be born a king? Never looked with a greedy eye on that augmented power that the rich necessarily hold in their hands and excused your ambition by asserting that you should put that power to so much better use? In his parlour every man has power. There can be no question of the force with which your influence acts upon the inmates of your dwelling. Let us try your capacity to be ruler over many things by your faithfulness over a few things. If you have learned to show piety at home, if you keep the purity of that sanctuary from contamination; if you have made it the holy fountain of generous and honourable habits; if prayer has been offered on the altar of God morning and evening; if its secret history could be opened to the world without regret or dishonour; then, fear not but God in the boundless future shall more than recompense your honest stewardship. Fear not but in the earth also, your reward shall be reaped. The same moral force that has dignified your character at home will surely give you standing and reverence abroad. The competence of a man is known to his neighbors. Your children will rise up and call you blessed. And God and man will provide you opportunity to do good to the farthest of your ability. But if alas! you are afraid to give account of your abode, if it has been the hiding place of folly and sin, if those that have grown up in it betray by the too certain sign of their life what pernicious lessons they learned in its precincts, then you have done what in you lay to combat the great cause which God created you to promote; you have abused all that power which he put in your keeping and it is surely with an ill grace you ask for more, with all this ground to believe that if you had more you would do worse.

III. God gave us our social affections not as instruments of pain, not as fetters to enslave us but as bands of strength wherewith we might better bear our burden by sharing it; to be sources of delight, to furnish new motives to industry in multiplying the powers of the body and the mind. By drawing us to each other by the strong cords of friendship and love he invested the fireside with its sacred delights, appointing therein to man the place to be born and the place to die, and surrounding the name of home with its sweet and solemn associations. Our gratitude to him should teach us its use and honor; should write his name on the best of his gifts. If his name is to be honoured anywhere let it be among our brothers and sisters, our parents and friends. Let us not hide our hopes and duties there, in dumb ingratitude. Let us bear one another's burdens. Let us aid each other in our difficult emergencies. When fortune has thrown us into foreign lands, when the tokens of affection we receive from afar make the eye wet and the heart yearn to that distant home, let its beautiful remembrance come over the soul with the force of religious recollection, animating us to duty, deterring us from sin. It will seem to us a new revelation sent to us from Heaven.

Death

My friends,[3] these ties are soon to be severed, for such is the lot of man. And it may aid us to form a just judgment upon the value of the character of these virtues if we consider what it is when death has stricken us that gives the best consolation to the bereaved. Inquire of those who mourn what they have found in the memory of the dead that was able to supply any comfort to the desolate heart. Was it the advantages of external prosperity, of advancing rank in society, of mortal beauty or success that saved the cherished image from being a source of hopeless sorrow? No! they are gone forever, and left no wreck behind. Was it the triumphs of genius? Alas! they gave but keener edge to disappointment. But was it not the remembrance of the private virtues of those we deplore, 'the daily beauty of their life' in that home of which they were the pride and honor? Is it not these recollections that slowly abate the poignancy of grief because we believe that the character of which these were the graces could not die and yet shines with the same in the purer light of a spiritual world?

My friends, let *us* learn to show piety at home. It will aid us in that work to keep always in view the difficulties that stand in the way. It is the want of a definite point to which we should direct our efforts. What is the history of every Sabbath? Men come to church and struck with the force of some divine truth which is here presented, their consciences also bearing it witness, they make on the spot a good resolution and mean to keep it. But the service is done, they go home and the old accustomed rooms suggest old and accustomed feelings. They are put off their guard and when the temptation comes their altered purpose has been forgotten and they break their vow. This danger is to be met by a correspondent care. Let us contract our purpose that we may concentrate our strength. Let us aim to spend a single hour of perfect purity and call God to our witness and aid. Let us aim to spend *one single hour* of every day without spot or blemish, without an error even in thought and give ourselves with our might to the performance.[4]

ON SHOWING PIETY AT HOME

God will bless the purpose. If it be sincerely attempted doubt not of success. Though you may labour with mortal infirmity, though you may fail once and again, you shall be backed by Omnipotence and shall not fail in the end. That hour you shall find the auspicious season that shall send out its good influences on every portion of your life and fortune. And when the clock strikes and tolls out its departure and you consider that the seal of your own praise is set to it, that one virtuous hour is safe beyond the reach of accident and it is gone to bear its unalterable witness to your character on high, it shall fill your breast with solemn gladness, it shall infuse the good contagion of its own virtue into the other hours of the day, it shall be blessed in your memory to the last hour of your life.

My friends, I should esteem myself most happy and successful if the doctrine I have attempted to recommend might weigh with any of you to set yourselves to this experiment, to make this small venture for your everlasting welfare. You will believe me, it will not subtract one moment of real enjoyment from the life it is to glorify, one individual pleasure that deserves the name from the home where it is tried. It will make that home you love, no matter how poor and unfurnished, no matter though the wind blows, the venerable home of all virtue and good hope, where angels shall visit, and the glory of the Almighty shall overshadow it with his wings. And when that day which comes to all shall come to you, of sickness and death, it shall bereave it of its pang and translate you to the resplendent home of all the good, of the innumerable armies of martyrs, of saints and angels and of God, the Judge of all.

The Christian Minister: Part I.

I am not ashamed of the Gospel of Christ: for it is the power of God unto salvation to every one that believeth.   Romans I, 16.

I AM NOT ashamed of the gospel of Christ, said the Apostle Paul; it was the declaration of a valiant heart. In him, it was no superfluous tender of adhesion to a cause already strong enough, nor arrogance of courage where no danger was. It was a challenge that a martyr gives to all terror of pain. It bid calamity do its worst — his part was taken, his soul was fixed. It was the pledge of mortifications to be borne; of advantages bravely given up; of infamy to be suffered in the place of renown; of indefatigable toils, of anxious days, of sleepless nights, of hourly exposure to death which would come at last in some hideous form. It was not alone that he undertook to be the patron of an opinion new and unknown, the brother of a low and obscure sect, the friend of the friendless, the lover of what men called vulgar and vile. Oh no, the world whose pride he insulted by his aversion and his doctrine was not to be appeased by a verdict of silent contempt. The Jew and the Pagan cried Blood! against the execrated schismatic, the lean beasts of the amphitheatre were unchained and let slip on him. And where he went, he heard the hisses of the world.[1]

The Apostle of the Gentiles made good his words with his life. He bore all. He overcame evil with good. He endured to the end. He came off more than conqueror from the field of his battle.

THE CHRISTIAN MINISTER: PART I

Paul of Tarsus died triumphing at Rome, his head being severed from his body by the command of Nero. My friends, I do not recall the memory of this sad life and this celebrated murder with any view of awakening in you an useless sympathy, a departed indignation. You look upon this story as I do. We do not count it any marvel that Paul was not ashamed of his faith. In our minds the association is familiar of seeming wretchedness with real glory. We know by heart from God's word what is the style of God's Providence. The mind leaps at once from the sufferings of virtue to its eternal reward. Why was not Paul ashamed of the gospel of Christ? Let us hear his answer — 'Because it is the power of God unto salvation.' Or in other words, 'because it hath a divine power for the salvation of every believer.'

My brethren, if we can conceive the feeling that animated Paul, it is easy to adopt the language of Paul. I am well aware that it is one thing for me at this day here in the bosom of my friends and the friends of Christianity to say I am not ashamed of the gospel and quite another thing for Paul to say so amidst timid friends and frantic foes and before the ragged front of Roman persecution. But for other reasons than the fear of danger and for reasons more cogent than fear in their action upon a well constituted mind — I take these words to myself. I believe that after eighteeen hundred years of exposition and diffusion and influence the effects of the Gospel are small and feeble; that is, small and feeble, considered in relation to the source from which it came, and the power that is in it. Christianity is the decent and reverend religion of our land, and therefore we support it. We are Christians by the same title as we are New England men, that herein we were born and reared. I know that men who do not love the Gospel do not know what it is; and I believe that many religious men do not derive from it all the comfort they could. I see the grossest ignorance and the most injurious prejudices existing in regard to that which I love and honour. I grieve to see men esteem as tyranny what

I feel to be a law of love. I am pained to remark a secret fear or dislike of what is full of beauty and full of glory. And now that the occasion to which all the years of my education have looked forward has come to me of bearing my testimony to the value of my faith, I wish to take up again these ancient words. I rejoice to perceive and to affirm that eighteen centuries justify the sentiment. What Paul said to the great and powerful of this world, I will say to the wise of this world — I am not ashamed of the Gospel of Christ, for it is the power of God unto salvation.

By the public services of the last week, my Christian brethren, a very interesting relation was established. You have called me to the pastoral office. I have accepted the charge. You have summoned the fathers and brethren of the churches to ordain me, by the ancient and simple rites of prayer and the imposition of hands, to the sacred work. I have been admonished of my responsibility and counselled in my course. The hand of the fellowship of the churches has been given me and I have been sent forth on my way with God's blessing invoked upon my head by the good and the wise.

I have attempted to weigh in the balance of an even judgment the advantages and the difficulties of this office and I embrace with alacrity this occasion of complying with a most reasonable usage which expects of the newly installed pastor some statement of his views of the duties which his engagements impose upon him.

The first and obvious distribution of the duties of a Christian minister, is into the two classes of public ministrations and of pastoral visits. I wish to speak to both these points.

The principal public performances of a minister are prayer and preaching.

Of the nature and reasonableness and of what constitutes a successful performance of the first of these offices, there is but one opinion among good men. How rarely the gift of prayer is possessed in any high degree of excellence, I am well aware.

THE CHRISTIAN MINISTER: PART I

It is a fruit of a frame of mind. It is to be sought in the affections and not in the intellect; to be compassed by the love of God rather than by the study of books. Most of you, my friends, have probably experienced at some time the power of a fervent prayer upon your mind. If you have, you know it to be singular in its excellence: it doth soothe and refresh and edify the soul as no other exercises can.[2]

But it is not so much by efforts to make good prayers that the minister is to succeed in producing the blessed effect at which he aims, as by leading a good life. That man who studies to act always with a secret reference to God — who finds God on his left hand and on his right in every place and in every event, who feels that when he muses in the silence of his own soul, God is there — can hardly fail to call his Father by names which he will acknowledge and in tones and sentiments that shall find their echo in every pious heart.

The second public duty of a Christian minister is *preaching*, — a high and difficult office. In prayer he is only the voice of the congregation, he merely utters the petitions which all feel.[3] In preaching he undertakes to instruct the congregation, himself an erring man, to deal out to his brethren the laws of the Almighty, to carry the conviction of duty home to their hearts, to encourage the faint hearted, to persuade the reluctant, to melt the obdurate, and to shake the sinner. That man has very low and humble views of this office who satisfies his conscience with uttering the commonplaces of religion for twenty or thirty minutes, reciting a lazy miscellany of quotations from Scripture[4] and then dismisses his unfed unedified audience, hugging himself that he has not spoken an offensive syllable, and that he has come off so cheaply from his Sabbath work.[5]

Even with this slovenly performance of his part, I know, many hearts will reap their own advantage from his words, because they are already in that devout frame that any holy text is sufficient to raise and fix their thoughts on heaven. But the preacher has not the less been unfaithful to his charge.

25

He has done much to exhaust the charity of the charitable, he has disgusted the intelligent, he has furnished an apology to the indifferent and a triumph to the scoffer. But it is not so much the evil he has done as the good he has failed to do, that I regard. He has missed an opportunity of perfecting good purposes that were ripening already; there were temptations that his breath might have blown away, there were apprehensions which he might have soothed, and doubts which he might have cleared. The mightiest engine which God has put into the hands of man to move man is eloquence.[6] I believe there is not one of us, my brethren, whose opportunities have been so abridged, living in this free state, as never to have witnessed its prodigious effects. When great sentiments call it out from a great mind and especially when it rises to topics of eternal interest, it is glorious to see how it masters the mind, how it bows the independence of a thousand to the reason of one; how it goes on with electrical swiftness from unobserved beginnings, lifting him that speaks and them that hear, above the dust and smoke of life, searching out every noble purpose, every sublime hope that lurks in the soul. Then is that sympathy lofty and pure; then the speaker and the hearer become the pipes on which a higher power speaketh. It is like the breath of the Almighty moving on the deep.

Now different men have the gifts essential to this divine art in very different measure. Yet in every man the principles of it lie, and every man who gives himself wholly up to a just sentiment which he lives to inculcate, will be eloquent. But the careless preacher leaves this weapon of matchless force to sleep in sloth and disuse. God keep me from this frigid indifference.

Brethren, when I consider the true nature and dignity of the office I have sought, whilst I am oppressed by the perception of my own incompetence I am animated to exertion by all the motives that can invigorate and gratify hope. There have been times and places where the name of a priest was opprobri-

THE CHRISTIAN MINISTER: PART I

What is wrong with pulpit

ous. The office must always have honour or shame from the manner in which it is borne. But the office of the priesthood was never made for contempt. To my eye when its duties are ably discharged it is the most august station which man can fill. But to be worthily filled — to be a preacher equal to the demands of the times and to the hope of the times, preaching must be manly and flexible and free beyond all the example of the times before us.

The reason why Christianity has found so many open enemies and so many lukewarm friends is not a defect in Christianity itself but a defect in its teaching. Christianity is true. What is true can never be ridiculous; it is falsehood and mistake that are ridiculous and mean. If Christianity were taught always in a manner as simple, absolute and universal as its truth is, nobody could look down upon it. In itself, no man can look down upon it. It is not the Christian faith but a vain imagination of his own, which the skeptic sees and rejects, — a poor, distorted copy which the ignorance of men has formed and which unfaithful teachers have confirmed. The world was wrong and the pulpit has not set it right. It seems to me that our usage of preaching is too straitened. It does not apply itself to all the good and evil that is in the human bosom. It walks in a narrow round; it harps on a few and ancient strings. It is much addicted to a few words: it holds on to phrases when the lapse of time has changed their meaning. Men imagine that the end and use of preaching is to expound a text and to unfold the divisions and subdivisions of meaning of *Grace*, of *Justification*, of *Atonement*, of *Sanctification*, and are permitted to forget that Christianity is an infinite and universal law which touches all action, all passion, all rational being; that it is the revelation of a Deity whose being the soul cannot reject without denying itself; that it is a rule of action that teaches us to attain the highest good of intelligent nature; a rule which penetrates into every moment, and into the smallest duty; that it is always seasonable; that it is our support, our comfort;

that it is our spiritual home; yes, religion is the *home of the mind,* from which man may wander, but he wanders unhappy, and bewails at every new departure his inability to return.

These views of Christianity should always be present to the mind of him who would preach as becomes those who bring the oracles of God.

I shall labour then, brethren, as far as my poor abilities will reach, to use a freedom in my preaching befitting the greatness of the Gospel and its universal application to all human concerns. I shall not be so much afraid of innovation [7] as to scruple about introducing new forms of address, new modes of illustration, and varied allusions into the pulpit, when I believe they can be introduced with advantage. I shall not certainly reject them simply because they are new. I must not be crippled in the exercise of my profession. If there is any talent, any learning, any resource, any accomplishment, which I can use and convert to the service of this Gospel, whose servant I am, I shall without hesitation avail myself of it. As there is not a grain of sand nor a wretched weed quaking in the wind, but contributes its part, an essential part, to the gravity of the globe, and the equipoise of the system; so all the facts in the universe, rightly seen, attest the truth of Religion. If to me were given that starlike vision which could see and make report how they all bear evidence to it, I cheerfully would. But I cannot. I am humbled at my ignorance. I see a few and dim parts. It would be silly to shut myself voluntarily within a yet narrower circle, and only use a part of my pittance of truth.

I have spoken thus at length upon this important part of clerical duty which more than any other marks and characterizes the minister because I was anxious to meet on the threshold an objection that I thought would lie in the minds of many cautious Christians against modes of preaching which I may think it prudent and they may think it bold to adopt. I am well aware that no apology however satisfactory, can ever make bad preaching useful,[8] and that good preaching of whatever cast will carry its own vindication. Still I am willing to fortify by the highest authority my opinions, if any one hereafter should object to me the want of sanctity in my style, and the want of solemnity in my illustrations.[9] I shall remind him, that the language and the images of Scripture which his ear requires, derive all their dignity from their association with divine truth; that they belonged once to what was low and familiar; that our Lord in his discourses condescended to explain himself by allusions to every homely fact, to the boys in the market, to the persons dropping into the custom offices; to the food on the board, to the civilities shown him by the hospitality of his entertainers; and would he not, let me ask, if he addressed himself to the men of this age and of this country, appeal with equal frequency to those arts and objects by which we are surrounded, to the printing press and the loom, to the phenomena of steam and of gas, to the magnificence of towns, to free institutions, and a petulant and vain nation?

It may be easily inferred that my views of my duty as a Christian teacher impose on me the necessity of giving to my own mind the highest cultivation, and that of every kind my manner of life will permit. *It imperiously demands the critical knowledge of the Christian Scriptures, which are to be considered the direct voice of the most High — the reason of God speaking to the reason of man.*[10] But does it less demand the contemplation of his benevolence and his might in his works? It demands a discipline of the intellect, but more than all it demands a training of the affections. Whatever else can be shared this is essential. Any defects can be excused but the defect of a pure heart and a good life.

Having thus expressed my views of what preaching should be, the same views must regulate my expectation of its fruits. The success must be of the same kind as the exertion. I do not plant a vine and gather corn. But as I plant, I hope to reap. It is a sad and meagre commendation of a Christian minister, when the departing congregation whisper to each other the praises of his manner, his language, and his voice and congratulate themselves on a skilful emphasis, or a musical period, and then go away and remember the service no more. Believe me, brethren, if this is the top of my success, I have miserably failed of my end. Far be it from me, both now and hereafter — that wretched vanity which sits down contented with the serenade of friendly praises on no better foundation than these accidental advantages. But if I can add any distinctness to your idea of God, any beauty to your notion of virtue; [11] if I can represent the life of Christ in such vivid and true colours as to exalt your love; if I can persuade one young man to check the running tide of sensual pleasure by the force of moral obligation; if I can prevail with one old man to forgive an injury that has rankled in his breast till hatred has grown into habit, out of regard to the example of Jesus and his law of love; if I can arrest one angry sarcasm of wounded pride in the moment of irritation, one syllable of slander as it trembles on the tongue, by the memory of the motives I have called to your aid; if a sermon of mine shall be remembered as a solace in the chamber of sorrow, if when the eye of one of you is closing forever on this world, your spirit, as it passes, shall thank me for one triumphant hope, — then, my brethren, it is praise enough, then I shall bless God that I have not been wholly wanting to his cause, that, by me, one mite is added to the sum of happiness.

The Christian Minister: Part II.

But we preach not ourselves but Christ Jesus the Lord, and ourselves your servants for Jesus' sake.   Second Corinthians IV, 5.

IN THE former part of this discourse I considered the two leading public offices of the Christian minister. There remain for our consideration his performance of the sacraments of matrimony, of baptism, and of the Lord's Supper, and his duties as a pastor. I shall then request your candour to some brief remarks upon the expectations a minister may form, founded on a faithful discharge of his own duties, of sympathy and cooperation in his purposes from the people of his charge.

He is called to bear a part in the most important and solemn occasions that belong to human life. It is his to tie the bands of wedlock, to bind on the part of heaven the league of affections between man and wife necessary to the existence and order of society, to turn the water of a civil into the wine of a holy union. It is his to sprinkle the newborn man with water, to mark the acquisition of one more intelligent being into the great family of the Father of the universe. There is nothing trifling, nothing insignificant in this event and baptism is the application of our faith to it. The account that we give of the existence of the human race is the benevolence of the Deity, who doth not sit in the solitude of his own perfections but rejoices in adding continually and infinitely to the amount of happiness and pouring forth around him the profusion of being and of joy. And surely nothing can be more suitable and right than to mix a religious feeling with the parents' gladness, to consecrate to God this his last creation, to set His name and His son's name on the forehead of the new moral agent now in the morning of the immeasurable day of his action and virtue.

Of a very different character and interest is the other rite of Christian usage. The Lord's Supper [1] is usually regarded, and I think not with sufficient reason, as a melancholy memorial. It commemorates, we say, the *dying love* of Christ. Yes, but he has conquered death, and he, the Head of the Church who bends over us as we sit at his board, is now our Friend and Intercessor at his Father's throne. But with whatever associations we come it commemorates his love and so comes with an aspect that to most minds the other injunctions of religion do not wear. This is the symbol of a holy affection. And so it opens the doors of the heart. He therefore who adventures to break the bread and pour out the waters of life should be himself susceptible of emotion. The minister should be a man of feeling, or I fear he will vainly endeavour to excite movements in other souls that have no archetypes in his own.

But, brethren, you have not called me only to read and unfold to you according to my ability the oracles of God and to discharge the customary public functions of marriage, of baptism and breaking of bread in the name of Christ; you have called me to affectionate and *domestic* relations as your pastor.

This day is in all things to me a day of hope. Whilst I am permitted to speak of myself I am rather describing to you my hopes than my expectations. I can easily conceive a perfection in the performance of a minister's duties which far exceeds the low limit of my powers. But we must aim high to secure any good. It is better to fail in our efforts in a good cause, than not to have striven in it. Suffer me then whilst I run over with curiosity and hope the scene that opens before me.

In order to be of any use to you as a pastor I must be regarded in a just light. It is fatal to that success which a good

THE CHRISTIAN MINISTER: PART II

pastor can look for when he is eyed as an austere zealot whose severe eye is always wary to pick flaws in your practice and error in your doctrine, who is always eager to bring you to the confessional, who strikes prattling childhood dumb with awe and disgusts lighthearted youth; a man whose mouth is full of menace; who is the tyrant of sick beds; and the tormentor of the dying. He forgets that he is the messenger of the Prince of Peace, the Herald of glad tidings of great joy, that whilst he knows the terrors of the law he should persuade men. Nor less when he is regarded as a man aloof from other men, a peculiar officer important when his own occasions come, but out of place where health and enterprise and friendship meet; whose form is contemned in the sunshine of ease and only grateful in the shade of a cloud.[2]

Not thus must the pastor be esteemed, who can hope to serve you in Jesus Christ, but as the mild and blameless friend who would win you to a life of purity by the shining example of his own; who does not affect to hate the good and the glory of this world, but has been led by the very lustre and harmony of things below, to the belief in something better; who sees with an affectionate eye your prosperity and seeing it harmonize with his views of a Providence always secretly directing the succession of human affairs, desires to come and tell you so and bid you thank God and not your own right hand; who sees with emotion your affliction and seeing by his own experience how it can be made to redound to your good, how, when a little time has passed, you may be made to bless God that it came to you, comes in, with sorrow as a man, for your pain, but with triumph as a Christian, in that clear and strong hope which conquers calamity and conquers death.

But the condition of man has one hour further of yet more solemn interest than the affliction that strikes nearest to us. The hour will come to yourself to die. (It will come to each of us. It belongs to God's order which we call nature as much as hunger or sleep. Here, under the canopy of heaven, we grow up, we ripen to manhood, and we decay.) In a few years or months or days the symptoms of that change will appear in you. The alarm will sound in the ear of your mind, that you have done with men, and men have done with you. You will be withdrawn by a weakness you cannot stimulate, from the living crowd that fill the street. In your various places of resort, you shall be sought but you shall not be found. In the shop, along the wharves, in the bank, in the exchange, in the courts, in social parties, in the church — you shall be missed. You have retreated to your chamber to a solitude which the world cannot relieve. I say you are alone; it is true you are nursed by the cares and assured of the sympathies of your friends. They knock at your door and they offer you — what men can. But alas, my brother, is that solitude less? When the system is convulsed with its last throbs; when all the aids of nature and art have been exhausted in vain — is not he alone who sees the shades of the last night shutting down over his senses, though the whole world environed his bed, and armies of friends cry out at his side? What would it avail? Can they hold him back? Ah, my brethren, at that hour wealth and poverty, genius, power and wretchedness, are all alike; even friendship bewails its weakness, and the dearest affection — what can it do? One medicine there is, one solace, one hope. Into that solitude the man of God shall introduce a sweeter society than the merriment of health has ever made; into that darkness of this world the good pastor shall let in the light of another. Yes, brethren, when God enables him to reach the ends of his blameless ambition the good pastor may illuminate with glory the gloom of the chamber of death.³ In that hour, at least, when trifles are neglected and ceremony is forgot I hope to be understood and esteemed as an effectual friend, that the tidings which I bring, that the cause in whose strength I come, will give power to my weakness. I that am your fellow in the same fate by God appointed will endeavour to quicken your faith by the same motives that sustain my own. We will talk of

THE CHRISTIAN MINISTER: PART II

the Resurrection from the Dead. We will call to mind the words of the Friend of the human race to his elder disciples, 'Yet a little while and ye shall see me.' We will think of the love he bore us. We will comfort one another by the thought of the benevolence of God which having encompassed us with so many blessings here, may surely be trusted with our future welfare. We will talk of the new heavens and the new earth, till the earth shall fade before the magnificence of the growing vision. Across the darkness so long dreaded of the valley of death, we will behold the Mount of our Hope lifting its everlasting summits into light. And though our flesh fail and our heart fail we will rejoice in the Lord, we will glory in the God of our salvation.

I dwell on this capital duty of the pastor because it is the reason why pastors are made.[4] For the hour of death all other hours prepare. Why are we here? What else is the motive of all this apparatus of a clergy and worship? Why do the sabbath bells sound and whence is the interest so bright and so tremendous of this Book? If we did not die, there were no need of religious monitors to prick us on to duty. If we did not die life in its long course would be sermon and monition enough; the moral laws of God would assert themselves by their effects: virtue would be seen to produce happiness, and the want of virtue to inflict woe, as undeniably as the sun produces light and the absence of the sun produces darkness. But life is short and we hardly get over its illusions before it is time to put on our shroud. God calls and eternity presses on whilst we lose our time in the ancient mistake, pursuing seeming for solid good. Hence the need of loud alarms, of bibles, of tracts, of prayers, of churches, of ministers, of afflictions, of pains.

These, brethren, are the scenes and occasions of pastoral duty and it is a consideration of much importance that the habits of the pastor are essential to a faithful and successful preacher. Human nature is so much the same in all its forms that a man who draws with any accuracy his pictures of virtue and vice from such a range of acquaintance as most men possess, will continually present traits and dispositions which you recognize as familiar to your own experience. When he drew the character of his friend it tallied with the character of yours. Still the preaching of a stranger must always be cold and unaffecting in comparison with the preaching of the pastor. For he sees only the outside of the people. He has no light to guide him in the selection of topics. Many of his exhortations must be aimed at random and when he has reached the heart, he is ignorant of his success, and again is ignorant that he has gone wide of the mark. But when he has come into your acquaintance, when he has sat by your fire and established relations of friendship and confidence with you, when he knows the story of your lives, what you suffer and what you hope, your reputation in the town and the prospects of your children, then he possesses a key to your hearts. He knows the good man's urgent motive, he knows the sinner's vulnerable side, he knows the doubt that perplexes you, what secret satisfaction you nourish and to what virtues you most incline. He will find the subjects of his exhortation in your sick chambers, and bereaved houses, in your parlour, and in the societies to which you belong. Besides, when he comes into the pulpit he comes into the midst of his friends; he knows their goodwill has prepared a welcome for his message, a kind interpretation to his remarks. He is sure of being understood, they are familiar with his modes of thought and will not complain of a vague and uncertain impression because they know he is to return from the pulpit to their fireside, and is always ready to explain in the parlour what was obscure in the desk.[5] It is abundantly plain what additional force and effect his preaching must derive from these facts.

It is usual on occasions like the present for the new pastor to disclose to his people his views of their duty in relation to himself. I have spoken so long upon my own duties that I have left myself little time to remind you of yours. It can be the

THE CHRISTIAN MINISTER: PART II

more easily excused because (to use that ancient and hallowed metaphor) [6] I do not come to reclaim sheep that wander in the wilderness without a shepherd — but I come to do in weakness what has been done in strength, to help, as I can, the spiritual progress of those who have loved their spiritual guide as he deserved to be loved, and have never been wanting to him.[7] I doubt not, brethren, of your readiness to extend to me every reasonable indulgence and all cordial cooperation in every good word and work. Still, there is an expectation that will operate unfavorably on my inexperience arising from the very signal merits which have created among you so warm a sympathy in your minister. I cannot leave this allusion without one remark. I am not permitted at this hour to indulge myself in dwelling on the virtues of my elder brother. It is well. They need no praise. I am permitted to congratulate you and myself that his counsel and sympathy are not withdrawn; to believe that whilst he exists his heart is here. His prayers and his hopes shall be blended with ours. But I must beseech you, brethren, to consider that no man can suddenly be a good pastor. It is an office in which experience is more necessary than any gifts. You must overlook many mistakes. You must forgive many seeming neglects, you must forgive many real omissions. You must impute a good purpose where you can, and the moment that even charity cannot find a palliation for an action of mine, you must frankly come and tell me my fault. Confidence invites confidence and I earnestly desire that between you and me no strangeness or reserve should ever exist. I hope to be received on the footing of familiar acquaintance in your houses, and to be sought without ceremony in mine.[8] Let it be considered by you, brethren, how essential it is to every hope of making me useful to you that the freest intercourse should subsist between us. If then the young have any project, any purpose which I can aid, let them be deterred by no mistimed scruples from coming to me as to a brother who is anxious to serve them. If those who have reached mature age, if those who are grown old have any counsel to impart, have any anxiety, any doubt, any coldness of faith, let them in kindness inform me, assured that my diligence shall not be wanting to them.

In fine, brethren, give me your countenance, your sympathy, your counsels, and your prayers. And forget the imperfections of the workman in your interest in his work, remembering that we are ambassadors for Christ as though God did beseech you, by us; that we pray you in Christ's stead, 'Be ye reconciled to God.'

And now, brethren, I enter on my duties with all good hope, but without levity and without presumption. I feel the force of the vows that are on me, to work the work of him that sends me, in prosperity and in adversity, in honour and in reproach, by speech and by action, from year to year, as long as God shall endue me with strength and opportunity. I feel the encouragements, I hear the warnings that come to me, as I approach, a youth and a stranger, to this ancient temple. I seem to tread on holy ground. I raise this day a feeble voice in walls that have echoed the voices of the elder saints and holy fathers of the New England church. Do we err, brethren, in deeming that their glorified spirits encompass our assembly, and delight in the places whence the incense of their prayers ascended? They call on you, they call on me, to make clean and holy the hands that are to lift up in our day and generation, the ark of their testimony. They call to us, to aspire to the glory they now partake, by the same steps on which they mounted, by faith, by obedience, by prayer, and by love.

Summer

The day is thine, the night also is thine: thou hast prepared the light, and the sun. Thou hast set all the borders of the earth, thou hast made summer. Psalm LXXIV, 16, 17.

IN THIS grateful season, the most careless eye is caught by the beauty of the external world. The most devoted of the sons of gain cannot help feeling that there is pleasure in the blowing of the southwest wind; that the green tree with its redundant foliage and its fragrant blossoms shows fairer than it did a few weeks since when its arms were naked and its trunk was sapless. The inhabitants of cities pay a high tax for their social advantages, their increased civilization, in their exclusion from the sight of the unlimited glory of the earth. Imprisoned in streets of brick and stone, in tainted air and hot and dusty corners, they only get glimpses of the glorious sun, of the ever changing glory of the clouds, of the firmament and of the face of the green pastoral earth which the great Father of all is now adorning with matchless beauty as one wide garden. Still something of the mighty process of vegetation forces itself on every human eye. The grass springs up between the pavements at our feet and the poplar and the elm send out as vigorous and as graceful branches to shade and to fan the town as in their native forest.

Those who yield themselves to these pleasant influences behold in the activity of vegetation a new expression from moment to moment of the Divine power and goodness.[1] They know that this excellent order did not come of itself, that this organized creation of every new year indicates the presence of God. They see him in the small leaf, in the wide meadow, in the sea and the cloud.

We are confident children, confident in God's goodness. Though we all of us know that the year's subsistence to us depends on the fidelity with which rain and sun shall act on the seed, we never doubt the permanence of the Order. We do not refer our own subsistence, especially in cities, to the rain and the sun and the soil. We do not refer the loaf in our basket, or the meats that smoke on our board to the last harvest. And when we do, we fail often to derive from the changes of nature that lesson which to a pious, to a Christian mind they ought to convey.

My brethren, all nature is a book on which one lesson is written and blessed are the eyes that can read it. On the glorious sky it is writ in characters of fire; on earth it is writ in the majesty of the green ocean; it is writ on the volcanoes of the south, and the icebergs of the polar sea; on the storm, in winter; in summer on every trembling leaf; on man in the motion of the limbs, and the changing expression of the face, in all his dealings, in all his language it is seen and may be read and pondered and practised in all. This lesson is the omnipresence of God [2] — the presence of a love that is tender and boundless. Yet man shuts his eyes to this sovereign goodness, thinks little of the evidence that comes from nature, and looks upon the great system of the world only in parcels as its order happens to affect his petty interest. In the seasons he thinks only whether a rain or sunshine will suit his convenience. In the regions of the world he thinks only of his farm or his town. Let us lift up our eyes to a more generous and thankful view of the earth and the seasons.

Do they not come from Heaven and go like Angels round the globe, scattering hope and pleasant toil and recompense and rest? Each righting the seeming disorders, supplying the defects

SUMMER

which the former left; converting its refuse into commodity, and drawing out of the ancient earth new treasures to swell the capital of human comfort. Each fulfils the errand on which it was sent. The faintness and despondence of a spring that never opened into summer; the languor of a constant summer; the satiety of an unceasing harvest; the torpor or the terror of a fourfold winter are not only prevented by the ordination of Providence, but they are not feared; and emotions of an opposite character are called forth as we hail the annual visits of these friendly changes at once too familiar to surprise and too distinct and distant to weary us. It is in these as they come and go, that we may recognize the steps of our heavenly Father. We may accustom our minds to discern his power and benevolence in the profusion and the beauty of his common gifts, as the wheat and the vine. Nor do these seem sufficiently appreciated. We look at the works of human art — a pyramid, a stately church, and do not conceal our pleasure and surprize at the skill and force of men to lift such masses and to create such magnificent forms, which skill after all does but remove, combine, and shape the works of God. For the granite, and the marble, and the hands that hewed them from the quarry, are his work.[3] But after they are builded, and the scaffolding is thrown down, and they stand in strength and beauty, there is more exquisite art goes to the formation of a strawberry [4] than is in the costliest palace that human pride has ever reared. In the constitution of that small fruit is an art that eagle eyed science cannot explore but sits down baffled. It cannot detect how the odour is formed and lodged in these minute vessels, or where the delicate life of the fruit resides.

Our patient science explores as it can, every process, opens its microscopes upon every fibre, and hunts every globule of sap that ascends in the stem but it never has detected the secret it seeks. It cannot restore the vegetable it has dissected and analyzed. Where should we go for an ear of corn if the earth refused her increase? With all our botany how should we trans-

41

form a seed into an ear, or make from the grain of one stalk the green promise and the full harvest that covers acres with its sheaves? The frequency of occurrence makes it expected that a little kernel properly sowed, will become at harvest time a great number of kernels. Because we have observed the same result on many trials, this multiplication is expected. But explain to me, man of learning! any part of this productiveness. There is no tale of metamorphosis in poetry, no fabulous transformation that children read in the Arabian Tales more unaccountable, none so benevolent as this constant natural process which is going on at this moment in every garden, in every foot of vacant land in three zones of the globe.

Go out into a garden and examine a seed; examine the same plant in the bud and in the fruit, and you must confess the whole process a miracle, a perpetual miracle. Take it at any period, make yourself as familiar with all the facts as you can at each period, and in each explanation there will be some step or appearance to be referred directly to the Great Creator; something not the effect of the sower's deposit, nor of the waterer's hope. It is not the loam, nor the gravel, it is not the furrow of the ploughshare nor the glare of the sun that calls greenness from the dust, it is the present power of Him who said 'Seed-time and harvest shall not fail.' Needs there, my brethren, any other book than this returning summer that reminds us of the first creation, to suggest the Presence of God? Shall we indulge our querulous temper in this earth where nature is fragrant with healthful odours and glowing with every pleasant colour? Man marks with emphatic pleasure or complaint the pleasant and the unpleasant days, as if he forgot the uses of the storm, the masses of vapour it collects and scatters over thirsty soil, and the plants that were hardened or moistened by that rough weather, forgot the ships that were borne homeward by the breeze that chills him, or in short as if he forgot that our Father is in Heaven, and the winds and the seas obey him.

SUMMER

We have been looking at Nature as an exhibition of God's benevolence. It will be felt the more to be so when it is considered that *the same results might have been brought about without this beauty.* The earth contains abundant materials for the nourishment of the human stomach, but they do not exist there in a state proper for our use. Now the tree, the vegetable may be properly considered as a machine by which the nutritious matter is separated from other elements, is taken up out of chalk, and clay, and manures, and prepared as by a culinary process into grateful forms and delicious flavours for the pleasure of our taste and for our sustenance. The little seed of the apple does not contain the large tree that shall spring from it; it is merely an assimilating engine which has the power to take from the ground whatever particles of water or manure it needs, and turn them to its own substance and give them its own arrangement.

For the nourishment of animal life this process goes on and to such incomputable activity and extent, not in one spot, not in one land, but on the whole surface of the globe. Each soil is finishing its own, and each a different fruit. Not only on the hard soil of New England, the oak, the potato and the corn are swelling their fruit but on the shores of the Red Sea the coffee tree is ripening its berries; on the hills of France and Spain the grape is gathering sweetness. The West Indies are covered with the green canes and the East with spices and the mulberries for the silkworm, the cotton plant is bursting its pod in the warm plantations of the south, and the orange and the fig bloom in the Mediterranean islands.

But all this food might have been prepared as well without this glorious show. To what end this unmeasured magnificence? It is for the soul of man.[5] For his eye the harvest waves, for him the landscape wears this glorious show. For to what end else can it be! Can the wheat admire its own tasselled top?[6] Or the oak in autumn its crimson embroidered foliage, or the rose and the lily their embroidery?[7] If there were no mind in the universe to what purpose this profusion of design? It is for the same reason as the rainbow is beautiful and the sun is bright. It is adapted to give pleasure to us. I cannot behold the cheering beauty of a country landscape at this season without believing that it was intended that I should derive from it this pleasure.

But there is more in nature than beauty; there is more to be seen than the outward eye perceives; there is more to be heard than the pleasant rustle of the corn. There is the language of its everlasting analogies,[8] by which it seems to be the prophet and the monitor of the race of man. The Scripture is always appealing to the tree and the flower and the grass as the emblems of our mortal estate. It was the history of man in the beginning, and it is the history of man now. Man is like the flower of the field. In the morning he is like grass that groweth up; in the evening he is cut down and withereth. There is nothing in external nature but is an emblem, a hieroglyphic of something in us. Youth is the spring, and manhood the summer, and age the autumn, and death the winter of man. My brethren, do you say these things are old and trite? That is their very value and warning; so is the harvest old — the apple that hangs on your tree, six thousand times has shown its white bloom, its green germ, and its ripening yellow since our period of the world begins. And this day as the fruit is as fresh so is its moral as fresh and significant to us as it was to Adam in the garden.[9]

I have spoken of the great system of external nature as exciting in our minds the perception of the benevolence of God by the wonderful contrivance their fruits exhibit; by the food they furnish us, and by the beauty that is added to them; and now, of the admonition they seem intended to convey of our short life.

But there is yet a louder and more solemn admonition which they convey to my mind as they do from year to year their appointed work. They speak to man as a moral being, and

Are we as dependable as nature

SUMMER

reproach his lassitude by their brute fidelity. Here we sit waiting the growing of the grain, with an undoubting reliance. If it is blasted in one field, we are sure it will thrive in another. Yet we know that if one harvest of the earth fails, the race must perish from the face of the earth. We have an expectation always of the proper performance of the vegetable functions that would not be increased if one rose from the dead.

Well now, whilst thus directly we depend on this process, on the punctuality of the sun, on the timely action of saps and seed vessels, and rivers and rains, *are we as punctual to our orbit?* Are we as trustworthy as the weed at our feet? Yet is that a poor machine — and I, besides the animal machinery that is given me, have been entrusted with a portion of the spirit that governs the material, Creation, that made and directs the machinery. — Are ye not much better than they? Shall we to whom the light of the Almighty has been given, shall we who have been raised in the scale of the creation to the power of self government, not govern ourselves? Shall the flower of the field reprove us and make it clear that it had been better for us to have wanted than to have received intelligence?

My friends, let us accustom ourselves thus to look at the fruits of the earth and the seasons of the year. Let all that we see without, only turn our attention with stricter scrutiny on all that is within us. In the beautiful order of the world, shall man alone, the highly endowed inhabitant, present a spectacle of disorder, the misrule of the passions, and rebellion against the laws of his Maker? Let us learn also the lesson they are appointed to teach of trust in God; that he will provide for us if we do his will; remembering the words of the Lord Jesus, who said — 'If God so clothe the grass of the field, which today is and tomorrow is cast into the oven, will he not much more care for you, O ye of little faith!' [10]

Sounds trite, but exactly what man has done with natural resources.

Trifles

Martha thou art careful and troubled about many things; but one thing is needful.   Luke X, 41, 42.

WE DERIVE very solid advantages from society. The greater number of men you collect together the greater is the chance of finding great talents and virtues.[1] And the presence of great men always elevates the tone of feeling of a whole community. So the larger the population the greater is the division of labor, and as this takes place in the production of the refinements as well as in the necessaries of life, civilization is pushed farther on, the means of knowledge are multiplied, generous projects meet attention, the means of religious improvement, the excitements of religious sympathy abound and exalt themselves. A solitary man of an ardent spirit who has felt all the inconvenience of remote residence in limiting his knowledge and depriving him of sympathy looks with delight and desire at these advantages and wonders that they are so little regarded by those who have them. He contrasts with his own confined means the ease of procuring information. [There is hardly any town on the globe so remote, no institution so obscure, almost no private individual living or dead — but in the next street or within sight of your door is some man able to give ample satisfaction to your curiosity.] [2]

But these advantages are purchased by some considerable disadvantages. One of the evils of social life is its tendency to give importance to trifles.³ When man dwells in solitude, he attends only to the supply of real wants, and consults no opinion but his own. So in the country, where intercourse is less frequent and plain fare is procured by plain labour — men are very independent of appearances, and are little disposed to give undue importance to little things. The farmer looks upon clothes as things of use, and not of ornament. He puts on woolens in the cold, and cottons in the heat, without much regard to the shape or the colour of his dress. But as you approach cities, and as people are crowded together, they naturally come to regard each other's opinion much more. *Fashion* becomes a consideration of importance. People live so near, and in such continual familiarity, that the eye seems to grow microscopic. Dress and ceremony and a most exaggerated regard to opinion takes the place of the former simplicity. Vice, at least in its more refined forms, begins to be thought a less enormity than awkwardness and vulgarity, and the soul is beset with new temptations.

It is a very remarkable property of the human mind, its range of action. It is capable of the most comprehensive views that regard God and eternity, and it can dedicate its whole force to the merest straws. It is like the range of vision of the eye that explores the atmosphere and catches the dim outline of a mountain a hundred miles distant and examines the anatomy of the smallest insect. [And this extent of power often resides in the same individual to a remarkable degree. It is related of Frederic of Prussia that so minute was his love of order and his economy that whilst he marshalled the armies of Europe, he knew the situation of every bottle in his cellar.]⁴ This range of which the mind is capable from the most grand to the most minute objects, is a valuable power and exceedingly useful to us in our condition in the world. It gives body and certainty to our knowledge, and at the same time gives it a great extent. It seems to us borrowed of that Power which in the preservation of the whole universe, is ever mindful of the parts, which cuts the fine notches in the petal of a dandelion and hurls the globe in its orbit.

But it is full of danger, very liable to abuse. If you busy the natural eye too exclusively on minute objects, it gradually loses its powers of distant vision; and more surely will the eye of the mind grow dull and incapable of great contemplation which is daily degraded to little studies. If you are careful about many small things, you cannot fix your thoughts upon the one thing needful.

That this is a strong tendency of social life I think none will deny. Men cease to regard great principles, they turn from looking after truth itself, they turn from seeking simple duty, to consider *what is agreeable to other people*. What will offend others, is more avoided than what is injurious to oneself. Men become studious of whatever the eyes of others will notice, they are very careful of their dress, of their manners, of their house, and are not easily convinced that these are not really matters of gravest consequence. There are many parents who would discover much more emotion if their children appear in soiled or ragged clothes, than if they had shown stupidity or gross ignorance and be more disturbed by the awkwardness of a boy before a well bred acquaintance than at detecting him in an untruth. Indeed so strong is this tendency of society to magnify trifles, that there is something that excites derision as hopeless and romantic in persevering attempts to denounce them. Scarcely any man you meet but has his foible of this kind, and (which is worse) is vain of his foible. One man is curious in trinkets, another in the texture of his garments, a third in his horse, a fourth in his furniture, or the binding of his books. There is nothing so absurd or insignificant but you shall find men of respectable powers who are agitated and piqued about it. You shall see it in loathsome calculations of selfishness. You shall see a person of a capacity for great and generous views who will sit and meditate on the means of getting his chair nearer to the fire than his who sits next him. And many a man who would unhesitatingly risk his life on a generous cause is afraid of being surprized in the performance of some little menial office. 'Ah! what will people think?' is the voice that is heard in our houses, — a low lived rule of action! They forget in this snug accommodated well reputed way of life that they were made for sublime attainments. They forget that the watch is only a measure of time, that clothes are only for a covering, that a house is only a shelter, and that these are all the mere supply of the labourer's outward necessities so that he may go forward with his labour for moral excellence, and that it is the wildest perversion to decline from the straight path of the great ends and waste his energies on these toys of petty comforts.

To feel what nothings they are, consider how they appear, when great occasions come, wherever the soul is strongly excited. If one were introduced into the presence of a man of great powers of mind would he feel it to be of any importance to that person, that his clothes should be rich? On the other hand, every body knows what pleasure men find in describing the contrasts between the plain or mean appearance of any very celebrated man and their heated expectation. Who cares whether Columbus was rich or poor, awkward or graceful when he opened his eyes upon the New World? or who does not feel the superiority of great simplicity of living, and dress, and simplicity of character, whenever it is coupled with real greatness, over ostentation and luxury?

Go into a company of strangers. The eye is caught by the fine personal appearance and tasteful dress of different individuals, and makes its guesses of their merits by their shows. But the moment conversation begins, let one of the company discover a surpassing wit and extensive information and the most unerring and weighty sense, all those shows are forgotten. A respect is felt for that person which throws all these appearances of others utterly into the shade. Can graceful form or costly dress protect a fool from your pity or contempt? And who does not remember in his own history hours of great diligence or concentrated thought, or of ardent piety when he rose above the low region where these insect influences reign? For a few blessed hours, or days, perchance weeks, the soul was so exercised within, that the world without was slightly esteemed. He did not accurately know the articles of his food or the times of taking it, the colour of the walls, the trifles of more or less attention he chanced to receive.

The folly and the danger of this overestimate will be felt when it is considered that you must degrade them from their importance or they will degrade you. If you give yourself up to the habit of exaggerating their value, of supposing certain indifferent things essential to your comfort, they unman and enslave you. Nothing so small an annoyance but give it attention enough and it will become insupportable. If the buzz of a fly or the step of a person in a neighboring room disturbs you and you give up to it, it will presently master the whole attention of your ear and eye and mind till the trivial sound swells on your trembling nerves to the noise of thunder, and produces the most uncontrollable vexation.

And so it is with all trivial things. The man that calculates too nicely on comfort will find the habit too strong for him. He is sowing thistles. He is embarrassing the path of life with additional perplexities, multiplying the sources of his own chagrin. He that observeth the wind shall not sow, he that regardeth the clouds shall not reap.

It becomes a Christian to despise trifles. The first mark and stamp of a great soul is a contempt of them. It should be our prayer that we might give every being and thing in the universe its just measure of importance. Do not be ravished with a little success or a poor jest or a feast or a frolic nor depressed by a rainy day or an affront, a headache. Let the soul feel its dignity and duties; feel that it is God's beloved child, made for the contemplation of himself, — his works, his moral perfections; made for continual self improvement, made to love worthy minds, and so let the soul stay at home in its holy rest, and not hurry out to every sounding brass and tinkling cymbal. It would ill become the general of an army to take a furious part in every chance scuffle that fell out between stragglers in the lines, and surely it is more indecent for the soul, the lord of an immense inheritance of life and power in earth and in heaven, to be thrown into ecstasies of joy or grief for nothing. The Christian is not too curious about the course of unimportant events, nor too anxious about their convenience or inconvenience to himself. He lets the world go on — satisfied that it is ordered by Wisdom, and that good shall result from all its arrangements. He gives his strength to his great duties, knowing that the less will easily follow. Jesus rebuked the officiousness of Martha, too careful of trifles, too careless of instruction. Martha, thou art troubled about many things but Mary has chosen the good part.

In urging this small esteem of small matters I am far from wishing to praise an eccentricity which sometimes has been affected under colour of this very magnanimity. It is mere pretence. It is very different to slight trifles and to go studiously wrong in trifles. Our Saviour was ever graceful and decent in his deportment. And the highest minds have been marked by their simplicity. Newton never did any thing odd; had no tricks. It is recorded of him that he was not distinguished by any singularity, natural or affected, from any other individual.

Especially should this subject interest those who have the education of a child intrusted to them. A great principle that should be early impressed on the child's mind is to *despise trifles*. And do not destroy the effect of this rule by your own example. Do not confound the guilt of selfishness or of deception in his mind with that of carelessness. If your son has soiled his coat, or spilled his supper, do not let him imagine by your deportment that it is all one as if he had broken his word. Do not let this child in his first faltering steps on the world he is entering, and which should be opened before him as a place of conflict on which highest things are depending, as presenting the means and occasions of the laborious exercise of the intellect, and of heroic virtue, as a world of which he may be made a guide and a benefactor — do not teach him to be dainty in his food or nice of his dress. Show him the world as God's work; as the house in which wise and great and brave men have dwelled, that with all the evil, almost every spot of it is made venerable by their history — the theatre of their virtues; show him its science, show him it as the platform on which Newton and the astronomers have measured in miles the magnitude of the sun, the pathway of the planets and written down the changes of the system for a thousand years to come. Show him the sacrifices that have been made; how low men have been born, and how high they have risen by the force of a good life. Let him trace in the earth with glowing reverence the footsteps of the Maker. Let him know that in this earth the unseen God has spoken to men. Then show him the glory, the moral interest to men and spirits which the death of Jesus Christ has shed over its history — and the Resurrection and its hope. Show him the great images of the Reformers of mankind, Numa and Socrates and the Stoics and the Christian Church and Alfred and Luther — and thus having given him an idea of the great purposes to which life may be spent, do not suffer him to fritter away his energies with such casual or wretched motives as children are permitted to act upon. Do not let him say, 'What will people think?' Do not let him be ashamed of poor dress, of mean occupation or obscure acquaintance or a deformed person but let him feel that there is that in him which can rear into respect all without him. Let his young heart beat to his Maker's name. O quench not his hope, O do not repress one impulse of enthusiasm by the mean spirited apprehensions of vulgar ridicule.

My friends, the question of the value we attach to trifles is not itself trifling. If we will steadily try to keep our attention on things truly great we shall find a great many things are trifling which now we think are important. I know it is difficult to walk in the world with these lofty views, for life is cast among little things. And society is full of superstitions and makes an outcry when its forms or its idols are contemned. And no general rules can be given that can apply to all practice as to what is to be slighted and what observed. But one central rule of life there is, which will guide us safe: the reference in every action of life, to God; the constant acknowledgement of his presence. In the words of our Saviour, Love the Lord your God with all your strength and your neighbour as yourself.

A Feast of Remembrance

This do in remembrance of me. Luke XXII, 19.

God has given to us, as to each generation in succession, the dominion of the world, the care of supporting and carrying forward the frame and institutions of society. We stand on the same ground, breathe the same air, are warmed by the same sun and have the same moral constitution as our fathers. We live in the influences of the same institutions — of society, of property, of government, of marriage, of the Sabbath.

And therefore are we in all respects in the same condition as they? No. The character of society is every moment undergoing a change. We stand on the same shores, but in different dress, with different laws, different customs, and new occupations. We read the same books but they speak to us a different sense. That which bears the same name and stands in the same place is not always the same thing. There has been a large town in Italy called Rome for now near twenty-five hundred years but it could only be a child that [would] think and speak alike of the Etrurian village and the city of the consuls and the city of the emperors and the city of the barbarians and the city of the Popes and the city of artists. No, it is the blessed law of heaven which makes the cheerfulness of this life and the hope of another that our nature should be progressive. The political economist has found out that the average term of human life is longer now than it was some ages since. Great truths which ages toiled to prove they did prove and we begin where they ended. The results of an old philosopher are the elements of his pupil. Their harvest is our seed. God has made the acorn such that it will grow to an oak and he has made his moral institutions capable of a far mightier growth. The governments, the laws, the customs into which we are born — they are like the shell or outer skin of many animals. If it do not admit of growth the animal will cast it.

So is it with the institutions of religion. Christianity, which at first seemed only calculated to break down the cumbrous ceremonies of the Jewish Law, was presently found to have set up a most forcible appeal against the systems of paganism. It was found fit to be the religion of nations, as the law it displaced was not. It is now found in the vast advancement of national intelligence to have made a contemporaneous advancement. As men think more and demand more Christianity is found to mean more, has more excitement and more consolation, and to be a nobler moral rule with more flexible application to life than a wise man who should have heard it expounded in the dark ages could have dreamed. And here it stands, brethren, in the veneration of our minds, shining on with its immortal and cheerful light, outliving a hundred schools of skeptics and now bringing in all the virtue and all the highest minds of this generation into its holy fold. Neither are we to imagine that we have seen all or comprehended all; but let us believe as our forefathers did, that God has yet much more light to impart.

So with the striking rite which its founder established, and which this day we celebrate. The time has been and that very early in the history of the Church, when gross superstition was combined with that ordinance. It was mixed, confounded by the new converts with the licentious feasts of the pagan worship which they had newly forsaken and turned to a scene of riot — which gave occasion to that word of Saint Paul, that he that eateth and drinketh unworthily. And when the doctrine of the divinity of Jesus at length grew up in the church, then arose the famous doctrine of transubstantiation or belief of the real presence of God in the bread and wine. The very statement of this notion seems erroneous to us and incredible, a proof how much we have truer notions than our ancestors.[1]

Still, I think it is very apt to be misunderstood and misused by us and it is important that we should occasionally give a formal consideration to the foundation and intent of the institution.

Jesus perceived that the hour was at hand when his ministry on earth should close. In the painful, boding interest of that hour, he was consoled by the good consciousness of the past and the prophetic glory of the future. No disappointment, no horrors of trial could wholly deject one who knew himself to be the Resurrection and the Life. Still there was much to sadden and create doubt. He had exhibited in proof of his mission a power that should amaze his nation. In the face of the sun, and in many places and before crowds he had realized the wondrous histories of their fathers. He had checked or changed the usual course of nature. He had healed the sick and calmed the sea, and those that had been dead stood before him, glowing with awe among the living multitude. In harmony with this stupendous display he had shown a life of moral perfection — as rare, as original in his time as his miracles. Yet with what success? All had well-nigh failed to attach credit to his revelation. The madness of the Jewish hope could not see their Messiah in the carpenter's son. The madness of the Roman scorn could not see a Saviour of the soul in the Jew and the Nazarite.

Therefore he groaned in spirit and might well doubt whether even in those nearest followers who had seen all and had heard all, the passage of time and the terrors of persecution and the temptations of sense might not shake even their convictions or relax their efforts to transmit the great reformation which was the object of his life.

A FEAST OF REMEMBRANCE

Perhaps it was with this feeling that he desired to give body and certainty to their recollection by appointing a feast of remembrance. He could not but foresee what perversions must be expected from the extreme ignorance of the world, to degrade the faith he would teach; but he knew that the devout affections of every time and of every heart that acknowledged him would meet round a table spread by him at so awful a moment of his life — that this feast would be a distinction, a badge, a pledge, a rebuke, a remembrance.

With his knowledge of men he could not but feel that this institution must have a meaning and an use changed and accommodated to every age to which it should descend, and not only so, but almost peculiar to the mind of every disciple.

He therefore requested his disciples to eat bread and drink wine in memory of him. He set no time, he fixed no number, he added no mystery. He left his ordinance loose to go down to all churches suitable to the wants of all.[2]

Having these views of the origin of the ordinance I feel no anxiety, brethren, that all men should think alike of its nature and intent. I am willing that every Christian should see it coloured by the complexion of his own mind. It seems to me that it will always seem to one mind an occasion of warning and alarm, to another of encouragement; to one of home, to another of remembrance; to one of pleasing sympathy, to another darkened by a deep shade of awful history. And further I think that the institution to all men is assuming, and with progress of men's minds will assume a more spiritual and useful character.

I said it was not important that men should think alike. Still, I think there are certain broad views of the Lord's Supper which are the result of the good sense and liberal thinking of the age and which ought, therefore, to influence our practice much more than they do. And mainly I think it should embrace all men who believe in the divine authority of Christianity and not as now, only a small minority.

I believe the whole end and aim of this ordinance is nothing

completely rejects the puritan view

but this, *to make those who partake of it better*.³ To join the church is not to say, I am good, or I have been, but *I desire to be*. It does not intimate, and this I pray you to observe, that a line runs through the world, dividing men into saints and sinners, that you have stood on one side and now stand on the other — but believing that there is no man wholly good or wholly bad, you manifest your wish to use this as you would use any and every means of strengthening your virtuous propensities. It is a means of warming your affections toward Jesus, God's highly authorized and highly honored servant and under God your most effectual friend; a means of quickening your moral perception and amending your character in its personal and social regards. And are not these things desirable and obligatory upon all? Why should not all come? There is no foundation, it seems generally agreed, in the rule or practice of the primitive Church for the division that now exists between church and congregation.⁴ All who named the Lord's name partook of his supper. And so should all now.

Therefore I would have no one feel himself unfit to come, because he is no more virtuous; and least of all would I see a Christian or a Christian Church put a bar in the way of any.⁵ Who is he to whom I shall deny the right to sit at the supper of the Lord? I cannot by strait covenants exclude any man, nor can I take it upon myself to say that any man's sin shall exclude him. If any man transgress, to him is the more need of Christ's aid; to him the closer application of Christ's address. He came not, he said, to call the righteous, but sinners.⁶ I would bring our use of his institutions into an unity with himself. I admire the character of the Saviour, not because I was taught to revere it but because as I have grown up and my mind opened, I saw in the history of the world none nobler or of softer humanity. And I should feel myself to offend grievously against all I understand of the spirit of his gospel, against all I love of the boundless generosity of his character, if I should lift my hand to hinder any from his fold. I should feel myself rebuked by the reproof which he addressed to his uncharitable disciples when they called for fire on his enemies.

No, brethren, it seems to me far more reasonable than that any should be shut out, that we should go to the prisons and bid the culprits come. As a matter of common expediency, what harm could result? There are no temptations to any to join the church among us except from good motives. And if the church had unworthy members every man's sin lieth at his own door.

My friends, I think this view of the ordinance, that it is simply a means of improvement just as attendance on public worship or the conversation of a wise man or the study of a good book or anything else that has a tendency to excite the affections or impart light — I think this view not only the true one but the one likely to be productive of the most benefit. It will most profitably direct our meditations around the table in the channel fittest for each. It will fill one mind with sorrow for sin and one with the fragrance of holy affections, one with contentment in his lot and one with ardent aspirations for union with the spiritual world. It will teach us to use this privilege with humility and prayer, that we may not dishonour it. It will teach us to walk in the world as having received the light of another, as the zealous yet unassuming followers of the meek and lowly son of the Almighty Father, who, coming out from Him and from the spiritual world brought to the human soul the hope of immortal life; the sanction of duty; and the joyful doctrine that man may do the will of God and grow to perfection in his love.

Oct. 18, 1829

Conversation

If any man offend not in word the same is a perfect man.   James III, 2.

IT IS good that we explore the value of common blessings and ponder the obligation of common duties. In our settled order of social life not many are called to martyrdoms or to opportunities of benefitting states. Our life runs on a beaten track and the only opportunity of greatness that is vouchsafed to us is that which is given to all, is not that of great place or events, but that of infusing great principles into plain and vulgar actions; the power of giving interest and respectability to the meanest offices — if heaven ordains our lot amidst such — by our way of doing them; the power of introducing the sacred relation of man to God into our use of every faculty.

One of our chief powers is that of speech. An old and familiar subject — but to what observer has it lost its interest? What we do so much we surely ought to do well. And I wish to invite your attention, my friends, to some reflexions on the use and enjoyment of this faculty and upon the duties that belong to conversation.

I do not wish to dwell upon the detail of wonderful contrivances by which this faculty is produced. It is the noble result that claims all my admiration, the power of articulate and rational speech — which is the foundation of society and the delight and the instruction of human life; this great bond of connexion between the seen and the unseen world — whereby the impenetrable darkness that covers the soul of man from man is taken away and I am made acquainted with the inaccessible soul of my brother. Speak that I may know thee, was an ancient proverb. We can only feel its worth by bringing to our imagination the state of man if this power had been denied. Suppose God had chosen to educate a race of moral agents apart or together in the solitude of the dumb. We have all seen some of those sufferers under this grievous infirmity — those poor outcasts from the sweet society of speaking men — and yet we see them under circumstances of great alleviation. In our institutions for the deaf and dumb the instructors, let it be remembered, are those who speak and are enabled to be of infinite service to those unfortunate persons by teaching them modes of communication that nothing but speech could have enabled them to invent. By their intercourse with those who speak as well as by particular instruction the calamity is lessened. And yet after all is done what a little it is. What slow and struggling conceptions they form, what a crippled mind is the mind of the dumb. Compare their existence and intercourse with the intercourse of witty, learned and wise among speaking men, and it seems as if Providence in denying them speech had withheld half the good of being.

Yet these, though almost shut out from the active world of men, have some imperfect communication, have their own inarticulate speech. To get the full conception of the value of the power we should try to contemplate the frightful solitude of those who should have none.

What were the state of minds that God had enclosed in unsocial bodies, with no language even of signs? You may place them side by side if you will in their appointed place and appointed duties, but they are separated more effectually than if oceans sundered them. The thought of one cannot penetrate to the thought of the other. They cannot cooperate. They cannot have affections. And the heart is oppressed by its pity for so forlorn a being.

Now compare this unformed sufferer with the finished man. He speaks — and is understood. The cheerful delight of a sympathy and common intelligence is let in upon the dark firmament in which his thoughts roll. Society is produced. Not only hand joins with hand in physical aid and support but the soul finds fellowship; discovers that in other souls the thoughts, the affections, the powers are formed and ordered upon the same springs, turn on the same poles as its own. Minds that confer together, heat and quicken each other to greater intensity of affection to that which both love. They modify and alter each other's opinion and purpose. The light that is in one mind is speedily imparted to the other without loss to the first. If one mind be superior, the other is benefitted in exact proportion to that superiority by the intercourse. And not only is there this mutual benefit by the exchange of knowledge by which in almost every case each man is a gainer, but a separate and remarkable advantage arises to each, that his own knowledge is increased by his efforts to impart it. Under the stimulus of conversation a man musters his thoughts more vigorously, and brings them out from their obscurity into air and light; observes their relation to other truth more narrowly than before; corrects them; and carries them to yet farther conclusions; 'and so feels himself to be wiser in conversation than he was in silence.' Bacon said, ' 'Twere better that a man should relate his thoughts to a statue than let them pass in smother.' [1]

It were a very interesting inquiry, though leading too far for the limits of this discourse, to trace the uses of conversation. It has one general use to which I will advert a moment. It is the natural institution for the diffusion of knowledge. The profound wisdom of one man and the rare opportunities of another are, by this easy process, brought into the common treasury of mankind, with advantage and pleasure to both the public and the individual. Any one may be satisfied of this benefit, who will consider how much practical wisdom passes current in the world in the shape of vulgar proverbs. These little maxims of

CONVERSATION

worldly prudence are a part of the inheritance that have come down to this age from all the past generations of men. They have given us their institutions, their inventions, their books, and, by means of conversation, have transmitted their commentary upon all the parts of life in these proverbs. They were originally doubtless the happy thoughts of sagacious men in very distant times and countries, in every employment and of every character. No single individual, with whatever penetration, could have attained by himself to that accurate knowledge of human life, which now floats through the conversation of all society, by means of these pithy sentences. We are all of us the wiser for them. They govern us in all our traffic, — in all our judgments of men, — in all our gravest actions.[2]

It is impossible not to notice the enjoyment as well as the advantage which our Heavenly Father has provided for us in this noble endowment of speech; not to feel how it diminishes the burden of life, and augments its pleasure; not to remember the happiness that is in the voice of a friend; not to remember how much stronger is truth when it is recommended by eloquence. There is a pleasure, a luxury, which is one of the most refined delights permitted to man which results from listening to the conversation of exalted minds when they possess this talent of communicating their thoughts to any high degree. Fine conversation is very rare. It is the fruit of talents and situation in society which are granted to but few — and the best eulogy of this art is in the convictions of them who have heard it. It is exhilarating to the soul beyond all other stimulus. It moves upon the mind with creative force. It gives heart and life to the listener and to a religious mind suggests the feeling of its immortality with a conviction sometimes beyond that of argument or evidence. But whilst I look with admiration and pleasure at this rare and costly fruit I am far from being insensible to the goodness of the Creator in that sweetness which all of us down to the least favoured of mankind derive from this faculty. It is the breath of social life. Solitary confinement is limited by our penal laws to a very short period as, if protracted, it is found to be a privation intolerable for human nature. How does this free expression of ourselves lighten labour and lessen pain. There is a consolation which the poor village gossip in the midst of her infirmities derives from treasuring up and relating her little anecdotes and feelings to attentive ears, which will not pass unnoticed by any observer of God's beneficence.

Having spoken of the excellence of the power of speech in regard to its use and of its pleasure I come now to speak a little of the duties that respect conversation.

With all the glory of this gift there is also a sadly sore side to conversation. The tongue instructs, consoles, pleases, rebukes, encourages; but also it rails, flatters, lies, and blasphemes. The virtues of man have made it their organ and his passions also may make it theirs.[3] It is important therefore to keep it to its right office and to find rules for its government. Our conversation is a very large part of life, and by our words therefore we shall be justified or condemned. It has every degree of merit. It may be wholly sinful or it may be so rich and pure as is the discourse of angels.

It is one of the secrets which conversation discloses to us that our minds are made after one model.[4] If it were not so, if every mind had different principles of right and wrong, different tastes; if that which was true to me, was false to my neighbor; and what one conscience condemned as mean, another extolled as heroic; — the faculty of speech would only be the organ of hopeless contradiction and perplexity. But we find there is a certain *standard idea of man* which we all have in our thoughts, in our conversation. In every dispute, we have tacit reference to it all along. If we talk on any question of speculation with a man who seems to us to be in great error, we always believe that at last, perhaps not in this life, but somewhere, sometime, he will come to the truth; he will see as we see; will come nearer to this standard-man, which we believe exists for both. This feeling amounts to so strong a confidence, when a man is very wrongheaded, that we do not feel it to be of great importance to set him right, sure that he will come right hereafter if left to himself.[5]

Now in that very standard, we have a rule, a guide, for the regulation of our discourse. Let us not come below that standard. Let us not offend against it. Let us not offend the man within the breast. Let it be remembered that in all our talk, truth is the end and aim. When therefore in argument you convince your opponent remember that it is truth and not you that wins, and so be not elate, but grateful that the attainment of it is given to you. But when you are overcome by fair argument and find your reasonings false and vain then if you keep your good humour it is you that win. There is high, a Christian nobleness in that victory over egotism, when a man in the zeal of debate doth frankly and joyfully yield himself to the manifest truth of his adversary.[6] It is brave and Christian to do so but not many men can. It was said of a celebrated American statesman that he was content to stand by and let truth and reason argue for him.

My brethren, the check upon conversation that will supersede all others is the religious feeling, the sense that we are God's children. It will elevate its tone above its frivolity or a criminal degradation.[7] It will take away its personality in which it is so prone to fall and supply all the courtesy to the persons and reverence to the topics that is due to them.

We can all of us form high ideas of the value and pleasure of social intercourse. But how poor is our practice. He that should go from house to house should find what low, unprofitable and quarrelsome talking, what degrading and embittering society; how ignorant. I would that men would consider that every injurious word we utter recoils on the head of him that utters it. In hot contention we are apt to forget ourselves. You were rudely assailed by him with whom you talk and you retaliate as sharply. But it is strange how entirely five minutes will sometimes change the complexion of a word. It appeared

E thinks other people have his tender conscience

just now a fair retort, a frolicsome sally — but now it appears a wanton and unfeeling taunt which you would give an estate to recall. I know there are sometimes outrages in conversation where indignation seems justifiable. Your feelings are wounded by unprovoked insult. But now, whilst your just anger trembles on your lips — consider. Revenge is mine, I will repay, saith the Lord. Fear not then that the cause of justice shall suffer by your forbearance and the transgressor go free. If in that moment you will be firm and silent he cannot go unpunished. 'The laws of God's justice in the universe will assert themselves.' If you meekly abstain from taking your own vengeance when the opportunity offers he will inflict it on himself. The recollection of his angry word will return to him by night, it will follow him by day. You shall see it in his altered apologising demeanor whenever you meet him, for months, for years. He feels the superiority, the divinity, of forgiveness and bends with all external advantages, despite of himself before your meek magnanimity. Thus you shall reform him but never by angry words.

The apostle in our text saith, If any man offend not in word the same is a perfect man. A great deal of good may be done in the world by good conversation, a great deal of harm by any other. We are all going to our homes to renew the conversation interrupted for a short space by the meditations of the sanctuary. Let us take heed to our words. God may have given to few or to none among us the power of wit or of eloquence but he has given to all the power to know the pure, the benevolent and the true from the impure, the selfish and the false.[8] Let us think before we speak and speak as unto God as well as unto men.

The Ministry: A Year's Retrospect

We then as workers together with him beseech you that ye receive not the grace of God in vain. Second Corinthians VI, 1.

During my recent absence from this place,[1] Christian friends, the year has been completed from the day of my ordination to the Christian ministry. I am unwilling to let the occasion pass without notice. Our life is hurrying to an end. And as we pass from stage to stage, we find a sad but wholesome admonition in the notice we take of these measures of time. Especially do these seasons demand attention when like this, they mark out periods of duty, when conscience, the truth teller, looks down on the poor performance of our imperfections and sternly points at the high requisition — all unfulfilled; when the hope and the vow of the first day of a year of time is put side by side with the remembrance of the last, when we come to see what a train of inconveniences, infirmities, private disappointments and sins come in to hinder and postpone the execution of our designs. In view of this contrast between what was proposed with what has been done, man eats the bitter herbs of regret and becomes acutely sensible of the sore side of his condition.

Suffer me then to offer you some remarks suggested by the occasion on some of the obligations that arise to you and to me out of the pastoral relation.

I have said that the first feeling on considering the sanguine hopes of a past year in close connexion with their defeat is the deepest regret at failure. And I, brethren, when I only look back on this span of time, which I had hoped would be rich with life and thought and action, when I see how the facts shrink from the promise — how little I have done and how little I have learned; even with the best hope I can dare to form of good derived from the connexion thus far established between you and me — I confess I am oppressed with doubt and sorrow, and if I stopped with this view, I should despond.

But this is not right. This is too limited a view. Why art thou cast down, oh my soul and why art thou disquieted within me? Hope thou in God. That we should deeply mourn and truly repent of our own negligence is most suitable to our condition and nature. But it is also suitable to our nature, and to the faith we hold fast as the children of God, and the disciples of Christ, that we should bate no jot of heart or hope. It would argue a self-sufficiency from which I pray to be preserved, to suppose because we have done little, that little has been done. What am I, that I should let my private contrition cloud my views of God and the doings of his Providence among men? What? that I should lament over the inefficacy of any one or more means of good as if the purposes of God's benevolence were obstructed thereby. It is true, God enables us to be of use to our fellow men, each according to his several gifts, — and rewards our goodness by making us see often the fruits of our exertions. But all the time, we are, in a strong sense, instruments in his hand, and it is reasonable to suppose he would have procured the same good for his children, whether we had acted or had forborne to act. Preaching, what Saint Paul calls 'the foolishness of preaching,' is but one voice in the choir of the world. The doctrines of the gospel, the spirit of Christ is preached to men not only by the tongues of ministers and the written Scriptures; but by the events that daily occur; by all the lives of those who live; by the remembrance of all those who are dead; by the connexions with society which trade, or curiosity, or pleasure, or want, or consanguinity, or love make

THE MINISTRY: A YEAR'S RETROSPECT

us form; by the development of the affections; in short, by all the parts of each man's personal experience. I take this to be an indisputable truth. For all men are at all times drawing insensibly a moral from what they see doing around them; and with this moral (as it appears to those who have deduced it most clearly) the precepts of Jesus strictly coincide. Now if the pulpit is silent these thousand teachers do not cease to speak; if the pulpit is false, if it is afraid, if it speaks smoothly, or superstitiously, — this ceaseless instruction of God's Providence *goes on*, and is never false or superstitious or afraid. It contradicts them and accuses them. Nor can these events nor can Religion ever want articulate voice. We may extol the individual merits of one man as much as we will, but the truth which he teaches perishes with no man. He was only a spectator[2] with more or less advantages for seeing the ways of God, but the same advantages exist and will commend themselves to other eyes who will also declare them. I do not think

> 'Though men were none, that Heaven
> Would want spectators, God want praise.'

This is the reason why our consciousness of imperfection and sin should not discourage us in our work.

Think not, my friends, that I find in this way of thinking any apology for remissness in a pastor or other teacher, for remissness in the discharge of his duty. I say it only as the just consolation of that comparison between what is required with what has been performed, a comparison which without this relief would lay on our shoulders a responsibility overwhelming. I make no apology for remissness. If I have neglected my duties I shall leave it in silence. I shall not add the guilt of excusing it. The minister of Christ will find motive and sermon in his name against all indolence. He must be instant in season and out of season. He must so serve the altar that he is never from it. He is to carry the light of God's presence with him always, not to wear a grave face or to talk from the Scriptures but to wear a pure heart out of which a good conversation, good manners, good actions shall proceed as naturally as clean water from a pure spring.

This leads me to another point. The activity which is the duty of a Christian minister in the discharge of his office, is of two kinds, preacher and pastor, and often in some measure incompatible.

He attempts with no better spiritual light than his brethren enjoy, to study the Scriptures and to explain God's laws and exhort them to comply therewith. A man who is presumed to have inclination and ability for the study of religious principles, is set apart for their discussion, because no man can discuss them without study, and all men are benefitted by having them discussed. But he must deserve the attention of those who come to him to be moved to the love of God by speaking wisely. He is the last who may be indulged in talking inconsiderately. He should not bring to the service of God what he would be ashamed to offer in the service of man. But every one at all accustomed to attend to what passes in his own mind may know that for the most part the thoughts which are greatest and truest, do not flash upon the soul in a moment in all their fulness, but are, first, remote possibilities, then, opinions, then, truth, as our knowledge increases; that different minds require different culture to bring them into action, that though the light of duty is always present to all, the reason of duty, is not; that sometimes silence and solitude; sometimes conversation; sometimes action; sometimes books; are necessary to repair the flagging powers of the soul, and enable it to carry on its inquiry. And just in proportion to a man's respect for the soul's good of his brethren will be his anxiety to prove all things, to hold fast that which is good and thence his care to do whatsoever he can to quicken and help the often uncontrollable faculties of his mind.

But the laws of thought are not accommodated to the divisions of time. The services of the church are periodical, but

THE MINISTRY: A YEAR'S RETROSPECT

the development of truth within the mind is not. Obviously then the minister who makes it an important aim to convey instruction must often stay at home in the search of it [3] when his parishioners may think he would be more usefully employed in cultivating an acquaintance with them. You will therefore have the charity to think when you do not see your pastor as often or at the times when you could wish it and desire it, that he may be employed with earnest endeavours to speak to you usefully in this place.[4]

Another subject of which I am naturally led to speak is the character of the exhortations of the pulpit. I believe none who hears me can be more sensible of their faults than I am. But I have spoken to you of our faith and duty as well as I could. We come often to church and our time is spent here in the same way. I certainly do not hope with each new day to engage your minds with new thoughts on the topics here treated — which are of immemorial meditation. The man who speaks to his fellows on the duties they owe and on the relations they sustain to God, must ever insist on those commandments which he thinks they have broken, whether those laws have been read to them one time, or a thousand. I do not think it necessary to say to you, Do not worship idols; for Christianity has shamed the idolater, and broken the image. I do not think it necessary to say to you, Do not kill; Do not steal; Do not commit adultery; because they who do thus are not often in this house, but I do think it important to say, Love the Lord thy God, with all thy heart. Love thy neighbor as thyself. Do not bear false witness; Be temperate; Pray; Give; because we are at all times liable to offend in some one of these points. Moreover some of these commandments touch those parts of action which never reach their limit, but admit of infinite improvement; and the spirits of just men in heaven may add fervor to each other's love and devotion, by exhorting each other to a celestial benevolence, to a seraphic prayer.

All spiritual truth is open to the investigation of all. But, as in our country, we all have our several and beloved home; among men, our select friends; among things indifferent, our own caprice; among innumerable books, our chosen pages; so is it here. Every mind hath its favourite resorts in the spacious domain of truth, its church of virtuous thoughts, whither it repairs morning and evening; — its own heaven where it takes calm but glorious surveys of God's Providence; where it finds solemn motives to do justly, love mercy, and walk humbly, where it best learns the lesson of serenity and trust.

I shall count it no reproach if I am reminded that my subjects have little variety.[5] I count it the great object of my life to explore the nature of God. For this I would read and think and converse and act and suffer, and if I shall succeed in enlarging in any degree your conceptions of the divine nature and government or confirming your convictions I shall praise him that he has permitted me to be so honoured an instrument in his hand.

To another point I must say a few words, namely, upon what is your duty in the observation of public worship. The difference in the attendance on church in the two parts of the same day you are aware is often very great. It cannot be that any very extensive changes have taken place in the situation of families. I fear we are doing ourselves great harm when we begin to relax, in any point, the fidelity of our religious observances, — and mainly the keeping of the Sabbath.[6] The duty of religious improvement is plain enough. It is every man's first and peculiar business. You have chosen me to aid in its public functions. I conceive it then becomes yours to make me as useful to you as possible by bringing hither a devout temper and hearing with what candor you can.[7] Of course I do not speak with any the least reference to personal feeling. I have no right and certainly no disposition to call upon you here for personal attention. But I do beseech you to give attention to your own spiritual habits and not permit any negligence of a

THE MINISTRY: A YEAR'S RETROSPECT

devout custom to grow into a habit with you. Believe me, it will grow fast to an alarming laxity and libertinism. Religion is a plant of that delicacy that will not bear the least tampering, as the costliest fruits are soonest spoiled. In the hour of youth and joy and self-confidence you may esteem these things as decorous customs, and neglect them in your own heart; — but, O, the hour will come and probably many before you go out of this world, when in sorrow, in danger, in anxiety, in solitude, the deep and eternal value of a religious faith shall make itself felt in your heart — when you shall weep at the long neglect that has estranged you from it and darkened your moral perception; and thrown an immovable shade over the evening of your days; or shall rejoice over every humble act of worship, every public offering, every closet prayer as the means that have brought the Spirit of God into your mind and fixed it an eternal inhabitant.

The year is gone and we remain. It has carried many of our brethren and sisters to the world of spirits who were wont to keep holy day with us and come up to the house of God in company. The old man is gone full of days, and the infant whose eye had not yet grown familiar with the sun. It has multiplied our days and advantages. And what have we done, my friends? Have we multiplied our connections with heaven, have we studied in the school of Christ? What proficiency have we made in our imitation of his example? Have we complied with his ordinances? Have we eaten of his bread and drunk of his cup? or have we done the same in a spiritual sense? I fear, brethren, the best of us would tremble if we should be called to a strict account, if it should be numbered against us how many duties we had neglected, how frivolous, how sensual, how selfish, how unjust we have been. Let us pray and let us strive that the year which has begun should be brightened by the proofs of our repentance and our piety. Let us consecrate anew these old walls that have heard the prayers of faithful men for three generations, — by coming duly under their holy shelter with the love of God in our hearts, that we may be able to contemplate the future with calm delight and may go away when God calls us from the means and exercises of his grace here to the boundless joy and glory of the spiritual world.

[handwritten: Thinks U.S. has best Gov. of all countries (comparatively) Ap. 8, 1830]

The Individual and the State

Happy is the people whose God is the Lord. Psalm CXLIV, 15.

RELIGION in its perpetual injunction of the social duties does not omit that important class of relations which we sustain to our country and to the world. In this country the existence of universal suffrage, the fact that every adult man by giving his vote for the laws and the officers exercises a portion of political power, has made good men feel more strongly the necessity of providing every young person with some systematic instruction in the history, the laws, and political institutions of the land. It has been thought desirable that text books should be introduced into our schools in which the constitution of the United States should be explained and the utility of its leading provisions illustrated. Undoubtedly this information would be valuable and ought to be provided. It is secured to some extent in the geographies and histories put into the hands of our children, and in some seminaries by special instruction.

But in my judgment a more important aid in a sense of moral responsibility should be awakened in the mind of every individual, that the individual should see the connexion between private and public duties; should be accustomed to extend the dominion of his conscience over these as much as over his secret actions.

I am very sensible brethren that it would be a violation of the plainest decorum, if the pulpit were made the vehicle of proclaiming or of insinuating opinions upon men and measures. In so doing the Christian preacher quits his true and dignified place and just as surely forfeits the confidence of those to whom he speaks.[1] But it *is* the office of the pulpit to warn men unceasingly of the universality of the law of duty, and to charge them that the state can never be in much danger as long as men vote for laws and for law makers according to their conscience and introduce into their political action the same regard to rectitude which they feel bound to exercise in dealing with their families and friends. But we are charged in this country with introducing into our political action a certain levity and recklessness, a negligence of the interests of the next generation in our violent grasping after an advantage of today, in short, a preference in all our parties of the expedient to the right, which is a dangerous symptom not only for the permanence of our civil institutions but for our own moral health as individual men. In this season of ferment and expectation, I shall not hesitate to ask your attention to the source of our social evils, that the heat of our civil and sectional strifes may be tempered by that humility and contrition which arise when we cease to see the mote in another's eye because we have found the beam in our own.[2]

When we consider the advantages derived to us in our passage through this world from living under a good form of government, the great influence which it may exert upon our characters, and our happiness; his civil relations become an object of serious attention to a Christian. All governments are mutable, and each man wields a portion of influence in determining their form. A bad government may check the progress of knowledge and indefinitely multiply the ordinary amount of temptation; it may have that degree of corruption that no man can act with it unless at a sacrifice of principle. And all the experience of man is, with few exceptions, a tragic tale of the pernicious connexion between the ruler and the ruled. In a well constituted state, the government itself will be out of sight,[3] will not be the prominent and exclusive object of attention whenever the country is considered. But all the past history of man is little more than a story of governments. The people, their occupations, their habits, their thoughts, their intellectual and religious condition are thrust aside, or only appear as they acted in relation to their ruler. It becomes then at all times to every thoughtful Christian a question of interest, what is the extent of his means of affecting the public mind; and a subject of devout gratitude, whenever Providence has ordered his lot in mercy in a country where the rights of men are recognized by the laws.

It has pleased God eminently to distinguish us with these civil advantages. We eat a harvest which we have not sowed. We are born to an inheritance which was paid for partly by the toil and suffering of the last generation and in part by earlier labourers, by the exertion of many an ardent soul in this country and in England for two or three centuries past.

But however procured, (and it was not procured by us) it exists to us the most perfect government — most perfectly answering to a Christian man the purposes of a state of any one on human record. The advantages of a government it is agreed must always be negative. It cannot do any good to the intellectual or religious character of the citizen. Such benefit must arise to him from himself; if it occasions him no harm, — if it leaves him in entire freedom, as long as he injures nobody, I call it a perfect government.

And this good condition of safety is certainly secured by our social system to every citizen. Unseen itself it envelopes him like the air. A man of retired habits may live ten years in the unmolested pursuit of his own calling and excepting the payment of his tax, and his service on a jury, never have his notice called to the fact that there is a government, and a code of laws.[4] But if his property or his rights are invaded either where he stands, or in another town, or another land, — he finds that this sleeping Law whose existence he had forgotten, hath an arm of power that can reach from sea to sea, from nation to nation, and demand redress for him all over the earth.

This good government we have. It is not yet to be procured. It is now possessed. All that rests with us is to preserve it. These institutions are far too excellent, and far too rare in the history of the world to be exposed to the slightest risk. Yet all men are impressed among us with a sense of their danger, of the uncertainty of their tenure. Thus far the evil operation, if there be any, has not reached the privileges of the citizens. If it is felt at all, it is not felt beyond the offices of the state, beyond the machinery of the Government itself. But as the number of the offices of the Government is many thousands, if any great evil should operate therein, its influence must needs be extensive, and must command the vigilance of all.

Then all men are sensible of the mischief of a licentious press as it is used for party purposes. All men are hurt and alarmed by the flood of slander that is every week and every day poured over the land by the madness of party spirit, destroying the peace and fame of good men, corrupting the ear of the people, and familiarizing the public mind with profligacy and avarice under the name and pretensions of patriotism.

There is yet another evil sign to our country in the strong tendency to disunion that blazes out in the discussion of every political question.[5] All things are seen with partial eye. The strong voice of self interest seems to be thought an over match for every other plea, and the abominable maxim of little calculators, 'The world will last our day' is almost avowed as the rule of political action. These evils all good men lament; and most have an impression that they are growing worse. Yet no one seems to imagine that he himself or his friends or his party are concerned in the guilt.

But how should it happen that in this virtuous nation such evil things should be done? It cannot be that a colony of bad men should have settled in the bosom of the land. There must be a traitor in the camp of Israel. It must be that the good are not good enough; it must be that the bad derive a countenance from the good. It must be that the standard of private virtue is nowhere very high; that God's commandments are disobeyed by his children; that those who are called Christians have not the spirit of Christ. Consider whilst we so readily repeat and deplore the fact of the increasing profligacy in the public morals if we ought not rather to lay our hands on our own breasts, and say, *We are the men.*

Let it be considered by us that a small amount of evil in those who are reckoned the good sort of people, becomes pretty coarse depravity when imitated on their authority in another class, — in a class where the restraints of opinion and of standing are less. The newspaper which is a scourge to the country[6] is only the common and tolerated degree of vice exhibited, — like the insensible motion of the hand of a watch made sensible by being lengthened onto the dial of a clock. People say as bad things of each other in good society as are printed in the worst papers. Then if people would not read bad papers, they would not be printed. But they are received by persons whom all would say are incapable of abetting a corrupt cause.

As it is with this ferocious calumny, so is it with the selfishness that appears in public measures. It is only the selfishness of private life magnified by being put on a great scale, and under the searching scrutiny of a nation's eye. They who act after this manner are not acting in any new and original way. They are following their habits. They are practising the lessons which they have learned in the common usages of trade, which men well-reputed in the world for virtue permit themselves to sanction. Indeed they are acting as they have always acted in their families and with their neighbours, and have not found that it injured them with any other persons than those whom it injured, or that it forfeited their place in society. They have had the instinct, it is true, not to show this fang to those whom it was important to conciliate, but only to such as might be overreached or oppressed. Moreover, whatever acts or attempts of a political character you most loudly condemn as sordid, did not by any means belong exclusively to those who were the agents, but had or expected the countenance of multitudes, or certainly they would not have been done.

It is thus that the political measures of this nation and of every nation may be regarded as an index whereon the average degree of private virtue is made known to the world.

It may be stated as a general law that the rulers of a country are a fair representation of the virtue of a country. In a virtuous community men of sense and of principle will always be placed at the head of affairs. In a declining state of public morals men will be so blinded to their true interests as to put the incapable and unworthy at the helm.[7] It is therefore vain to complain of the follies or crimes of a government. We must lay our hands on our own hearts and say, Here is the sin that makes the public sin.

And it should be felt by us also that this average public virtue is never a fixed amount but always fluctuating; that it depends not on masses, but on individuals; and that each of us every day does somewhat to raise or to depress it. Let no man shelter himself under a false modesty, as if what he did or said could be of insignificant consequence in the vast aggregate of action. Every one knows that when men come in their business to consider how far they may honourably go in this or that transaction, a few opinions, the names of half a dozen men who would approve or condemn the course, are quoted as authority and commonly decide the question in each man's mind.

Nothing in this world ends in itself. High virtue will surely be attended with deep respect. It is of God and cannot be overlooked. It will prove a stimulus and encouragement to goodness wherever it goes. It will confirm the wavering purpose and rebuke the new born sin. Virtue tends to create virtue

THE INDIVIDUAL AND THE STATE

as surely as vice to beget vice. Let it be deeply felt by you that however you may despair — a solitary individual — to do any thing of importance to stay the public degeneracy, yet when it is directed to your own character not a single exertion is without effect. This is the true way to reform states.[8] You compel people to be better by being better yourself. For you do something to raise the standard of virtue in the world, which is always the average of the virtue of individuals. What said the Saviour? Let your light so shine before men, that others seeing your good works may glorify your Father which is in Heaven.

Whilst thus you fulfil the duty of Patriotism let it never be forgotten by us that our duties are appointed to us here only for a little time. We are citizens of the heavenly country.[9] Are you unable to control your sorrow at witnessing the corruptions of the state? Rejoice that the hour cometh when God will release you from your service here and join you to a purer society — a peculiar people. But do not therefore relax your zeal to improve the character of your fellow men. The privileges, the high places of that state, are given to those who have most efficiently laboured in their place and duty on earth — according to God's commandments. Thus hath Godliness the promise of the life that now is and of that which is to come. It should give us pleasure to reflect that the piety which we owe to one country enjoins the patriotism which we owe to the other and that God has so harmoniously joined together the good of this temporal and of that eternal world, that every effort which we make with a pure heart to deserve his favor, every struggle with temptation, is so much done to purify and so to perpetuate the civil institutions of our land.

Religious Liberalism and Rigidity

Let every man prove his own work and then shall he have rejoicing in himself alone and not in another, for every man shall bear his own burden.
Galatians VI, 4, 5.

THE times in which we live are much agitated by the discussion of religious questions, and the community is, for the most part, distributed into two great parties, by a line which runs between sect and sect, or divides the same sect into two parts.[1] One of these may be called the *rigid* and one the *liberal* party.[2] This is by no means a casual or temporary division. He is much mistaken who thinks this warfare is transient or is confined to this country or this age. Its seeds are as old as the human mind. Both parties are founded on principles inherent in our nature, and both build their system upon unquestionable facts. Indeed the same division of opinion may be traced beyond theology into the discussion of every question, upon which men take sides with any degree of zeal. There is a rigid and a liberal party on ethical and metaphysical questions, on questions of education, on the questions of free trade and of civil government.

I propose to consider what are the great principles that lie at the foundation of the two prominent parties of the Christian world. This consideration will lead us to see what dangers and what duties arise out of this controversy.

There is in the nature of man a distinct and strong feeling

of approbation at the sight of a good action in himself or in another. There is also in his nature a distinct and strong feeling of disapprobation at the sight of a bad action.

On these two principles, which are not at variance, but both true, the two parties severally stand. The *liberal* party take the principle of *man's capacity for virtue* and from that ground survey the creation.[3] The *rigid* party take the principle of *man's liability to sin*, and from that ground survey the creation.[4] From these two fountains flow their feelings towards God and man. The rigid party in the church, alarmed with the contrast between the grievous guilt that is in man, and the perfections of God, look up to him with dread, and conceive him as the Judge of action, and the punisher of sin. The virtues on which they most insist are penitence, renouncement of worldly pleasure, and prayer.

The liberal class of Christians, touched with the benevolence that appears in the Universe, and with the great powers and desires of man and with the signs of a moral Providence which appear — delight in conceiving God under the parental relation, as holding out encouragements to human virtue and as being Himself an object worthy of endless study and love, whom to know aright is life eternal. And they commend naturally the virtues of gratitude, of resignation and of diligence.

If we consider it still more particularly we shall easily perceive how naturally each of these systems can flow from one of these partial views and how close a mutual relation the different doctrines of each system have within itself.

Thus if any one of us should be led to an exclusive or only a disproportionate attention to the single feeling of remorse for sin, — (that feeling which is peculiar to rational nature), it is not difficult to analyze the process by which he is led to adopt the popular doctrines of the stricter church. First, he feels that an indefinable evil hangs over him. He has offended God, a being of unknown power and unknown purposes. There may be no bounds to his displeasure and to the bad consequences to himself. Of course his soul is oppressed with *fear*. Its active powers are paralyzed, its affections cramped, and all its energy directed to an anxious exploring of ways of escape, a way of atonement. Great sacredness attaches to all opinions concerning it. Fear makes the spirit passive. It only asks what it must do. It makes no conditions. It questions nothing. This is the state of mind most apt for unlimited credulity. And this may account for the remarkable fact that this stricter class of Christians have always set so high a value upon Faith — because a strong faith indicated a strong sense of sin. The spirit, bowed by a consciousness of its guilt and of God's anger, counts it presumptuous to cavil at the statements of the Scriptures concerning his nature and laws. The conditions of any law are better, it says, than it deserves and whatever it receives from him, it will reverence.

I do not conceive that all the doctrines usually held by this class of Christians have a necessary connexion with their first principles. Thus the doctrine of the Trinity is, I think, *accidentally* a part of their creed. An Arian might be a member of the rigid party for all his views of the inferiority of Christ to the Father. Yet with this foremost feeling of the sinfulness of the heart, they appear to have read the Scriptures with a devout if with an erring eye, and to have made a systematic but partial application of its language to the support of their opinions.

It is just as easy to follow the steps taken by another mind which, setting out from a consideration of the pleasure we take in the right use of our powers, arrives at conclusions very far remote from the former. A mind of generous nature is early taught to contemplate with delight and reverence its own faculties, — to reverence them for their use; to believe, that, as God gave them, they are imperfect copies of his own perfections; and that he is well pleased in the good they produce; that the purposes of God are best deduced from his works;

that, as the world is full of contrivances for use and pleasure, and not one for pain, (pain only resulting from some ignorance or abuse of nature) it is reasonable to think that he designed always the happiness of his children; that as we possess freedom and as all those powers are extremely susceptible of cultivation, that nothing can be more manifest than that we should become more wise, more true, more just, more temperate, more kind, and so more happy, every day; that a day is full of duties; life a term of education.[5] What blessings, opportunities, hopes, and truth, exist in this world, to those who will seek them! Then what unspeakable cheerfulness and dignity has the gospel of eternal life poured over the future! And if the good, the exaltation, the felicity of man is the object of God's arrangements concerning him, and none so noble, so divine can be imagined by us, then a sufficient reason is given for the existence of all pain, because it is all of use; and a sufficient reason is given for the interference of the special economy of the Christian Revelation, because we cannot conceive a richer gift from God than the announcement of the future life on such conditions as it is offered.

From these views they are naturally led to give all their views of God a degree of trust and love becoming more perfect as they are sure their actions please him; they are also induced to put their whole reliance in order to obtain his favor upon their works, including all voluntary action. Believing the end he had in view was their happiness, and knowing that only in one way can that be secured, by doing right, they come to value states of mind only as they are marked by that surest index, the deeds.

These views also claim in their behalf the strong testimony of the Scriptures. But as the human mind must always be the interpreter of Scripture, they explain the Scripture in conformity with the laws of the mind; they appeal from the letter to the spirit and find one meaning in the word and the works of God.

These two great systems of religious opinion being once established, the well known disposition of the human mind to magnify its own, ensures to each the total force of its espousers. Each advocate labours in his own cause with all his means. He strengthens its argument, adorns it with his genius, and rejoices by his goodness to show its good effect. Each will have in course of time its fair proportion of powerful thinkers. Many men have dedicated their entire life to the cause of a religious creed, men of great minds and best dispositions,

> 'Who, born for the universe, narrowed their mind
> And to party gave up what was meant for mankind.'

In this way, each cause in the course of one or two centuries, does its best; shows all that influence it can exert; what height of virtue it can sustain in its followers; what scope it gives to action; what life they lead, and what martyrdom they can bear. Thus a chapter of man's history is unrolled before us, from which valuable instruction may be drawn. (If we have eyes, let us see it. If we have ears let us hear what the Spirit saith unto the Churches.)

Now the first great objection to the state of the church [is] that it is the effect of a party spirit and all party is exclusive. Each of these opinions we have seen is based in a great truth; and, of course, the Christian character must embrace the foundations of both.[6] But, by the operation of this jealous warfare, by adopting one opinion you are understood by the multitude, and are in the greatest danger to be understood by yourself, as branding the other opinion, and excluding yourself from the peculiar good fruits of it.[7] The majority of men do not make nice distinctions, and the moment a line is drawn between sects they show their zeal by pushing as far from it as they can into the unsafe extreme of the part they have chosen. This makes the objection which good men have to the use of names whenever they can be avoided. It is an objection to the denomination Unitarian[8] that it tends to make those who do

RELIGIOUS LIBERALISM AND RIGIDITY

not hold their general sentiments, Trinitarians. For it is but too true a maxim that people generally end with being, what they are accused of being. And who is there in our times who has had opportunity of extensive observation, but can name not individuals but families, and communities, with every opportunity of being enlightened, who have actually been kept out of the progress to which they had every right and hope by the deep trenches that have been digged and the stakes that have been set in the field of thought that have made it a party consideration to think thus and so?[9] The question is not — What did God intend? — What saith the human heart? But, How do the Unitarians believe? And what must I as a Calvinist say?

Now, my friends, an active and honest mind that loves God and is truly anxious to do his Will, will take its place in the middle ground, and borrow something of eternal truth from both of these opinions. Whilst one usurps the Christian name to consecrate the rancour of bigotry, and another turns the liberty wherewith the gospel has made him free into a cloak of licentiousness,[10] this humble disciple rejoices with trembling. He feels deeply the weight of his sins; he deplores the power of temptation; with prayer, with tears, with terror he watches over himself and his occasional backslidings, he dares not think lightly of a crime or presume on the mercy of God. But though he is cast down he is not destroyed. A more perfect love casteth out the fear. He is buoyed up with an infinite satisfaction when he considers that the arm of omnipotence is enlisted on the side of Virtue. When he sees the munificence with which his Father hath endowed the race, in their intellectual, moral and social gifts, the gentleness with which he leads them upward, and lastly, in the great hope he hath disclosed, abolishing death. Life to him is far too dear, too solemn a preparation to be soured by hatred, or dishonoured by folly, or wasted in speculation, which was given for virtue.

The next great mischief that comes of the controversy is

not only losing the portion of truth which is contended for by that party you oppose, but begetting in you a disposition of all others the most adverse to true religion. The very front of the Christian religion hath this maxim, *Love the Lord your God with all your heart and thy neighbor as thyself*. But the banding ourselves in religious parties hath a strong tendency to make us dislike and denounce our neighbor, if he does not think as we do. And so out of your devotion to a Christian denomination you forfeit the blessings of the Christian religion. To some men it is almost impossible to speak with kind feelings of the other religious party. There is the greatest difference I know in this respect in constitutional self-command. And it becomes an important duty to govern ourselves by our knowledge of this circumstance. If you are always in perfect good humour when you talk of your opponents; if you can reckon with perfect confidence on your principles and prudence that you will utter no expression which a cooler reflexion might condemn — why then you may venture on that question with as little scruple as on any other. But if you cannot — do not touch it — turn from it and pass away. The principle God implanted in us to use to others, was *love*, and to use toward ourselves, *jealousy*. But this evil habit makes us reverse them, and be jealous of others, and indulge ourselves.

Brethren, these things ought to be considered by us, that in the warm discussions of the day, we may not miss the substance whilst we grasp the shadow. Every man ought carefully to ponder the evils of party spirit, that he may be a partisan, when he must be, without them. I do not think it is possible entirely to keep aloof from these communities of opinion. When a persecution arises against an opinion which you hold, you must avow your sentiment, and join the weaker party in their defence. We are to use all our means to spread the knowledge of true religion, and we must unite with others to make our efforts of any avail.[11]

But let us cleave, in the midst of parties, to an independence of party. If your education and temper dispose you to some austerity in your religious views — if you incline to revere God with awe rather than to love him — let that fear of him and the fear of sin make you abhor to judge your brother for his trust and his gratitude. And if you fear most the extremes of the rigid Christians and their propensity to a faith without knowledge, yet be careful that you frankly own the good that adorns them. Let us love and copy their seriousness, their bounty, their fear of sin; and join to it an affectionate trust in God, an ardent progress from virtue to virtue, an undaunted resolution to seek and maintain the truth and a hope of good hereafter which no evil nor disappointment nor failure can take away.

The Authority of Jesus

He taught them as one having authority and not as the scribes.
Matthew VII, 29.

THESE words are not only remarkable as they express the feeling produced by the instructions of Jesus in the promiscuous assembly of his countrymen, but also, as they are descriptive of the impression made by him as a moral teacher on all succeeding times. In the present discourse, I shall attempt to show the nature of this distinction, and, as in all respects he was an example [1] for us, to show how far we may hope by imitating his virtues, to share in his power.

Let us inquire into the means by which he gave dignity to his instructions.

He was not learned. He does not appear to have received any better education than a Jewish peasant. And there is no display of science or various reading in his discourses, nor does he ever refer to any other books than the Jewish Scriptures.

He was not a subtile reasoner. It is the fame of a few men that they have analyzed every thought and emotion of the human mind into its elements, that they have received nothing until it was proved, that they have shaken the evidence of the best authenticated facts and have introduced doubt under the foundation of every opinion. Others there are, who have applied the same ingenuity to better purpose, and have done what they could to fortify with impregnable reason every useful

THE AUTHORITY OF JESUS

custom, and every important truth. Neither of these sorts of skill, was the merit of Jesus, of whose instructions it is one of the most remarkable features that he does not reason at all. He proves nothing by argument.

He simply asserts, on the ground of his divine commission.[2] Every one of his declarations is a naked appeal to every man's consciousness whether the fact be so or not. Christianity could not be defended, if it looked to its author for a systematic account of its evidences arranged by the rules of logic.

Nor was it by powerful declamation, nor insinuating arts of address, that he attained this end. Nothing can be more simple than the style of his discourses. It is the style of conversation. Nor was it by means very acceptable to his countrymen, the charm of a great name, or the stately manners of a Rabbi. He came among them the reputed son of Joseph, and the story of his life shows us how free were his habits of intercourse with men. It is true that many passages incidentally show the singular deference with which he was approached; yet so entirely did this spring from other causes than such external accomplishments, that no pen has transmitted one syllable respecting the personal appearance, or the manners, or the voice of so remarkable a personage.

On these considerations, the enquiry returns with new force, how was it, if he was not learned, or subtile, or of noble family, or of popular arts, like many of his later disciples, that he spoke with an authority which they have never obtained?

I conceive it was because he taught truth, and the supreme kind of truth, (that which relates to man's moral nature) with greater fidelity and distinctness than any other; because he taught more truth, and (if I may say so) more truly; because he did not, as other teachers, drop here and there a good hint, a valuable fragment, but plainly announced the leading principles by which whilst the soul exists, it must be governed; because, speaking on his own convictions, he expressed with unexampled force, the great laws to which the human understanding must always bow, whilst it retains its own constitution; the great laws, which, after all our doubts, after running the round of skepticism, we return to acknowledge with new conviction.

He spoke of God in a new tongue, not as the philosophers had done, as an intellectual principle, nor as the vulgar had done, as a cruel or sensual demon, but in terms of earnest affection as being best understood by us as the Father of the human soul, the grand object of all thought, and that the end of life was a preparation of the soul to approach him by likeness of character. Humility, love, self denial, were the means of approaching him, — were the true glories of man. To have them was to have life. They make the natural felicity of a good mind, the real heaven after which men should seek. And as these cannot die, the mind that was clothed in them should not die.

And he summed up his instructions in the rule, Be ye perfect even as your father in heaven is perfect.

These sublime and salutary lessons found a willing entrance into such hearts as were not shut up against the truth by sin. The candid and virtuous were astonished at the gracious words that proceeded out of his mouth. Their hearts burned within them as he opened to them the Scriptures.

I would speak a little more particularly of the nature and reason of this superiority of Jesus over other teachers. There are different sorts of truth and various ways of possessing it and of communicating it; and it is quite important here to discriminate. You say the same truth is now possessed; we have the very words of Jesus, yet how ineffectual they prove from so many lips as utter them, and only rarely are they spoken in the spirit of our Common Teacher.[3]

In the first place, then, it was in Jesus *living* truth. There is a wide difference between the power of two teachers ordinarily classed under the same name and understood to teach the same faith. The reason is that in one his doctrine is to himself *living* truth, and he speaks it as he sees it; and in the other, it is dead truth, it is passively taken and taught at second hand; it is like a lump of indigestible matter in his animal system, separate and of no nourishment or use. It is, compared with the same truth quickened in another mind, like a fact in a child's lesson in geography, as it lies unconnected and useless in his memory, compared with the same fact as it enters into the knowledge of the surveyor or the shipmaster.

This is a distinction which I apprehend every one at all attentive to his own thoughts will readily understand. Every one will remember how often he heard in youth without heeding it any one of the common proverbs that pass from mouth to mouth and the lively satisfaction he derived from the perception of its truth the first time that his own experience led him to express the same fact in similar language. And he smiled at saying anew so trite a sentence. Hence, too, the common remark upon the new force which a man gives to a trivial thought when it is the fresh result of his own observation. Truth is always new from the mind that perceives it. But much more impressive is this property in the case of moral than of intellectual or physical facts.

First, then, it was living truth.[4]

In the next place, this truth which lived in him was *moral* truth. That truth whose distinguishing mark is that as soon as it is perceived, it commands. This introduces us into a new world. What is moral truth? moral law? or the authority of Virtue?

'It is that which all ages and all countries have made profession of in public; it is that which every man you meet puts on the show of; it is that which the primary and fundamental laws of all civil constitutions over the face of the earth make it their business and endeavor to enforce the practice of upon mankind, viz. justice, veracity and a regard to common good.'[5] It is God's mark upon every moral act that it tends to produce good; upon every immoral act that it tends to produce harm.

Obedience to it is that way of life to which all good is promised and the contrary of which all nature fights against. But what more concerns us at this time is that it is essential to the perfection of the faculties. It opens the eye, it sharpens the sight. It is the door to wisdom; it is the cause of love; it is the means of power.

'Since the world, (says Hartley) is a system of benevolence and consequently its author the object of unbounded love and adoration, benevolence and piety are the only true guides in our inquiries into it, the only keys which will unlock the mysteries of nature and clues which will lead through her labyrinths.'

And certainly every man will admit that a good man is a better judge of truth in any question than a bad man of the same abilities.

But in the next place there is a vital connexion between moral truth and right action, that where the truth is vividly seen, it leads directly to action, and when the actions are done, they lead directly to better knowledge, and so there is a constant reciprocal action of the opinions on the will, and of the will on the opinions; so that they cannot be separated in the thought of the observer, but the words are enforced by his veneration for the character, and the character is exalted by the dignity of the sentiments it is accustomed to express. This is what we mean to say by the expression *living truth*, when applied to morals. And this it will be admitted was true (if then only) in the character of Christ.[6] His character was consistent, part with part, and the mighty work of his hand was justified by the gracious word of his mouth. We may even say his miraculous powers were not separate but harmonized into his character. Rather say his hand was strong because his soul was filled with angelic virtue.

In the third place, a necessary accompaniment of moral truth is its authority. This belongs to it in the nature of man. It always speaks with a voice of command which all other desires feel it right to obey. This is not a rhetorical expression but a scientific fact. There is no man but perceives a difference between the natural reverence that belongs to this and to any other. The feeling is very different with which we hear that the sky is blue, the earth is a globe, three plus two equals five, or any speculative opinion or mathematical law, and that with which we hear, Blessed are the meek, Love God, Serve all men, Judge not, and the like, for here comes in the new relation, *I ought* and *I ought not*. Here comes in that new relation of command and obedience. Thus, I want food, or power, or praise, or society, but the moral faculty forbids me to seek them at my neighbor's expense — and all those desires feel the right of that command and the propriety of their obedience. 'Had it strength as it has right it would govern the world.' (Butler) Whosoever, therefore, teaches this truth participates of its authority, whosoever speaks it out of a soul over which it has full dominion, must speak as a God unto men, for he utters the word of God.

It is remarkable how this mastery which belongs to it shows itself in the tone that is taken by its teacher as much as in the facts that are presented. A tone of authority cannot be taken without truths of authority. It is impossible to mimick it. It proceeds directly from the perception of great principles. It is powerful because truth always convinces, and people always know whether they have been convinced or not. There is therefore no artifice possible in dealing with truth. He that hath it in himself will move you. He will speak with authority. He that hath it not will labor with his rhetoric and his learning in vain.

It is this truth more than miracles that moves the whole frame of human nature. It is not the power to make surprizing changes in matter, to heal the sick, to wake the dead, that can act on the soul of man with most effect.[7] These things would be prodigious indeed, but what then? Beyond the temporary convenience afforded to the individual they would effect no-

Down-plays miracles

thing but a blind wonder. No, real power is in that command of truth which can pour light through the soul. He that can reveal to me the great secrets of my own nature which I see to be true the moment they are disclosed, will have a deeper influence on me than he who chains my limbs or feeds me or who heals my disease. Because he holds the lamp by which I walk, he determines the course of my thoughts and actions and all the happiness I attain looks back to him under God as its author. This is what is meant by saying that Jesus is the author and finisher of our salvation.

Jesus then was distinguished from other teachers by the possession of living moral truth which he held according to its just conditions, that of being the principle of his own life.

1. The subject suggests two general considerations. A great error to which we are liable on this subject, is, that we are apt to separate the truth taught by Jesus from his office, and suppose that it was his divine authority, his peculiar designation to the office of Messiah that gives authority to his words, and not his words that mark him out as the Messiah. The utterance of that truth is his office. It is his truth that made him Messiah. (And it is his goodness that revealed to him so much truth.) He is our Saviour or Redeemer not because oil was poured on his head, nor because he descended by his mother of the line of David, nor because prophets predicted him or miracles attended him nor for all of these reasons but because he declared for the first time fully and intelligibly those truths on which the welfare of the human soul depends; because he declared them not as formal propositions but in a full apprehension of their commanding importance, — he lived by them; because in short they were so vitally his own that he has identified his own memory almost with the conscience of good men from that day to this.

Now there had been many other moral teachers before him yet had no one devoted himself with this entireness to the highest interests of the human race or expressed the rule of life

THE AUTHORITY OF JESUS

in anything like so just and comprehensive and significant a manner. Filled and empowered by this truth, his words have gone through the whole earth and his spirit has moved and continues to move the human family [8] to the renouncement of their sin and conversion to God. And therefore and thus is he the Messiah, the Saviour of men.

2. The next consideration of much importance is that as this authority belonged to this truth and not to any person, so it is not confined to the pure and benevolent Founder of Christianity but may and must belong to all his disciples in that measure in which they possess themselves of the truth which was in him. Jesus has not monopolized it. His mission was to communicate it and precisely in the same measure with it he communicates his power over men. There is no stint or jealousy or grudge in the divine bounty. God's thoughts are not like man's thoughts. Jesus is loved and followed in proportion not as men cower at his name and obey the letter of his commands in a slavish spirit, but as they generously embark in the same cause by word and by act; open the elementary truth he gave them; carry it out to farther conclusions; and each be to their own age and circumstances as nearly as they can the excellent benefactor which he has been to so many ages and nations.[9]

And thus many a disciple in different ages of the Church hath learned of Christ so much of his truth, hath had infused into his soul so much of his master's spirit that he hath spoken with a large measure of his master's authority. And these are they who have been the lights of the world and whose precepts and memory prompt all men to virtue. And all of us receive and understand and impart the same truth as we keep his commandments.

My friends, let us not be the last to receive this instruction. We can do nothing against his truth. It is the law and mould wherein God made the heavens and the earth and them that dwell therein. Let us not be slower than the multitude who first heard him, but let us pluck out of ourselves the only enemies his words can find in the human heart, our own sins; our false estimates of earthly good; our sensual, selfish, uncharitable thoughts; and we shall find, that, as we do this, the voice of our Saviour becomes the voice of a Friend;[10] — sounds to us full of consolation, of promise, of praise. At last when truth has had its whole effect on our minds, it will gain its fulness of authority by becoming to us simply the echo of our own thought. We shall find we think as Christ thought. Thus we shall be one with him, and with him are with the Father.

Sept. 5, 1830

Self-Culture

I beseech you therefore, brethren, by the mercies of God that ye present your bodies a living sacrifice, holy, acceptable unto God, which is your reasonable service. Romans XII, 1.

The shortness of life and the importance of improving it are old topics but as they get a new and increased interest from every hour they are the more seasonable, the oftener we have heard them. The great art which religion teaches, is the art of conducting life well, not only in a view to future well-being, but in the very best manner, if there were no future state. Every serious man looks to religion for the supply of wants which he deeply feels. We want such views of life and duty as shall harmonize all we do and suffer; as shall present us with motives worthy of our nature, and objects sufficient for our powers of action. We want principles which shall give the greatest strength to our social union, and the greatest efficacy to social action. We want principles which shall guide us in every transaction of life; that shall go into the shop, and the factory; that shall make contracts, and project enterprizes, and give gifts, and receive favours. We want principles that shall direct our education when we are young, and select our profession and control its exercise when we are mature; that shall assist us in forming our friendships, and connexions in life. We want principles that will bear the scrutiny of solitude, of doubt, of experience; that will fortify us against disaster; that will enable us to overcome every temptation, and every fear; and make us respectable and happy in ourselves when we have nothing and hope nothing on earth.

The Revelation of Jesus Christ discovers in us such principles and appeals to them. It withdraws man from looking for his motives to the world, outward, and directs him to look within. It shows him a Divine Eye that cannot be deceived, that fixed within his soul, commands a perfect prospect of his whole being, all he does, and all he wills, — and passes judgment upon all. It teaches him to conform all his actions to this superior will; for this is God working in him, both to will and to do. It teaches him that some things perish, and that other things never die. It shows him that truth and right are of God everlasting, and impart their own eternity to the soul that embraces them with its affections. It is in the power of man, so far as, obeying this voice, he puts aside the force of vulgar motives, and refusing the service of his senses, subjects himself to the law of his mind, — puts off, so to speak, his human nature, and puts on the divine nature, — it is in his power to obtain a degree of participation (I speak it with reverence) in the attributes of God; to enter into that peace and joy, that unmixed delight in goodness and that universal love which are in Him; and, so entirely to apply his own spirit to the Divine Mind, that he shall be, as it has been expressed, a drop in that Ocean, moving with him, acting with him, partaking of his felicity.

Blessed among men be the name of Jesus of Nazareth! illustrious and beautiful his history! This immense elevation of Man from his capricious, low, and too often descending course of action to this interest in and cooperation with the Providence of God, is suggested directly to our minds from his gospel. He gave his doctrine the authority of his life. In a degenerate age, in a degraded country, himself of low birth and suffering a malefactor's death, he spent his few years in conformity with these principles in such manner as to exemplify to all time their infinite superiority.

SELF-CULTURE

It is in the spirit of that master whose principles of life he is expounding that the apostle Paul enjoins us to present ourselves living sacrifices. The duty to which we are called is nothing less [than] an unceasing effort at self-culture,[1] or, in the words of the apostle, a patient continuance in well doing. We are endowed with the power of voluntary action [2] and taught to turn our freedom to this end. Our present condition, is one extreme from which we are to depart, and this height of a divine nature the other extreme towards which we are to aspire. We are to present ourselves living sacrifices. This is our work, and it admits of no delay. It is our first and present business. I shall offer, my brethren, a few of the more urgent reasons which speak to every mind, of whatever power, or condition, in behalf of the life to come, — in behalf of an immediate, unceasing labour to become better.

I. Let it be considered by us that there is a retribution in every hour for past action and therefore no time must be lost. Already our good and our evil actions are gone before into judgment, and their rewards are visited on our heads. We interpret the Scriptures when they speak of judgment as always referring to God's award upon character after this life, and so are apt to forget that the laws of God are eternal, and, as they have no end, *so they have no beginning.*[3] Whenever there is moral action, these laws take place. Wherever there is character, there is judgment. It will be admitted by all who have thought much upon life, that, in a great degree a compensation takes place in our condition for all the qualities of the man. Go where you will, you shall work out with great fidelity your own effect.[4] Every hand shall hold a whip to your vices, and a laurel for your virtues. Such is the force of spiritual nature that every thing takes the hue of our thought. The peevish man finds his way full of crosses; the benevolent man full of charities. The world is but a mirror in which every mind sees its own image reflected. Everything speaks wisdom to the wise, and sensuality to the sensual, and worldly hope to the ambitious, folly to the frivolous, and God to the good. As a man thinketh so he is and so he receives. This seems to hold through all our intellectual and moral properties. It is so with our possession of truth. Let a man have a strong grasp of truth and everywhere he shall find confirmation. If a man have clear and pious perceptions of the Unity of God, of the tender love of the Universal Father and have learned to live with him in prayer and in action as his child, if in these views his heart delights — let him go where he will, he shall not find strange Gods. In the churches of his brethren of other persuasions, Catholic or Calvinistic brethren, in the temple of heathen, the Unity of God and his parental love shall be preached to him, and new and unexpected conviction of the truth will dawn upon his mind out of arguments offered against it. And if he surrender his understanding and receive error his errors shall seem to him to be confirmed by the world. So is this the law of all action. All things are double, one against another.[5] Love and you shall be loved. Hate and you shall be hated. Judge not and ye shall not be judged, saith our Saviour, for whatsoever measure ye mete, it shall be measured to you again. And as truth finds light, so error finds its own darkness in all the creation.

A Retribution, however imperfect it may be, does thus run into every moment of life, so that prosperity cannot give peace to the bad man, nor adversity take it away from the good man. It will not therefore do to neglect your soul a moment, lest you reap a harvest of thistles for a harvest of wheat. Brethren, if these things are so, if even very imperfect justice takes place, it is plainly no world for careless and improvident persons. It will not do to live by accident, we must live by design. We must do nothing without intention. Everything admonishes us never to slacken our heed but always watch. We must have intention in manners, we must watch our conversation, watch pleasure, watch in the streets, watch in the closet, in all things to make the voluntary offer of ourselves to our Maker.

II. But a second reason why we ought to hasten to make our sacrifice is our constant liability to changes and care, to disease and death.[6] Look back, brethren, at any of your deliberate purposes of improvement and recollect the sad interruptions that intervened between the design and the performance. A thousand cares besiege the most favored condition. There are always mistakes to be corrected, there are difficulties to be encountered, a livelihood to be earned, relations to be assisted, there are losses to be repaired, and public as well as private duties to tax your time. Then sickness comes and cuts down in a moment the vast projects of hope, and suspends the labours of benevolence. He lays his grievous hand it may be, on the best years of our life and turns to nothing the most manly and prudent schemes, puts a stop to labor, and to study and bids you wait, whilst he loosens the sinews of strength, and drains the blood, and puts pain and weariness into the bones and makes the heart sick with hope deferred. And what is sickness, but the forerunner of death? We are of that feeble frame that every accident threatens our being, the wound of a pin will let out our life; a fever, a humour, a draft of cold air will destroy it, and put a final period to all our intercourse with men, all our repentance, our perseverance, our enthusiasm, our faith, our hope on earth.

Tomorrow, today, the next moment, it may be the turn of any of us, the strongest, the youngest. It will not do then for such manner of persons as we are, brethren, to postpone for an hour any serious purpose, much less the main purpose for which we live.

There are other considerations that speak loudly to us but these two will suffice to the wise, that every moment is already reaping the consequences of action, and the fact that we have not a warrant on our being for another hour. These facts should prevail with us to give our utmost heed to use what ease and health and talents and means we have in a present obedience to the commandments, a pressing toward the mark of perfection, [a] surrender of ourselves to God.

Every one of us should give that he has. The way is plain — the work is simple — we are to give ourselves in every moment living sacrifices. We are to give *ourselves*, that is, all that we have. We are to give *ourselves*, that is, the whole of our being, the present as well as the future. We must give not what we would, but what we can. Some of us have the trial of sickness; that need not prevent; we are to give our sickness. There is perhaps no more costly and acceptable offering than the obedience of a holy life on a sick bed. It is easy to be resigned to God's will when that will gives us prosperity and usefulness but in the loitering months and years of sickness, to bring the reluctant spirit to feel a cheerful submission, to be left out of the race, to send up thanksgivings to him that has stricken us, to feel glad that he doth not need our service, to feel that thousands at his bidding speed and that they also serve who only stand and wait,[7] — that is a severe and difficult duty, but that also is to present ourselves living sacrifices, holy and acceptable to God. It may please him to reward such virtue upon earth. It may please him to restore us to new and wider usefulness in his service, but surely he will reward us in our character and eternal condition.

Finally, brethren, in whatever condition we are, in fear, in misfortune, in ease, in youth, in age, let us present ourselves to God, let us not be conformed to this world, but be transformed into the likeness of the eternal world. Here on earth let us keep the laws and observe the customs and think the thoughts, and speak the language of Heaven, and God shall administer every aid, and shall make us pass with joy from this present world to the world of spirits.

Trust Yourself

For what is a man profited, if he gain the whole world and lose his own soul?   Matthew XVI, 26.

All the instructions which religion addresses to man imply a supposition of the utmost importance, which is, that every human mind is capable of receiving and acting upon these sublime principles. That which is made for an immortal life must be of an infinite nature.[1] That which is taught that its daily duty lies in overcoming the pleasures of sense, and in being superior to all the shows and power of this world, must indeed have something real and noble in its own possessions. And that which can sustain such relations to God as will justify the uniform language of the Scripture in speaking of good men must have costly and venerable attributes. It is no small trust to have the keeping of a soul. And compared with their capacity men are not such as they ought to be.

It is the effect of religion to produce a higher self-respect, a greater confidence in what God has done for each of our minds than is commonly felt among men.[2] It seems to me, brethren, that a great calamity with which men are contending after all the preaching of Christianity is their distrust of themselves. They do not know, because they have not tried, the spiritual force that belongs to them. If a man has a soul, he has an infinite spiritual estate, he has a responsibility that is tremendous, simply in the view of the duration of its being; but far more so in the view of its nature and connexions. If God has made us with such intention as revelation discloses, then it must be that there are in each of us all the elements of moral and intellectual excellence, that is to say, if you act out yourself, you will attain and exhibit a perfect character. Our Saviour in the confidence of all the worth which his instructions supposed in human nature, says to his disciples, What is a man profited though he gain the whole world, and lose his own soul? The lesson that may be gathered from this Scripture, is, to value our own souls, to have them in such estimation as never to offend them. And this is the theme of the present discourse.

I wish to enforce the doctrine that a man should trust himself; should have a perfect confidence that there is no defect or inferiority in his nature; that when he discovers in himself different powers, or opinions, or manners, from others whom he loves and respects, he should not think himself in that degree inferior, but only different;[3] and that for every defect there is some compensation provided in his system; and that wherever there is manifest imperfection in his character, it springs from his own neglect to cultivate some part of his mind. I am afraid of this great tendency to uniformity of action and conversation among men.[4] I am afraid of the great evil done to so sacred a property as a man's own soul by an imitation arising out of an unthinking admiration of others. I believe God gave to every man the germ of a peculiar character. The ends of action are the same, but the means and the manner are infinitely various. As every man occupies a position in some respects singular, every man has probably thoughts that never entered the mind of any other man. Cast your thoughts round upon your different acquaintances, and see if any two present the same character to your imagination. And the more finished the character the more striking is its individuality; and the better is the state of the world, the more unlike will be men's characters, and the more similar their purposes. If you name over men that have created the most decided greatness you will find that they present very dissimilar ideas to your thought. Abraham, Moses, Socrates, Milton, Fénelon, these are all eminently good men yet how wholly unlike. But instead of society's exhibiting this striking variety of mind, there may be noticed everywhere a tame resemblance of one man's thoughts and conversation to another's. The gardeners say[5] that the reason why vines were thought to fail in this country, was that they tried to get out of one soil the flavor that belonged to another soil; they would raise Madeira grapes in America when often the fruit is very different that grows on either side of the same fence, and much more in different latitudes and continents. But cultivate in every soil the grape of that soil. In like manner, men fail in neglecting the intimations of their own inborn intelligence out of an unlimited deference to other characters. Let them on the contrary have greater confidence in the plan yet to them unknown which the moral Architect has traced for them. If he has appointed to it some present defect or less measure than he has given another, as will doubtless be true, he has also given it its own excellences. Explore the mine and make it yield such ores as are in it. Be sure that nothing therein was made in vain.

It is not uncommon to hear a man express with great interest his regret that he possesses some particular manner of intellectual superiority or some quickness of feeling which, though reckoned advantages, he thinks rather stand in the way of greatness. It seems to me this self-condemnation is ungrateful and injurious. He thinks this quality is not good, because others who are great do not have it. Let him rather trust the wisdom of God and extort from these faculties all their treasury of good. When I look at the vegetable world, I admire a tree, a flower, and see that each oak and each lily is perfect in its kind though different in its proportions and number and arrangement of branches and leaves from every other oak and lily in the field. And shall I not believe as much of every mind; that it has its own beauty and character and was never meant to resemble any other one and that God pronounced it good after its own kind. Every man has his own voice, manner, eloquence, and, just as much, his own sort of love, and grief, and imagination, and action. He has some power over other men that arises to him from his peculiar education and the cast of his circumstances and the complexion of his mind; and it were the extreme of folly if he forbears to use it, because he has never seen it used by any body else. Let him scorn to *imitate* any being. Let him scorn to be a secondary man. Let him fully trust his own share of God's goodness, that if used to the uttermost, it will lead him on to a perfection which has no type yet in the universe, save only in the Divine Mind.

One measure of a man's character is his effect upon his fellowmen. And any one who will steadily observe his own experience will I think become convinced, that every false word he has uttered, that is to say, every departure from his own convictions, out of deference to others has been a sacrifice of a certain amount of his power over other men. For every man knows whether he has been accustomed to receive truth or falsehood, — valuable opinion or foolish talking, from his brother, and this knowledge must inevitably determine his respect.

Now what is it to speak from one's own conviction, to trust yourself, — what is it but to keep one's mind ever awake, to use the senses and the reason, to rely on your birthright of powers which God bestowed? But how little of this virtue enters into conversation. Men speak not from themselves but from the floating parlance of the time; they think, — What is expected to be said? What others have said? — What is safest to be said? — instead of what they hold to be true. Is it not wonderful that they do not see the infinite advantage that he must possess who always listens only to himself? [6] I think this cannot be illustrated better than by comparing the looseness of men's discourse upon these questions most deeply interesting to our nature with the cogency of their talk in common affairs. How clear and strong is the language of a man speaking the truth in things concerning his ordinary business, that a commodity sold for so much, that a stage runs on such a road, the wind blows from such a quarter, or such were the numbers of a contested vote. No ingenuity, no sophism that the learning or eloquence of a man would intrude in such a conversation could be any match to the force of their speech. It would be ridiculous weakness. For when men converse on their pressing affairs they do not so much seem to speak as to become mere organs through which facts themselves speak. Now that is precisely the way in which God seems to justify those who withdraw their eyes from everything else, and fix them on their own thoughts only. They become, as it were passive, and are merely the voice of things. If a man would always as exclusively consult his own thoughts as men do in these things, he would always speak with the same force, a force which would be felt to be far greater than belonged to him or to any mortal, but was proper to immortal truth.

It is important to observe that this self-reliance which grows out of the Scripture doctrine of the value of the soul is not inconsistent either with our duties to our fellow men or to God. Some will say, to press on a man the necessity of guiding himself only by the unaided light of his own understanding, and to shun as dangerous the imitation of other men seems inconsistent with the Scripture commandments that enjoin self-abasement and unlimited love to others, and also with our natural relations to other men who are older and wiser and better than we are. Certainly it is our duty to prefer another's good always to our own, and gratefully to borrow all the light of his understanding as far as it agrees with ours, but the duty is quite as plain the moment our own convictions of duty contradict another's, we ought to forsake his leading, let him be of what wisdom or condition he will, and without fear to follow our own.[7] Brethren,

I beg each of you to remember, whether, when you have in any instance forsaken your first impressions of a book, or a character, or a question of duty, and adopted new ones from complaisance, you have not by and by been compelled to receive your own again, with the mortification of being overcome by your own weapons. Certainly other men, especially good men, are entitled from a good man to all respect. I honour the modesty and benevolence which is respectful to men of worth and thinks there is soundness in all their opinions. But I honour more this image of God in human nature which has placed a standard of character in every human breast, which is above the highest copy of living excellence. Every man has an idea of a greatness that was never realized. Take the history of a great and good man, of Newton, or Franklin, or Washington, and explain all its details to the most obscure and ignorant wretch that wears the human form, you shall find that whilst he understands all its elevation he will be able to put his finger upon imperfections in that life. Which shows that in his heart there is a greater man than any that has lived in the world.

Nor on the other hand let it be thought that there is in this self-reliance anything of presumption, anything inconsistent with a spirit of dependence and piety toward God. In listening more intently to our own soul we are not becoming in the ordinary sense more selfish, but are departing farther from what is low and falling back upon truth and upon God. For the whole value of the soul depends on the fact that it contains a divine principle, that it is a house of God, and the voice of the eternal inhabitant may always be heard within it.[8]

A good man, says Solomon, is satisfied from himself. An original mind is not an eccentric mind.[9] To be wholly independent of other men's judgments does not mean to come under their censure by any extravagance of action. But it is only those who are so that can bear the severest scrutiny of other men's judgments. It is by following other men's opinions that we are misled and depraved. It is those who have steadily listened to their own who have found out the great truths of religion which are the salvation of the human soul. My friends, let me beseech you to remember that it is only by looking inward that the outward means of knowledge can be made of any avail. The soul, the soul is full of truth. The bible is a sealed book to him who has not first heard its laws from his soul. The drunkard and the voluptuary might as well read it in an unknown language as in their mother tongue. And it is this fact that gives such immense meaning to the precept, Know thyself. To him who has reached this wisdom how ridiculous is Caesar and Bonaparte wandering from one extreme of civilization to the other to conquer men, — himself, the while, unconquered, unexplored, almost wholly unsuspected to himself. Yet Europe and Asia are not so broad and deep, have nothing so splendid, so durable as the possessions of this empire. What shall it profit a man though he gain the whole world and lose his own soul?

My friends, the deep religious interest of this question is apparent to you. The body we inhabit shall shortly be laid in the dust, but the soul assures us, with the voice of God to confirm it, that it will not die. Let this strange and awful being that we possess have that reverence that is due from us. Let us leave this immoderate regard to meats and drinks, to dress and pleasure and to unfounded praise, and let us go alone and converse with ourselves, and the word of God in us. What that bids us do let us do with unshaken firmness and what it bids us forbear, let us forbear. Let us love and respect each other as those who can assist us in understanding ourselves and let us hear the distinct voice of Scripture which has taught us to forsake the world and its vanities and deceptions, and seek God who is to be worshipped in our hearts.[10]

How Old art Thou?

How old art thou? Genesis XLVII, 8.

THIS is the inquiry which in the natural world may be made of all objects, for all are growing old. And old age is the approach of dissolution to animated and to inanimate beings. Every science is the record of the progressive changes or steps toward dissolution in the objects it considers. Geology shows us how the ball we dwell upon has been rent and its central beds of granite lifted to be the ragged peaks of the Andes and Alps; how these have been worn and crumbled into common soil; what races of vast and shapeless animals have roamed over the earth and been buried under new convulsions; how populous cities of men have been whelmed, now under floods of the sea, now under inundations of melted stone from volcanic hills, now have been swallowed by the yawning of the earth itself. These are the great graveyards that intomb their thousands in a moment. But every moment is as fatal as these dreadful catastrophes; every moment kills some part of life in all the children of nature. In our own race it is plain enough. Every face, every feature we behold betrays marks of its destiny. All history is an epitaph. All life is but a progress toward death. It is computed that in ordinary times when the plague is stayed in Asia and war in Europe and only the common causes of mortality operate, 2400 of the human race die in an hour, so that almost every pulse is the knell of a brother. The world is but a large urn. The glorious sun itself, burning in his bright-

HOW OLD ART THOU?

ness at the heart of the system, and pouring out the incessant floods of heat and light, to all his tributary planets, seems but a funeral fire operating the destruction of all that he shines upon and lighting men and animals and plants to their graves.

All things are so constituted that they perish in using. The lamp burns out, the causes of destruction lie so thick and numberless that the gentlest wind that brings the perfume of the fields proves poisonous to some frame and checks the tides of the blood and sets the seed of fever or rheumatism. In this scene of wreck and fear the natural man hears on every side the question, How old art thou? that is to say, How soon is your turn to die?

The true asylum from these apprehensions of mortality is the church.[1] It is the only refuge from this fear. In the mouldering of nature we flee to the gospel. The soul escapes to God affrighted by the decays of the universe. (To the natural man all things decay and himself also. To the spiritual man all things are eternal and himself also in God.) What is it that working ever in the soul of man has constrained him in every place to build his temple, altar, church or meetinghouse? What is that grander nature which everywhere separates him at short periods from his day labor to think and to pray? A conviction swells in his heart, which all the decays of the senses will not put down, that within this decay there is a germ that decays not. Whilst all things are thus flitting away there is a duration to which a century is but the turning of an hour glass. Whilst all perishes, there is a creation as fresh as it was in its morning prime, before the stars were launched on their orbits, and that shall be as fresh when they are swept out of the heaven. There is a natural world and there is a spiritual world.

My friends, the church takes a different view of almost all seasons and events from that which is taken in the street or the exchange or the statehouse. It surveys man and his life from quite another side.

There is a spiritual world which is immutable, the kingdom

of love, of purity, of righteousness, of truth, the kingdom of God — which is incorruptible and cannot grow old. The cause of all order, the source of all good it is in the world and the world is made by it, yet the world knows it not. But the soul of man must live in it or it hath no life. As the body was born into this world, so must the soul be born into that, not in some future time but now. This is the Scripture doctrine of the Regeneration.[2] The Scripture is the message from that world to the soul of man to call him to that, his true home. It teaches the necessity of this new birth. It teaches that in the closing the senses to the exclusive commerce with outward things and in the opening of the interior senses to the acknowledgment of this better kingdom does true life consist. In the spiritual world only can we live. In this world we die daily. It calls nothing else, *life*, but that life. It calls the entering on that state by men, a *passage from death unto life*. It looks round on men struggling in vain care and keen competitions of this world, the pursuit of fame and office, the labor for perishing meat, as all laborious trifling no better than the toys of children. It teaches the soul to seek for life in itself as the Father hath life in Himself. And what is the life that Jesus means? His truth alone. 'The words that I speak unto you,' said he, '*they are spirit* and they are life.' That soul only has entered into life that has found out, that God's will is better than its own; that humility is better than pride; that to seek another's good is better than to seek its own; that to be good is to do good; that a perfect trust in God gives more contentment than the greatest possessions. (These facts are the years of the soul.) Therefore as soon as man has received these truths, not into his ear, for then they are mere sounds; not into his memory, for there also it may be a dead stock, but into his soul as a part of his soul as we receive bread into our bodies and it becomes flesh, so when this has become mind and soul in us, then is his second life begun. Then does man emerge out of the finite into the infinite; out of time into eternity.[3] Then really does his

HOW OLD ART THOU?

life begin. Now, *How old art thou?* Judge by this measure. Let the question come home to each of us. Do not run back to the month nor the year when your parents say you were born; if you are in any true sense, *of age* 'ask yourself'; take the New Testament for your Almanack. How long have you *lived?*[4] that is to say, how long have you lived in any other way than to the senses? How long has the word of God been to you anything but a dull book? Has light begun to break forth from it? How long has Jesus Christ been the Son of God in your mind? Take the New Testament and read it thoughtfully and observe how many of its rules yet seem disagreeable to you. See if you do not stop with the first recorded teaching of the Lord, *Blessed are the poor in spirit for theirs is the Kingdom of heaven.* I am afraid it will seem to you mean, burdensome and unworthy, not finding through the darkness of your soul any correspondent sentiment reflecting it as a mirror in your mind. Read on. Find the summary of the new law, *Love the Lord your God with all your heart and strength and mind.* Here is the great law of moral nature. And does it find its full echo in yours? Read the next, *Love your neighbour as yourself.* Is this your rule? Have you shared your means and toil between the good of others and your own good? How many months have been filled with the love of others and how many have been spent upon yourself? Stop now and think — *how old is your soul?* Is it ten years old? Is it one year old? Is it one month old? Has it yet burst its bondage? Has it yet awoke from the womb of worldly life to the light of Heaven, and the sight of the face of God? And yet twenty, thirty, forty, fifty, sixty ungrateful years of self-love, of impurity, of sloth and covetousness have been counted on the family register and every one has ample vouchers in the memories of your companions, perhaps in the too faithful imitation of your children.

My friends, we received the words of the gospel with our mothers' milk; we call ourselves Christians, that is to say, receivers of the word of God that came by Christ, — and yet if we deduct all those days of our life that have not been lived in this faith; if we reckon up only those hours that have proved our adherence to the truth, add up all the good, and take out all the evil, I am afraid these years that have been so busily spent and have brought us so near to the grave would shrink to a hand's breadth — the compass of a few hours — perhaps to less. Honourable age is not that which standeth in length of time, nor that is measured by number of years but wisdom is grey hair unto a man and unspotted life is old age.

These principles must be the law of our action. Just as in the natural world we conform ourselves to natural laws and do not try to walk on the water nor to fly into the air nor to live without food or without motion, so in the spiritual world if really we enter it by a new birth we shall studiously conform ourselves to these principles which Jesus declared. I do not think we are old at all until the Christian law flows unobstructed through the channels of our life. It seems to me there should be no Christian who should not hold himself amenable for all his acts and words to every other Christian. I desire to do nothing that I cannot justify. If anything can be shown us in our practice inconsistent with what we receive as truth we are bound to alter our action. It is the perfection of free agency to be as faithful to the law as brute matter is. We believe it impossible for God to do wrong because he is perfectly wise. There is not a leaf nor a fibre in all the vast economy of nature that breaks a law of matter, so neither should one thought in all the world of souls. When we are old truly, old in love, old in truth, old in God, we shall thus find our perfect freedom, a perfect law, and move 'impelled by strict necessity along the path of order and of good.'

Is it not fit, O my friends, that we should make the life of the soul in us or the life of God in the soul coextensive with the term of our natural life? That whole term is a span. Seventy or sixty or thirty such rounds as this make up human life. Twelve of those few years are taken up in childhood; then follow the heats and temptations of youth, that are apt to make the real life yet shorter, and so much of maturity is apt to be consumed in the cares of this world, that the main business of man is shoved aside from day to day and remains at the last undone. Now it is too soon and then it is too late. This delay has been the rock on which the former men have been shipwrecked. Our time is yet present. That span out of his measureless eternity which the Almighty Father allows to each, to be tried and instructed, to hear his name and to read his commandments, to make friends, to deal with men, to choose our part and make our character, that time which is nearly equal in all, (a few years making little difference when compared with the boundless duration out of which it rose and into which it recedes,) — is now ours. It is all that the great and the wise have had. It is all that saints and heroes had. It is all that Paul or Luther or Newton or Washington had, to lift themselves by humility and the love of truth and sublime energy into the spiritual world and help the human race. It is now our turn of life. It is a singular proof of the independence of spiritual nature on space and time that this life is long enough for the vast purposes to be answered by it. It is long enough for useful men to work their ends. It is long enough to the wise to instruct men. It has been long enough for tyrants to enslave men. It has been long enough for the patriots to free nations. A truth may be announced in a moment that shall go down to all ages and affect all human society.[5] Finally, it is long enough, as all experience shows, for men to be saved or to be lost. And now it is our turn to make our election; all for which the soul of a man can exist, the choice of all the future, of the love of God, and of all souls, and unceasing advancement towards the infinitude of wisdom and love, or the rejection of all these, are on the right hand and on the left hand, of each of us. We are to choose principles for the rule of our souls on the one part or we are to prefer the little gratifications that begin and end in this nook of earth where our bodies were born and where they will moulder. This is our alternative. It is pressed on our minds at a season like this with unwonted force.

Whilst the occasion calls us to this consideration there is another fact worthy of our most intense attention, the care God has manifested that we must make this choice for ourselves. It is the stern call of his moral order that each must be wise for himself. Every soul is jealously excluded from the salvation or the death of the rest. The knowledge that has been accumulated by others is of no use until it has been verified by us. For all the learning and sound judgment and rich experience that has been in the world no man is wiser by one poor thought who is not wise in himself. And yet more clear is this truth respecting another's virtue. He is virtuous to himself. But whilst wisdom cannot pass into folly nor one man's goodness into another who is vicious, yet these are means of helping those who help themselves. To him that hath is given. If it were not for this law the vast burden of evidence arising into one voice from the history of every individual man, would teach every other that a Christian life leads to peace and a worldly life to ruin and leave us no room to doubt. The convictions of all would be accumulated on him and the gospel would be demonstrated in his faith. But there is no such lazy wisdom allowed us. None can by any means redeem his brother, all past wisdom is nothing but as far as it is identified in our own. Our own is nothing till our will directs it. But God is continually presenting excitements, suggestions to startle us into attention and beseech men as Christ besought them to be reconciled to God.

One of these excitements, one of these occasions that are the trumpets and thunders of God is this which now speaks to us. The shadows of the last hours of the year are come upon us. They speak to us of change and death. They hush the passions, the worldly hopes, they outspeak our temptations even, and procure a moment's silence for their question. They ask if the time has any terror to you; if you have any fear of what time and death can do or whether you have passed from death into life through the power of that quickening truth which Jesus revealed. If you have any fear of death, it is a pretty plain mark that you have not yet read your title clear to a place in the new heavens and the new earth, wherein dwelleth righteousness; that the flesh has yet a great part in you. Let us, my friends, not be deaf to this voice, let us save these fleeting moments with a divine economy by making them bind us to God for the next year. Let us repent of our sins. Let us love one another; let us be humble; let us be resigned to God's will; let us sin no more. These are the signs of the Regeneration, of our birth and adoption into that world, of which God is the everlasting light, where is no age but immortal youth [6] and no change but from glory to glory.

Miracles

The same came to Jesus by night and said unto him, Rabbi, we know that thou art a teacher sent from God, for no man can do these miracles that thou doest, except God be with him.   John III, 2.

It is my purpose to offer to your consideration a plain account of the reasons which make the miracles recorded in the New Testament credible. It will be admitted by all that as soon as one miracle has been shown to be credible it is enough for our faith. The point of importance in the question, therefore, has always been felt to be, to show that in some circumstances it is not unreasonable to expect a miracle and that such circumstances existed in the age of Jesus Christ. I shall therefore proceed to consider first the considerations which show a miracle is not incredible.

1. The first consideration is that a miracle is the only means by which God can make a communication to men, that shall be known to be from God.[1] For to suppose that he should speak directly to each mind is only to suppose millions of miracles instead of one. The speaking to each mind in any unusual way would be a miracle or else would not be believed by that mind, a peculiar communication from God. To deny, therefore, that there has ever been or ever can be any miracle is to deny that there has ever been or ever can be any communication from God to men.

2. The second consideration requires more words in the statement. It is a certain want that arises from the nature of things to mankind, the human mind, and which only a miracle can supply. It seems to be the inevitable effect of the invariable order of God's operations, to withdraw the human mind from the contemplation of God. For the unceasing procession of events without any interruption, or any sign of intelligence beyond what the infinite beauty of the whole furnishes, without a hand outstretched, or a word spoken in heaven or on earth, makes man doubt the existence of a cause that is never shown to his senses.[2] It is only the very thoughtful that see the necessity of something more. The multitudes, seeing the laws of nature uniform, stop at the law and take that for cause enough. Now the only way by which men's attention can be aroused to the thought that there is a presiding Intelligence, is to startle them by a plain departure from the common order, as by causing the blind to see and the dead to arise.[3] There are thousands of men who, if there were no histories and if the order of natural events had never been broken, would never ask in the course of their lives for anything beyond a secondary cause and never ask for a first. It is enough for them to say that a stone falls or the earth falls in its orbit by Gravity; that a man walks and speaks by reason of his Life, without asking whence Gravity and whence Life? But astonish them with a miracle and their minds instantly inquire why things keep one order rather than another, and the same inquiry instantly suggests itself to every mind who hears of the miracle.

Now does not this furnish a suitable occasion for the particular interpositions of that Providence which consults always for the good of his offspring? If truth and religion are good for us, will not God interpose to prevent us from losing both?

3. Another consideration that makes a miracle not incredible is this, that it supposes no more power than we have already seen every day exerted in and around us; and no more

inconceivable power. The existence of God is necessarily suggested to the reasoning man by what he now beholds and a miracle suggests no more.[4] Does the unbeliever who doubts of a miracle suppose that by giving up that superstition he has made all plain? that he shall now be troubled by nothing for which he cannot assign a cause? Far otherwise. To an instructed eye the most common facts are the most wonderful. It is not so surprising to a wise man that there should be volcanoes and earthquakes and meteors and cannibals and monsters, as that he himself should live from day to day. A wise man perceives that there is really nothing more incredible in the story that reason should be restored to an insane man by a word than that he himself should be able by a mere thought to raise his own arm; or that he can communicate such vibrations to the air by his tongue as shall make his thoughts known to another man; or that by an effort of recollection he can summon up events in which he took part twenty years ago. All our life is a miracle. Ourselves are the greatest wonder of all. Our own being is a far more astounding and inexplicable fact, than, after life has once been exercised, could be the resurrection of a man from the tomb.

The ordinary course of nature indicates an intelligence capable of the alleged works, for it can require no greater power to suspend than to originate the operations of nature. In other words, I can believe a miracle, because I can raise my own arm.[5] I can believe a miracle because I can remember. I can believe it because I can speak and be understood by you. I can believe in a manifestation of power beyond my own, because I am such a manifestation.

4. In the fourth place, as a miracle does not transcend the power, so neither does it depart from the character of the Intelligence that presides over ordinary nature, in being an evidence of a moral truth. Our constitution is moral, and so is the constitution of the universe. All things preach the moral law, that is to say, a life in conformity to nature is a moral life.

Health is to be sought by temperance. Safety is got by abstaining to offend. The love of others is gained by loving them. All benevolent feelings are pleasant to him that exercises them. All malevolent feelings are painful. And the moral law with no essential variation reigns in the bosom of every man. The character of the Deity that presides over the world is thus ascertained to be moral. And therefore a miracle, which is a special act of his power for a moral purpose, conforms with what we know of him.

I take notice of this fact that from the constitution of things we should expect a miracle *would have a moral purpose*, because it seems to be necessary to the idea of a miracle that it should be *moral*. A miracle must be to a moral end, to have any effect. A miracle could not prove a falsehood. It cannot approve a vicious act. Let it be suggested that here before our eyes a man should pretend to declare from God that hatred and murder were agreeable to his will and should cause stones to speak or storms to rise to confirm his word,— it could never engage us to think that it was right to hate and kill men and that the messenger came from God. It might bewilder us with horrible doubts, but the miracle would be ascribed to an evil spirit and not to the same power which made our moral constitution. To make a miracle of any effect as evidence, it must accompany the revelation of a truth which, when made known, is agreeable to the laws of the mind. Then the truth and the miracle mutually confirm each other.

These considerations may serve to show in general the credibility of a miracle. The history of a particular miracle must always show to what degree of credibility it is entitled.

We ought to weigh with extreme caution the evidence of any alleged miracle, for though a pious man will always be ready on good evidence to admit a miraculous agency, yet we feel that the same wisdom which may sometimes interrupt its customary order, for the special benefit of man, will for the same reason, very seldom interrupt it. Some may ask, if there have been miracles, why are they not common? Why have not I seen them? For this reason, that their often occurrence would be fatal to knowledge which the human mind stores up and reasons on the expectation of the permanence of the laws of nature. Any uncertainty in the operation of the laws of nature would defeat entirely the purposes of that wisdom which formed him and them. If it were in the least uncertain whether the sun would rise tomorrow or whether wheat on being sown should come up wheat or hemlock, all prudence, all experience, would be of no use. And not only so but the order on which we found our beliefs of the Unity and Providence of the presiding cause would be broken. And not only so but the miracle, it is plain, would no longer answer the use of a miracle.

I wish now to speak of the peculiar credibility of the miracles of the New Testament. In so doing I shall confine myself to a single general consideration, which seems to be conclusive on the subject, that is, the claim to miraculous power considered in connection with the nature of the revelation. It ought to be considered that a miracle is a lower species of evidence. It speaks to unbelief. It speaks to ignorance.[6] It is not (even on the foundation on which it stands now) the favorite evidence of wise and pious Christians. Internal evidence far outweighs all miracles to the soul. A reasoning Christian would think himself injured by the fortifying too scrupulously the outward evidence of Christianity. If the whole history of the New Testament had perished and only its teachings remained, the discourses of our Lord, the authority of holiness, and the heavenly standard of Jesus, the ardour and spirituality of Paul, the grave and self-examining advice of James would take the same rank with me that now they do. I should say, as now I say, that this certainly is the greatest height to which the religious principle of human nature has ever been carried and it has the total suffrage of my soul to its truth, whether the miracle was wrought, as is pretended, or not. If I did not acknowledge the doctrine as true, I should yield to the skeptic that this story of miracles, like other such stories, was false. But as the doctrine is true the miracle falls in with and confirms it.[7]

The truths taught in the New Testament will stand by themselves. In other words, many minds will not want the miracle, but to all it is such truth as might be expected to be accompanied by miraculous power. Now we put the question to every reasoning mind whether the great peculiarity of the Christian miracles is not decisive in their favor, viz. that the moral truths which they are alleged to have accompanied are not utterly incompatible with the supposition of imposture in those who declared them and lived by them. There is nothing in the teaching of Jesus or of his apostles that would encourage what is called *pious* frauds, but all that abhors them. They were teachers of sincerity, of contempt of worldly honour, of the fear of God and the fear of hurting the soul, beyond any earthly evil, and they kept their own rules and exhibited the principle in practice. Yet these persons appeal distinctly to the knowledge of persons they address respecting miracles done by their hands; and since I perceive the divine truth of the doctrine, I know the miracle must have been wrought which they say was wrought. This is an evidence so strong that I ask no other. It is impossible that the principles which these men reasoned out and lived out, as all external testimony declares, should permit the least imposture. To suppose it is to admit a miracle far more confounding than the miracle of the Resurrection.

There are many allowances to be made for anything that seems improbable in the records of these transactions which will always be considered by sincere seekers for truth. Thus it should be considered that the books of the Evangelists are not the revelation but the record of the Revelation and that many things may have come to their ears by common rumor which were false. One miracle performed will make a multitude credible, as one clap of thunder has a hundred echoes. I am not therefore made uneasy by a plausible account that gives a natural origin to an event related as miraculous, or to any number of such events. All I ask is a single miracle, a single fact to show that such power was evinced by the teachers of such wisdom.

The question to be asked concerning them (I now quote the words of an eloquent English writer, Mr. Coleridge) is, 'Was it an appropriate mean to a necessary end? Has it been attested by lovers of truth? Has it been believed by lovers of wisdom? Do we see throughout all nature the occasional intervention of particular agencies in countercheck of universal laws? (And of what other definition is a miracle susceptible?) These are the questions and if to these our answers must be affirmative, then we too will acquiesce in the traditions of humanity, and yielding as to a high interest of our own being, will discipline ourselves to the reverential and kindly faith that the guides and teachers of mankind were the hands of power no less than the voices of inspiration; and little anxious concerning the particular forms and circumstances of each manifestation, we will give an historic credence to the historic fact that men sent by God have come with signs and wonders on the earth.'

Self and Others

Thou shalt love the Lord thy God with all thy heart, and thy neighbor as thyself. Luke X, 27.

It is my design in the present discourse to present the principle on which the great class of social duties depends. There is something at all times refreshing and elevating in the contemplation of the social duties. All selfish passions are mean and all social ones, that is, all that seek the good of another for his own sake, are noble.

The fear of death is unworthy of a man. Would you know the remedy? Go and see the death of one who spends the last breath in devoted serving of others and you see the ruins of human nature clothed with beauty and all the meanness of death taken away. It may be recommended to us as a practical rule, the golden rule of Christ, that when unawares we are surprised with any cowardice either in the apprehension of death or of evils on this side of it, let us take refuge in immediately applying ourselves to an active interest in the welfare of those persons who have the nearest claims upon us. It will bring more than angels to our side. It will bring courage and conscience and God to our aid.[1]

Especially should these thoughts reinforce us amidst anxious and difficult times. 'To keep yourself temperate at a feast,' says an old moralist, 'you have two expedients, to carve or to discourse.' And how shall you more gratefully awaken your heart and your conscience amid the present despondency² than by reflexions on the perfection of that web of relations to all beings into which your own lot is woven, and which makes it impossible for you to act without affecting many more than one; which enables you to touch so many hearts with joy or sorrow; which therefore teaches you that you are born to promote happiness; to add to the sum of good?

Let us proceed to consider the false answers and the true that have been offered to the question, What is the principle on which our duty to serve our fellow men depends?

I. In the first place, it has been answered that it flows from self-love but a long sighted self-love.³ 'Benevolence,' according to a proverb of false philosophy, 'is self-love well calculated.' This is not true. Self-love, short sighted or long sighted, is not benevolence. In any common use of the word self, in any sense less than that infinite sense in which self-love loses itself in the love of God and the universe, this answer is not true. Self-love and Benevolence may prompt the same outward act. They are not the same action, as is proved by its not having the same effect. Self-interest never prompted a sincere service of others. From a polluted source a pure act cannot flow.

It is true indeed that it is the interest of man to be the friend of man. It was an early discovery of political economy that in no form could labor be exerted to less advantage than in an attempt to confine its fruits to the laborer. The man who should set himself to build his own house, weave his own clothes, make his own shoes, teach his own children and so prevent the price of these works from enriching his neighbours, would presently find himself the poorest of all.⁴ It is easy to show that united men live easier, richer and happier than hating men. A striking illustration of this may be seen in history, whenever small contiguous countries have been united under one government. The small territories of England,

Scotland and Wales, included in the island of Great Britain, were once separate nations, and their continued separation cost them each a perpetual garrison upon all their frontier, beside endless wars and all the expenditure of life, comfort and virtue, which war involves. It is all saved by the simple discovery that they can be one nation; a fact so cheap that it costs nothing. And in general it is easy to show that a well calculated self-love would dictate a punctual discharge of duty to others, as pride is civil to others to keep others from treading upon its skirts; or as covetousness relieves the starving multitude with part of its store, to hinder the starving multitude from relieving themselves; or as the wise statesman educates the lowest class of the population in order that God's restraints of knowledge and virtue may keep down the turbulence which an armed police cannot keep down.

It is true then that it is the interest of men to be benevolent. Is it, therefore, the true foundation of our duty to others? What a motive were this! I am to go to my brother with relief for his wants, with kind words in his distress, with instruction in his ignorance and say, Brother, I find that such are the laws of Providence that I cannot get and keep all the bread without your aid. I therefore give you some. I find you can do me great mischief; I therefore speak you fair. I instruct you, to keep you from assailing my life, or burning my barn, or being the pirate of my ship.

What sort of gratitude will this excite? What hatred rather will it not inflame? It is fear. It is concession and deserves no honor or love and will find none. It neither benefits you nor him. And in so far as it now operates, it begets the disposition which just this language would create in individuals. It exists and it creates that murmuring which is so often heard against the rich.

That the interest of the individual and society are one is most true and much more than this is true, and yet all together do not yet constitute the true motive of our social duty. It might be shown that it is an indispensable part of a finished character to comply with the law of charity. It might be shown that he who withholds his aid from his fellow man is more a loser than his fellow man from whom he withholds it; that the soul of man was made to act for others as much as his body was made to breathe the air; that speech and reason and knowledge and grace and beauty and power are all worthless whilst they are confined to one, and were given to be communicated; that all his improvement is from a selfish to a social life — a development of power to act with and for others.

I look upon all these facts as of great importance, as illustrations of the perfect wisdom with which the world is framed, so that the good of others is promoted involuntarily and against his will by the most selfish man in his most selfish action, yet this is all their value to our present purpose. Let self-love be instructed and exalted as much as possible, it can never become the principle from which the good of others should be sought, nor can it be proposed to Christians by Christians as a proper motive.[5]

II. Nor, in the second place, will it do to say that the manifest wants of our nature make the obligation to serve our fellow men. It is not a sufficient reason. It needs a foundation itself. The question may still be asked, And why must I supply my neighbor's wants?

Nor can the love of our neighbor in that degree of strength in which the sentiment is ordinarily found, be safely trusted as the support of such various and incessantly returning duties as we owe to others. It is too capricious and discriminating — too selfish. It is to be considered that although love is a universal passion and no man can be found but his heart warms to some fellow being, yet very few men love all their fellow beings.

Especially how is it to prompt us to that important part of duty we owe to the inferior and to the wretched?[6] Would it do to trust the supply of the wants of the poor to this partial selecting passion? Some men hate the poor. Some men lock their gates and a great many lock their hearts against the poor. We love the lovely, the modest, the good, the eloquent, the poetical, the well educated, the well mannered, the elegant.

But that class of persons who most need the assistance of their fellow men are commonly unlovely, uneducated, many of them stupid, often vicious, offensive frequently from the filth of their habitations, and sometimes much more so from loathsome diseases.[7] And the very fact of their wants is apt to make the selfishness of men hostile to them. The love of man in those who have no higher principle, the love of man in the atheist, would be a bad dispensary, I fear, to the sickly, hungry, shivering wretch who ventured to appeal to it. Who has not heard the oft repeated refusals of the selfish that the beggar is a nuisance; that all charity is a bounty to vice? There was mismanagement somewhere, or there never would be want. I am sorry they suffer, but follow it up and you shall find it was their own fault.[8] The love of our neighbour is a principle of wonderful force where it really acts, as in the relations of parent and child, of husband and wife, of friend and friend, and will prompt the noblest actions and the greatest sacrifices, but it will not serve as a principle whereon to found the whole system of social duty.

III. It appears, then, that the love of self is unworthy and the love of the neighbour is not sufficient to be the principle on which our duty to our fellow creatures is built. The Scriptures, both in the old and new Testaments, furnish us with the true principle, in the language of my text. Thou shalt love the Lord thy God, with all thy heart. The love of God is the principle on which the love of our neighbor stands. The reason why I must help him when I can, is because he is God's child, as I am. His claim on me is through God. God is my Father. All I have is his and I am wholly bound to his will. His will is the good of the Universe, and that I must promote, and my neighbor's as a part of it.[9]

Does this seem too vague and distant a principle for the motive of actions that are to be done every day? The love of God, some will say, is a sublime theory which makes the happiness of heaven, but few men in this world attain to anything beyond low degrees of the sentiment, and certainly the duties of every hour ought to meet us with all the force of the plainest commandments. Yes, and it is because we are so much separated from God that we so ill understand our relation to our fellowmen and so poorly discharge our social duties. This objection, which is continually made in the world, this awful distance at which God is placed from our minds, this uncertainty with which men speak of him, accuses our evil life and dims the evidence of the truth but cannot alter the truth itself. We are sad aliens from the heavenly life, we grievously break the commandments, if we are thus strangers to Him. The Scriptures teach us that nothing is more intimate than our relation to Him. They teach that we are God's children, not by any metaphor but in a far stricter sense than we are the children of men. We are made of him. We live but in him, as the leaf lives in the tree. 'Know ye not that the spirit of God dwelleth in you. God worketh in us, both to will and to do, of his own good pleasure.' We are his children in a manner, that as we keep his commandments, shall all but identify us with him. We shall be parts of God, as the hand is part of the body, if only the hand had a will. We are made of God as the urn is made of clay, but separated from our great Parent by our free agency, and separated farther from him by it perhaps day by day. Whenever we act from self, we separate ourselves from God; when we do right, we consent to his action by our hands.

When we do right, it is not our act, it is that we receive God into our souls and submit to be his organ. We are then conscious of acting upon a greater will and to a greater end than self good. It is I that do wrong; it is God in me who does right. And it is the perception of thus living in God, that makes the propriety of the commandment to the Jews, Be ye Holy because I am Holy; and that by Jesus Christ, Be ye merciful as your Father is merciful, Be ye perfect as your father in Heaven is perfect, — commandments which would be wholly incomprehensible but for the great truth that men, in the words of Saint Peter, are partakers of the divine nature. This truth is so invaluable to the mind that I wish it may receive the consideration of every one who hears me. For all great souls, when they have given themselves up to their duty, have found this conviction grow in them, that in God only they had life. As Paul said, The spirit beareth witness with our spirit that we are the children of God.

This great doctrine that God dwells in the human heart in a manner so intimate that it is because he there is present, that we exist, so that a man is not so much an individual as a manifestation of the Eternal and Universal One, is no new or peculiar doctrine. It does not belong to any church but to a certain elevation of mind in all churches. It is not the doctrine of any sect but of all devout Christians. I may say, not the property of Christians but of men. For before Christ had declared the character of God and his relations to the human mind, humble and thoughtful men had yet communed with their Maker and rejoiced in the conviction that God dwelt within them. The pious men of the Stoic sect received this faith, saying that the wise man differed from God in nothing but duration. It was also a maxim of their school that mind was God in man. The devout Fénelon, a bishop of the church of Rome, declares that God is in our souls as our soul is in our bodies.

Archbishop Leighton, one of the most esteemed and one of the best divines of the Church of England, writes that 'by the love of God the soul is made divine and one with him'; and quotes with approbation the language of Saint Austin, 'If you love the earth, you become earth; if you love God — shall I not say? — you become God.'

And that great light of the Calvinistic Church, Henry Scougal, says in his sermon on the Excellency of the Religious,

'Learn to adore your nature.' It was the favourite doctrine of George Fox, and William Penn and of the society of Friends, that the whole growth of man was by direct communication imparting of the Divine Spirit.

Now whilst I see this to be true in my nature, I see that my fellow man is made in the same mould and of the same substance. Every man you meet seems to repeat yourself, to be another of the same. We never converse without seeking, if I may use the expression, to find ourselves in each other, guided always by the conviction that we were made to think alike. Especially as men are good do they understand each other, for then the spirit of God in them is less and less disguised and they feel that they are inspired by one soul.

Now is not this the principle of charity? Is not this the principle that must regulate all our dealings with mankind? Is it not that we are everywhere to acknowledge the present God? Must not all my intercourse with my brother, poor or rich, be governed by this tender reverence for our mutual nature, divine in its origin, however disguised by selfishness in both of us? Are we not to deal with the most obscure and sinful wretch as only a perverted wreck and ruin of a mansion in which God has dwelt and perchance is already returning to dwell through these very storms of misery by which he is preparing his entrance? [10] I see at once that there are nobler ends to be sought by me than giving him bread. I am not to relieve his wants as an end, but by means of relieving his wants I would justify myself to himself, or produce a full consent between God in him and God in me. I am to show him that I know and own this our sacred relation as children of one God. I would not forget the glorious attributes that are obscured by the necessities of his circumstances and by his sin. I would search for them under his rags and under his sin. I would love him as myself. I would love him for the same reason that can alone justify and regulate the love of myself, that, in both of us, is the spirit of the living God. It will be seen at once that this principle will exclude all selfishness. I shall be seeking, in every exertion to benefit another, the good of the Universe; and it will serve in all places throughout the sphere of human action. It begins with the nearest relation and reaches to the farthest. It dictates our intercourse at the fireside and it reaches our conduct to our country, to other nations, and to the brute creation.

Let me add now a few remarks as to the extent of this claim. It lays its grasp on your whole being. It says you are bound to the will of God because all you are is from him. What hast thou which thou didst not receive? There is not a man in the world, who has got a piece of bread for himself. He got it by the hands which he never made, and by the head he never made, and by aids that he never made. And if you should strip the most powerful and opulent and accomplished person on earth of all that he has received, you would leave him nothing but his sins. To the same extent then does the claim on us reach. In the eye of the Christian law, 'No man liveth to himself and no man dieth to himself but whether living or dying we are the Lord's.' There is not an inch of ground in the Creation left for self-love to stand upon. We are not our own. And our business is the love of all. We are to hold all our possessions and all our powers of body and mind *in trust* for the utmost good they can be made to accomplish.

Brethren, I have stated, as I hope truly and plainly, the principle on which Christianity founds our duty to others. I cannot stop to show its applications to the multitude of human circumstances. It rebukes the spirit of war, the spirit of party, the spirit of covetousness, and every form of self seeking. It says to the human race with an angel's voice, Little children, love one another. It says, Whoso would be chief among you let him be the servant of all.[11]

The doctrine of the New Testament which I have endeavored to illustrate is that because God is our Father and all we are brethren, therefore we are dearly bound to seek each other's good. And to whom does it speak? to some Jews and Romans long departed from this world? or to our fathers who are also departed? or to us? To you and to me in whatever state we are, of joy or sorrow, alone or in families. To you and to me does this sublime doctrine come home, — and if we can open our eyes to see it — with such power of consolation and of command as to make adversity no longer adverse, the fears and vexations of time no disturbance of our peace, and human life a part of the Eternity of God. My friend, (and I speak to each one in this house) have you never suspected a greater inmate in your frail body than a frail animal life? Have you never perceived that while all things change, a soul possesses you which changes not; which amid doubts, doubts not; which amidst dejection, intimates that all will be well; a soul which amid the clamors of temptation, breathes the low thunders of his admonition; a soul which though disregarded and forgotten in the din of affairs still meets you again with its unruffled supremacy on its own occasions when you are alone; a soul before which you are known though you wear a mask to all the world; a soul which never participates in your guilt, but as God in Heaven beholds it all from an infinite superiority; a soul which assures you that integrity and truth and love can never be a loss, nor crime a gain?

My friend, have you this soul and has it never seemed to you that an Eternal Voice speaks through it to you, and an Eternal Eye looks through it upon you? 'Know ye not that ye are the Temple of the Holy Ghost, and the Spirit of God dwelleth in you?' It commands you with the whole of its authority, to use all the occasions that are presented of serving your fellow man who is also a Temple, however disguised by evil influences and his own will, of the Divine Presence. The manner of our being, the strange mystery of our greatness and our littleness we may not understand, but these duties he hath written in light. Because God is, and for God's sake, let us love and serve his children, our fellowmen. In the name of God, if your brother has wronged you, forgive him; and so conspire with all that is good at the bottom of his own heart. And if you have entertained an unkind purpose against him, O see that it is a warfare against yourself and God in you. It is the suggestion of an evil spirit. Why should you make the happiness that is in the world less? O, for our own sake, let us be just; then, where we can, let us be merciful; and, with fixed resolutions to make others happier that we have lived, let us purchase by kind, forgiving thoughts, and helping intercessions and affectionate wishes a little permanent happiness amid the sorrows and sins of this transitory life.

Feb. 20, 1831

Consolation for the Mourner

For we know that if our earthly house of this tabernacle were dissolved, we have a building of God, an house not made with hands, eternal in the heavens.   II Corinthians, V, 1.

THE truth of God brought by Jesus Christ is related to all our being, to all its changes, to life and death, to two worlds. Its main fact is the immortality of the human soul. It teaches us, that when we descend by age or disease to the tomb, it is a change and not a termination of our being; that the Providence of God reaches through all space, and lasts through all time, and upholds this feeble spirit of man through that extent; and administers to it eternal justice; and makes it capable of receiving all truth, and all goodness. It is made of God, and it is made to find its perfection in resembling him, in knowing and doing his will.

But these sublime ends are begun to be sought with means how small! We have this treasure in earthen vessels. The immortal soul is lodged in a dwelling most frail and painful, that in its greatest strength will last eighty summers — sometimes not twenty — sometimes not one.

A thousand causes of pain beset every one in this great company of pilgrims, and the heart aches to enumerate them. And to this child of sorrow and fear, this human soul imprisoned in flesh, God sends the consolation of the truth and promises of the New Testament.

CONSOLATION FOR THE MOURNER

My friends, I wish to speak, though I fear very unworthily of my theme, of the consolation that Christianity offers to those who mourn. Let me speak as I feel. Let me give utterance, if I can, to some of those thoughts that crowd in succession into the heart of those who have seen the life that made their own life pleasant come to an end. Which of us has no interest in these consolations? Which of us has not needed them, or is not likely to need them?[1]

And first, I cannot pass without notice one or two counsels that are habitually in men's mouths when they condole with the afflicted, but which in most cases are thrown away because they are not founded in truth, and can only give unnecessary pain. It is usual to warn the bereaved man to be still, and not repine at the decree of the Almighty. Let me say, that *it never occurs to* a mind at all enlarged by religion, at all accustomed to observe and admire the uniform and universal provisions for good that on every hand reach far out of his sight, when he meets with a distressing event, *it never comes into his heart to murmur and repine*. To repine is to believe that though he who reigns in all is called a God, it is only a man ignorant, and severe, or partial, that administers events; and as a well ordered mind is incapable of receiving such an idea of the infinite Divinity, to charge him not to repine is like telling him not to fly, or that he must not imagine the earth to be a plane, nor believe that the sun is annihilated when it sets, or anything else which would never come into his thoughts. If called upon in that moment when grief has sharpened into anguish, when heaven and earth grow dark in his eye, because the life of his body is only regarded as the wall of separation that hinders him from his desires, — even in that moment, and as often as it returns, if called upon, he would bear witness with the same conviction as in his brighter hour, to the perfection of the Providence in which his only hope is.[2] Is it not plain that then more than ever he needs the whole support of that central faith? For except in that belief he has no prospect of relighting his extinguished lamp. And for the world he would not utter a word that could have a tendency to shake his own confidence in the Divine love.

Neither is there to a mind that seeks truth the least unkindness in its grief. Sorrow is called selfish, but it is because it is occupied at home, and not that it covets or reproaches the happiness of others. It cannot leave its own thought, it is out of the power of man when prostrated by calamity to get up with cheerful social face, and interest himself to his usual degree in the condition of his friends and neighborhood. He is so entirely disheartened by an event which changes the whole aspect of life to him that he broods on that event, and has no spirit to act or to think. He is unstrung, debilitated by grief, and so neglects others as he neglects himself, but do not imagine that he who well deserves all your pity, nourishes a secret malevolence at pleasures which he can not enjoy.

I have said that the mind that is used in all times to recognize God, and in any worthy degree to keep his commandments, will not charge God foolishly, nor grieve at the happiness of others. But if this were all the peace the gospel brought, it would hardly touch the evil of sorrow. The truth and the resurrection of Christ have done more for his disciples. The blessing of the Christian hope enters with alleviation into every degree and every thought of sorrow. The Christian faith teaches us that the soul does not die but is separated from the body and enters into a nearer relation to the Father of Spirits. The Christian faith teaches this, and the Christian soul, as it departs out of life, affirms it cheerfully to those who weep.[3]

I proceed now to say that the Christian faith removes the dread from the grave, first, in regard to those who die, and then to those who survive. 1. The pure and the wise who leave this world receive the natural reward of goodness and wisdom, in the removal of all doubt as to the course and the end of their secret journey. We follow them down to the last gate of life, but our unaided eye cannot explore one step into the gloom beyond.[4] Yet they go in a courage not their own, and above nature. They follow their Lord. They are gone with him into the house, and the door is shut. Jesus says, 'My Father's house hath many mansions,' and we easily believe that the 'mansion,' i.e. the happiness of every soul will be different, and measured by the progress it has already made. Every element of evil it has indulged in itself is so much diminution of its peace. Every truth it has understood, every act of humility, of love, of devotion, is a new star in its crown. All that part of man which we call *the character*, survives and ascends.[5] Not a shade, not a thought of it cleaves to the cold clay we have put in the ground. And let me ask of those who have been called to part with some dear image of human worth, whether they find any difficulty in separating the soul from the body in their thought; whether the being that has been forming under their eye for years, acquiring truth, adopting habits, and beginning to disclose hints and glimmerings of an unknown abyss of thought within itself, putting forth the marks of magnanimity, of fortitude, of inexhaustible kindness, and lastly of a great trust in God, — I ask if you think this being is one with the body, and all these signs of corruption? If you think so, you do not understand the language God speaks by his works to your soul, and you have not kept the commandments of Christ, for those who obey them, insensibly receive the thought of this happy future. Yes, they teach us better — the pious dead — whose hope in God grew stronger as the heart it agitated was ceasing to beat. They went down to the tomb with prayer and praise on their lips, and the thoughts of heaven found their way in to the convulsions of death. We will sing the hallelujahs of faith over their ashes. We will leave the soul with God, sure that his wisdom shall find action and enjoyment suited to the soul in the resurrection.[6] A wise and good man may think he sees enough in this life, to suggest to him the fates and actions of an unbodied spirit. But far more gladly we trust the promise of the Scriptures,[7] that 'Eye hath not seen nor ear heard, nor hath entered the heart of man, the glory that God has prepared for them that love him.'

2. The faith of Christ removes the dread of the grave, secondly, in regard to those who are yet alive in the body. It abolishes the power of death. It peoples every solitude; it animates every silence with the conviction in the mind of the mourner that the dead are present. They speak to him out of the darkness words of comfort which the living could never utter. He is assured of their sympathy, of their prayer, and of whatsoever aid the spirit out of the body can give to the spirit in the body. By the living he may be neglected, he may be affronted, he may be misunderstood; he appeals from their imperfect judgments with a swelling spirit to the clearer sight and to the unmixed and now glorified affection of the dead, and he finds comfort and increasing conviction in this invisible sympathy.[8]

He may find temptations multiplied in his path, he may feel deeply his own unworthiness, his uselessness to his fellowmen, his guilt before God. But in this holy society which he finds in his closet or in the open day, with the virtuous dead, he is calmed and strengthened. They present the remembrance of a pure example, and the suggestions of approbation and succour to every good intention. They remind him that he is not alone or unpitied when his house seems most lonely, and his duty most difficult; for the Father of all Spirits who made him at first the gift of these affections, and of their objects, has not lost sight of his afflicted child.[9] Jesus will not forget a humble disciple, for his promise was, 'Lo, I am with you always, even unto the end of the world.' And, in these our friends who are gone, we now seem to possess a *personal interest of love, of intercession in the spiritual society.* The soul that has thought with us, and preferred our interest to its own, and known well what was in our heart, is now only a step removed from us, and we believe, looks back with more than earthly love, mixing the recent knowledge of human wants, with the newness of the revelations now

CONSOLATION FOR THE MOURNER

made to it by change of state. In a pure love for the departed it is very easy to bring home to the soul the vision of their joy and love. And it is these contemplations which make what have been well called 'the sublime attraction of the grave.' Soothed by these thoughts, we wonder how the grave was ever frightful to us. When we have explored our desolate house for what shall never there be seen, we return with an eagerness to the tomb as the only place of healing and peace. It seems to us that willingly — oh yes, joyfully, we would, if permitted, lay down our head also on the same pillow, so that God would restore us to the society we have lost.

But does any one say this is extravagant, unreasonable sorrow? This is a spirit of bitterness which would disqualify man for his place in society; the loss of a friend would then by the indulgence of these fruitless desires, be the loss of usefulness to the survivor, and death would be a far greater evil in the world than now it is. Does any one say this? So in our ear say the dead also. Reason and virtue do not change their language by change of state; the virtuous dead utter the same sentiment with the virtuous living. This is what I would chiefly observe in commending the blessedness of the Christian faith, that it does not permit even these holy affections to mislead us. It keeps *Duty, the soul's everlasting object, always uppermost*. When the love and desire of departed excellence makes us eager to quit the places and offices of earthly duty, the same love and desire corrects this disgust of life. It makes us consider that it is not death, but life that we are seeking, and that an inglorious quitting of our post, a neglect of any of our appointed trusts, a life of inaction, a death of grief, would disqualify us for that very happiness we aim at; would bring down upon us the displeasure and sorrow of those very friends who watch over us; would be unfaithful to their counsels and to their devoted love; would alienate us from their hearts instead of cementing us with them, because the only true and enduring bond that can unite souls is the love of the same excellence, the love of truth and goodness — the love of God who is their source.

When therefore we first feel that the claims of others upon us are irksome, and are disposed to lie down in useless despondency, let us feel that then the eye of love begins to grow severe, that we are departing from the friendship of the pure, that the best tribute the living can offer to the dead is to be faithful in our place as they were faithful in theirs, to keep up the courage and good hope that will always spring from earnest endeavours to do right even against the embarrassments of disappointment, of defeat, of reproach, of poverty, of sickness, of old age. Thus may the connections of nature and friendship become yet more sacred, and as may reasonably be thought, I hope, by Christians, the tie may really grow stronger between one on earth and one in heaven.

These are the feelings that by direct inference from the New Testament mix with our sad thoughts and lead them toward heaven. By them and by the spectacle of triumphant faith the dying chamber of youth where a thousand expectations are shattered may infuse more sweetness and joy into the soul than ever prosperity or praise could give. In the wreck of earthly good the goods of the soul show a lustre and permanence divine. Blessed be God that there are these consolations, these remembrances, these hopes. Blessed be his name, that he has provided every soul among us in the truth of the New Testament with the means of depriving death of its sting.

Hymn Books

Sing praises with understanding.   Psalm XLVII, 7.

It is a natural idea that has always occurred to the pious man, that man is the tongue of the creation and is to utter praise not only for himself, but in behalf of all the irrational creatures, and of the inanimate works of God. He alone hath the music of speech. He alone can form the thought of praise into words. It is very hard to analyze music and say how much is intellectual and how much is material.

It is harder yet to analyze poetry and tell where the charm is lodged that pleases us in its measures. After the experiment is tried, after verses are made, we can tell what measures please and what offend, we can make rules describing them.[1] But who can go into the chambers of the ear, and tell why one order of syllables should be harmonious, and any change should hurt it; hardest of all to analyze the joys of sentiment and imagination which make the soul of poetry? Only he that made the throbbing heart, the hearing ear and the speaking tongue, and the vibrating air. And to him let the music which results from them all be paid.

Music and poetry have come down together from an immemorial time. And from the earliest notices of them they were consecrated to religious service. The oldest records of every literature are religious odes. In every nation there appear to have been bards who were priests. The historians who take up the veil of time and show us the long pathway of our race leading back to the first seats of the human family, introduce us to the fathers of mankind, a simple race of shepherds and husbandmen duly meeting to honour the Deity in a true or false worship with hymns and dances. In ancient Egypt and in Europe it was a costly and gorgeous ceremonial. When purer religion displaced their idolatry, this natural species of worship remained; it has survived every revolution of opinion and held its place among Catholics and Protestants, among Episcopalians and Dissenters, among Methodists and Shakers.

Some of the finest powers of genius have been exercised in providing this beautiful entertainment for the mind of the worshipper both in music and in poetry. For those who understand both it unites the finest pleasures of the sense to the finest pleasures of the soul. Psalmody is the union of sacred poetry to sacred music. I am wholly incompetent to speak of the last [2] of which few I believe understand less. But I am much interested in the first. I wish to bring to your attention the subject of hymn books. I am anxious that our sacred poetry should be good; should be a worthy expression of our sentiments to the Creator. I am anxious that we should sing hymns which we can feel, and which can do the office of sacred poetry upon our minds — can arouse, thrill, cheer, soothe, solemnize or melt us. I desire that we should not sing hymns to God that we should be ashamed to compose in the praise of a man, flat, prosaic, unaffecting productions such as too many have been and are. I desire that on the altar of God whilst eloquence brings its deepest truths poetry should exhaust its powers. It is but reasonable that the hymns which make so large a part of our religious service should be chosen and good ones. It must be perceived by any one who considers the subject that this part of our service admits of being made much more interesting than it is. A large number of every congregation have some taste for sacred poetry and perhaps a much larger number for sacred music. If this taste were taken advantage of in all cases by a diligent collection of the best hymns and a careful rejection of all inferior ones, the hymn would do much good in exalting devout feelings. Almost every person has at some time had opportunity to observe a very great effect produced upon an assembly by a pertinent hymn aided by the effect of fine music. This effect might be greater and more frequent if our hymn books were better.

It is very singular that in the English language which contains some of the sublimest strains of poetry and of sacred poetry the hymns sung in churches should have been until the last century so low and inharmonious, sunk indeed almost below criticism. One would have thought it would have moved the ambition of great geniuses, of many a holy successor of David and Miriam, to give utterance to a nation's praise and pious rapture. What work of learning or of imagination could ever hope for such permanent and precious fame, ever hope to enter into the heart and faith of a nation like the simple religious song that is in their mouth every Sunday, aided in its effect by the reverence of the Bible, the power of music, the associations of the place, and the sympathy of a congregation? The best poet[3] should have written hymns for those who speak the English tongue and whatever sublime bard has sung to any people could best have instructed them by doing this office, instead of permitting the unskilful versifiers who with whatever good intentions first turned the psalms of David into English metre.

Very great improvement, however, though not so good as we could hope, has taken place. The stiff and wretched verses used in old times have disappeared. Very many persons, some of them highly gifted, have turned their talents in this direction and some noble strains of devotion have been heard. Dr. Watts, though his mind was imprisoned in a dark and barbarous system of religious faith, did yet by the fervor of his piety and the freedom of his thought wonderfully raise the downtrodden muse of the English churches. Addison, Mrs. Steele, Doddridge, Cowper, Mrs. Barbauld — have enriched our collections and now many living authors have added to our stock.

The collection of the late Doctor Belknap,[4] which is in use in this church, was received with great satisfaction by the enlightened men of the American churches at the time of its appearance near forty years ago, as being a very marked improvement upon the gloomy Calvinism of the old books. But many years have since elapsed in which the public attention has been intensely fixed upon theological questions and many errors then strongly suspected have been fully exposed. Much of its theology is therefore antiquated. No enlightened Christian can read many pages in that book without meeting confused views of God and many bad or at best ambiguous expressions concerning the offices of Christ, his Deity, his sacrifice and atonement, and his now exaltation as the central object of adoration to all beings in heaven, as in the 122nd hymn

> 'Jesus, my God, I know his name;
> His name is all my trust.
> Nor will he put my soul to shame,
> Nor let my hope be lost.'

My friends, it does not become us to whom God in his mercy has given his word in simplicity and in freedom, to worship him with doubtful heart or with double lips. Let us not confound the reason he has given us by making two Gods, or three; or two in one, or three in one. If we cannot measure the dignity of Jesus, and do not feel that our duty requires us to know of any other dignity than his truth and goodness, so let our hymn say, and let not our hymn book break the first commandment.

But besides this occasional Trinitarianism, sometimes express and sometimes by allusion, as grave a charge lies against many of these pieces as injurious to the character of God. Language is there applied to the Supreme Being that cannot be repeated without dishonouring him. He is represented as vindictive, greedy of praise, and uttering threats in the poor passion of a man.[5]

Next to these great errors which ought not to be found in a book selected for such an use, I may remark a confusion of thought and of expression concerning the great doctrine of Christianity, namely, the immortality of the soul, which in some of the psalms seems to be forgotten and in some misunderstood.

Another fault is a prevalence of unchristian sentiments of denunciation and bitterness, which never flowed from the law of love. See 101 Psalm, called A Psalm for a Master of a Family. Again, besides this utterance of unchristian sentiment there is a defect running through a great many of the hymns, that of a very gross material imagery. Heaven is always described as a land of rivers, of luxuries, of music, of crowns; God as a king sitting on a throne; Christ as a conqueror with sword and chariot; and the life of the saint is painted in military hymns; and the mean descriptions of angels, — all which have a most pernicious tendency to mislead the mind in its understanding of spiritual things.

Let us not be unjust to this book so long and so generally used in the liberal churches of New England. It contains many excellent hymns which have served a pious purpose to many worshipping assemblies and many a private heart. But it contains numbers of indifferent and some bad ones, and does not contain a great many which ought to be introduced into our church. Much that is objectionable in it arises from the division, now disused, into Psalms and Hymns.[6] It is not wise to attempt to wrest and accommodate the peculiar language of David, originally suited to many temporary and private occasions, to the present wants of the Christian Church. In the attempt to do this, a great many inapplicable verses are made and, what is worse, a great many sentiments expressed utterly inconsistent with the Christian religion. The effect of this has been that one half of the versions of the Psalms in Belknap are now grown obsolete — are never or very rarely sung in our church. An obvious improvement would be to select the good versions of the many fine passages in the Psalms and incorporate them with other hymns adapted to our peculiar wants or to the wants of the church in every age.[7]

The practical ill effect of these objections is of course not so obvious to any one in the church as to the preacher. It costs him much time to select pieces to be read and sung, and again out of the suitable pieces, to select what is unobjectionable. These faults exclude from use a very large number of the hymns and psalms in the book, so that out of four hundred and sixty not many more than two hundred are commonly used, and our church is as yet a stranger to a large number of excellent hymns, not included in this collection. And we fear that in our meetings the reading and singing of hymns grown so familiar to the ear fails of its desired effect.

I have thought it well to make these remarks to you, brethren, because it is in my opinion a great blemish on our service, and one admitting an easy remedy, and because, as you know, the expediency of introducing a new hymnbook has long been and is before a committee of the Society; and the evil complained of is not mended by time. And before the report of the Committee is presented for your action I desired to make a plain statement of what I esteem the faults of our service and what advantages we might hope to gain by a change.

There has now been for about a year a new Collection before the Christian public compiled by the Pastor of the Stone Chapel in this city.[8] It has the suffrage of many good judges and almost of all sects in its favor. It is free from all the objections that lie against the old collections and contains near six hundred hymns. I hope in these circumstances it may receive the examination, and if found worthy, the approbation of every worshipper in our ancient temple.[9]

We worship in plain walls. We have no tapestry, no pictures, no marble, no gold, no sacrifices, no incense. Let us at least have truth and piety. Let us have hymns worthy of God the subject, and suitable for man, the singer. Let us not think this a light matter. Let us sing praises with understanding.

The Choice of Theisms

Choose ye this day whom ye will serve; as for me and my house, we will serve the Lord.   Joshua XXIV, 15.

The sentiment of Love to God is the highest that can fill the soul. It is a question which every thinking being may well ask himself, What principle shall govern me? It is a question, not whether any love shall govern him but what love. Shall it be idolatory or shall it be religion? It is not to choose whether he will serve or not, but whom he will serve. I say it is not a question whether any love shall govern him, but what love. The human heart requires a God. Some God, a true or a false one, it will and must have. There exists no mind but is possessed with love either of good or of evil. It will make a God of conscience, or of riches, or of power, or of science, or of honor, or of hatred, or of the belly. It was made through all its faculties to love, as a tree was made to bear fruit. For everyone may see, who will look at the mind as a philosopher, that whoever made us, we were made not for ourselves, but from the beginning to the end of our structure and of our progress, do plainly discover a reference to something else than ourselves.

The keenest and noblest of our pleasures is admiration.[1] We are eager to admire. All men admire. To be without admiration of anything is to be destitute of the mainspring of our progressive nature.[2] We are so prone to this habit that we make good which we do not find, and grow very dexterous in decking our idols. Every one must have noticed the eager disposition to admire that runs through almost all conversation. How fast does any wonderful story concerning any man's performance get abroad. It is repeated from mouth to mouth a hundred or a thousand times, and the story never loses in one. If you have heard an eloquent oration, or seen a good book, or a beautiful face, or a fine landscape, or a worthy man, how prone are men to say not, it is good, or fair, or upright, but it is the best, the fairest, the greatest they ever saw in their lives. Why do they say so? Not from an intention to deceive, but because for the time they really think so, not taking the pains to reflect, and because it is natural to the heart to give itself up to unbounded praise. Considerate persons gradually correct this habit in themselves and become more parsimonious of their praise. Why? Because they love less to admire? Oh no. But because they have corrected and extended their views of what is truly grand and beautiful. It is because they have refined on their admiration and a more admiration has supplanted a less.

The fact is that the human heart is impatient of things finite, of a small limited merit of which it can see the beginning and the end, and loves to lose itself in the contemplation of the vast and unbounded. Did ever anybody read or hear an eulogy which did not break over the frail edges of truth? Did ever anybody read an essay upon a man of genius such as Shakespeare or Newton or upon a hero as Tell or Wallace or Washington that did not discover a disposition to magnify the genius or the prowess of the man? This proneness to admiration, to an unlimited love of others, is a conspicuous peculiarity in man. It flows directly from his religious nature. It proves him to possess a religious nature. He is formed through all his faculties to love, to venerate, to adore. The improper direction of these feelings is idolatry. The right direction is true religion. It has always seemed to me that much light upon the true intent of our faculties is got by some of those remarkable sentiments which in all ages have exercised the strongest and the best influence over

THE CHOICE OF THEISMS

men, and whose only fault is that they have called out a strength of affection altogether disproportionate to their objects. The most familiar and striking example of this tendency of the mind is in the passion of love. In young and ardent minds, as is well known, this passion increases by indulgence, and from slight preference proceeds to warm attachment, and then to extravagant devotion. The growing affection clothes its object in ideal perfections and cannot speak without hyperbole. It utters itself in expressions of self devotion which seem ridiculous to others, and if strictly applied to the actual characters concerned, would be so. The language of love approaches very near to the language of worship. But however extravagant the language, the feeling is genuine in the mind of the lover. He really adores the excellences which he contemplates, though they are only attributes of his own mind, and do not exist, to that extent he supposes, in the character of his friend.

Every one knows too, what heroic energy of thought and action this passion has imparted to the mind. It ennobles and blesses the mind which feels it. 'The lover,' it is said, 'is made happier by his affection, than the object of it can be. Like the song of the bird it cheers his own heart.'[3] And it was avowed by a keen observer of human nature, that 'were it not for the shame that attends an unrequited affection, he should prefer to love without any hope of return for the mere pleasure of loving.'

Now what is it that excites this sentiment? Is it the beauty of the skin? Is it a little color or form or motion? Never. These catch the outward eye but never satisfied the human affection. These are not the objects of the true love. Its objects are certain amiable and excellent qualities supposed to reside in the person beloved; purity, truth, kindness, self-command and wisdom. And if these qualities should increase to a great, to an infinite degree, would it not increase our attachment?

On the contrary, if the opposite qualities of cruelty, falsehood, hatred, impurity, meanness should appear in one whom we love would it not alter our feelings?

I say then that the natural object of this sentiment of love in us is infinite goodness and though the objects on which it rests in this world are imperfect, yet the passion is true and noble.

Another example of the force with which the human spirit delights to go out of itself and give itself up to another is found in the sentiment of *loyalty* or fidelity to a King, or to the Chief of a clan, a passion which has given rise to some of the noblest incidents in history, and has been a very powerful spring of action.[4] Whilst it was a graceful friendship or private attachment in the higher classes who came into personal acquaintance with the Sovereign, in the great body of people it has been frequently a far stronger principle and became a species of worship; and hundreds of times men have marched in companies or alone to certain death, without flinching, yea, and with ardor, in the cause and for the love of a man whom perhaps they had never seen but once, perhaps never, of no great merit, possibly a person of loathsome vices.

It is related by an eye witness of Buonaparte's Russian Campaign,[5] that, in crossing a frozen river, the ice broke, and many of the troops were lost. One soldier, after struggling a long time, being benumbed with cold, and unable to extricate himself, yet found strength to wave his cap, and cry, 'Long live the Emperor,' and then sunk in the icy waters. The history of Europe abounds with instances of similar devotedness and perhaps oftener lavished on men of blood and crime, than upon virtuous princes. We read these incidents with a mixture of admiration and pity; admiration for the glorious dis-interestedness of the sufferer; and pity for the unworthy direction it had taken. We say the sentiment is right, but the direction of it is not right. These facts show plainly the truth of the old observation that a man wants to feel himself backed by a superior nature, as one of the lower animals, a dog or a horse, will exert powers in the presence of man they would never exhibit for their own advantage. They show that the mind was made with this intent — to go out of itself and apply its affections to some

THE CHOICE OF THEISMS

other being. This hungering admiration which rather than not indulge itself will live and glow all unreturned, — what is it but the rudiments of pure religion, the first efforts and directions of that affection which the Maker of the Mind demands for himself?

The Reality of which these admirations are the poor shadow, is God. Nothing else but Himself can satisfy the desire of what is vast and great, which haunts it. In both these instances, in the sentiment of love and of loyalty, the object of regard is a poor fellow creature — in the first, with a nearer view of personal satisfaction and advantage; in the second, a much more remote and contingent good. But neither of these can ever furnish the mind with a rule of action. The soul wants a pilot, a star, a stronghold amidst the vicissitudes of life to which it can repair continually for refreshment and instruction. In short it wants an object as great as its love.

But there is a third sentiment of which the mind has made a deity, which is more elevated and unexceptionable than either of those to which I have alluded and which seems to be a yet nearer approach to religion or the worship of God, — I mean Honor. Here we get a more spiritual devotion. This is not a homage paid to any man or any woman, but to a simple sentiment. It is a respect paid by proud men to what they think is graceful and becoming; what is approved in the judgment of honest and generous men. It was a delicate sense of right which, when seated in a noble breast, quick and correct in its judgments, was no unfit representative of the law of God. For, take the high definition of Honor which a true poet has given:

> 'Say what is Honor? 'Tis the finest Sense
> Of justice which the human mind can frame,
> Intent each lurking frailty to disclaim
> And guard the way of life from all offence
> Suffered or done.' [6]

If it were so, — if, in the hearts of all who appeal to it, it were this pure tribunal, then it were sacred, and its decisions would chime, as far as they went, with the decisions of the gospel. Far be it from me, — it is not in my heart, to breathe one word of disparagement against this pure sentiment wherever it has been refined of vulgar error and has extended its jurisdiction over all the parts of life. It was said of Andrew Fletcher, in whose heart it ruled, that 'he would give his life to serve his country but would not do a mean action to save it.' And in a dark age I rejoice that it had honor to form single characters, an image of courtesy and truth, a man without fear and without reproach. There are memorable words and sacrifices which it hath dictated, which make our hearts glow within us and which I will not cavil at because of the name honor. In noble breasts it rises often to a religion, though without the name of Jesus of Nazareth. And then arises an unexpected coincidence of sentiment between these heroes of the world and the heroes of the gospel. Anthony Collins, an unbeliever in the Christian miracles, was accustomed to confess his unqualified admiration for the character of Saint Paul, whom he said had the sentiments of a true and perfect gentleman. And if any man of honor shall tell me that his code is such to him as to exclude every action that the sternest morality would exclude, I shall think he is a Christian without knowing it. Though the misfortunes of education may have given him false associations with the Bible, he has read the original edition of it in his heart. I shall say to him,

> 'Here you stand,
> Adore and worship when you know it not, —
> Pious beyond the intention of your thought,
> Devout above the meaning of your will.'

But whilst this sentiment of Honor, like the other sentiments we have considered, shows the natural tendency of the soul and whilst it has prompted such pure and lofty sacrifices, yet considered as a Rule of life it is open to very serious objection. It is not in all men what it is in the purest bosoms. Though it may be a religion to one man, it is a worship of devils to another.

THE CHOICE OF THEISMS

The service of it in Sidney's mind is the service of God, but in Buckingham it is lust and pride. This arises from its uncertain foundation. For who is the umpire that determines what is and what is not consistent with honor? It is the collective sense of the great multitude of persons of standing in the world. It is the speech of men exalted into a god. Of course it is liable to all the caprices and imperfections and vices of society. And beside its uncertainty it very rarely extends its authority to all classes of actions. It has been found that they who held this law in respect and would die rather than do a cowardly or a miserly action, have yet been intemperate and licentious. It is insufficient to the wants of the heart and of the life of man. It is good in the street but what can it do in the closet? It will serve it may be in laborious and perplexed action, — but how will it urge and sustain the mind in intellectual labors, in the acquisition of truth? It is good to act with the brave and the industrious, — but what can it do for those who are excluded from action, who are only called to suffer?

It is remarkable that all these sentiments are of the most beneficent and unexceptionable character, that they exalt the soul which feels them but the direction of them all is unworthy. The sentiment is infinite and so always outruns and belies the object which is finite. One worships a friend of another sex. One worships a King. One worships the speech of his fellow-men.[7]

These sentiments which we have considered are powerful and in their degree noble principles. They have produced and are producing the welfare of society; they shame our selfishness, but their objects are not equal to the capacity and destiny of the human soul. It seems to me they serve a higher use than to make the present order and advantage of society, they acquaint us with our own powers and wants. From the delight and the superior efficiency which we find in surrendering ourselves to a sentiment, we discover that the soul was made to go beyond itself for its objects; to apply itself to more than its own benefit;

157

[handwritten: Extend love of honor to love of God]

to lose itself in the love and seeking of infinite good. They point at and prophesy a higher principle to be the love and object of devotion to the soul, that is, God. The sentiments are natural and they are infinite, but the objects to which they are applied are finite and very unworthy. Our earthly friends baulk and disappoint our affection. We have invested them with perfections that are not theirs, much more so the great men whom we choose for our leaders and patrons. The extremist spirit of party would not now teach us to die for the cause of a political leader. And as to honor, its foundation is too narrow and its being too artificial and limited to fill the desires and exercise the faculties of the soul. But carry out these sentiments to their greatest extent, enlarge these desires and exercise these faculties to the utmost, and they become the love of God.

[handwritten: 4) Faith] Let me then present to your thoughts another sentiment by which the human mind can be controlled, that of faith in God, and compare it with these imperfect sentiments.

My friends, you are so familiar with the words 'faith in God' and so accustomed to hear as things of course what is said in the pulpit, that I hardly can hope to get for this thought that freshness of effect which even the oldest thought will derive from the effort to bring it home to our own mind. Yet I could wish that this sentiment might be compared by you as a principle, a rule of action, with the confessedly beneficent sentiments to which I have alluded. I could wish that every soul that hears me would explore the sense of that word 'faith in God' and see whether possibly it do not contain a beauty and value as yet unknown to you.

If it seem to any ardent mind a noble devotion to be in heart and in soul the bondsman of your friend, or of some great man, or of your honor, I entreat that one to come with me and visit an infinite and immortal beauty — a most intimate and perfect Friend, a law which is the fountain of Honor — to accompany me within the doors of his own soul and by humble watching, he shall find there is a source of all truth, of all generous

THE CHOICE OF THEISMS

humane affections, a source of power to produce great and beneficent changes in the world. There, in the soul, in the eternal Temple of God [8] — he who watches his thoughts will find that he can at once make a calm solitude in the midst of the thickest multitude, yes, and the sweetest society in total solitude.

I believe there are degrees of this feeling known in great hearts which have something more heroic, more truly sublime than anything which the sentiments of love, of loyalty, of honor ever dictated. Consider how the pious man worships. He seeks not the approbation of one or two erring creatures but invigorates himself with the thought that the Eye which fills the universe with light and searches the darkest secret of space, rests benignantly upon him, sees in his mind with approbation every good intention, long before yet it has bloomed into action. He considers that a powerful and earnest Benevolence watches in the creation and sends its bounty as in ceaseless waves of light from the centre to the circumference of things. He steadies his steps with the thought that in all the immensity of nature there is no lawless particle, there is no decay, there is no malice, that is not watched and overruled. But the perception of God's power is the least affecting thought to those that know him best. The heart must have the relation of personal love. 'I fear God' said the pious Thomas Browne, 'I fear God, but I am not afraid of him.' Nothing is known of him until we have become acquainted with the serious and sublime pleasure of opening to him the council chamber of our own thoughts, of treating him as the holy Friend [9] whose praise atones for all censure and whose censure spoils all praise; to whom we make a solemn appeal whenever we are injured by men, and feel that, — come what suffering soever, — even unto death, his power and justice will make all things equal, and justify us in the end.

Then when this faith hath got rooted — when it has become the ruling motive, it fast becomes an object of exclusive attachment. Then it comforts the wretched, it unchains the slave, it is father, mother, friend, house, and home to them who are destitute of all.

The heart in the sight of God feels that all earthly distinctions are annihilated. What are the greatest inequalities in human lot, before him, but varieties of discipline? And moreover his sight converts the worst losses and pains into angels and helpers; for the happiest man, in God's eye, is the man of humblest and sweetest temper, and that perfection is formed in obscurity, and dependance, and disappointment. The heart that is touched with this celestial impulse amid its own afflictions rises with gratitude to its Author and without one repining thought asks for higher blessings upon those who are better endowed and better placed in life. To feel that he is low, causes him no regret; for the thought springs in his mind — Can the favoured child of his election love him so well or cling to his will with the submission of the shrunken sufferer pinched by poverty and sensitive to the touch of error and shame? No, an angel knows not the height and depth and breadth of resignation like him who, stript of all and satisfied that in him is no strength, yet exults in all that is good and fair; he has a property in all through his relation to God. The peace and joy that belong to deepest suffering are the miracles of faith. I find in the book of the Acts one of the sublimest passages in human history. 'At midnight in the prison Paul and Silas prayed and sang praises unto God.' [10]

And is it not a practical principle as it affects our active powers for the good man, leans upon omnipotence, yes and borrows of omnipotence in the prosecution of his undertakings? I mean what I say. Surely the future will wear a new face to him who considers that he may rely on a Divine help in every virtuous design, that a good cause is always strong with more than the help of man, that unexpected succors spring up from a thousand quarters, and, mainly, out of his own faculties; — in a right cause they multiply themselves, they grow wiser than they were; there is more fire in his eye; more activity in his imagination; his understanding hath a greater reach; new truth opens, greater courage appears, until he discovers in his own experience the truth that a humble man in the single service of conscience hath literally infinite force and becomes the voice and the hand of God.

Finally, faith in God opens the understanding of the mind and explains the seeming contradictions of the Gospel. It shows how the poor in spirit have the kingdom of heaven or true happiness, how the pure in heart see God, how they that mourn are comforted by lasting consolations, how the hungry are filled and the persecuted triumph. For the greatest sacrifice requires the highest faith and the highest faith is the most intimate union with God.

And as this faith increases, it continually makes the conscience more clear-sighted and the affections more pure. An observation of the secrets of nature does not operate to diminish our admiration of her laws nor does an affectionate watching of the moral laws lessen our wonder or our love.

My friends, there are two questions which a sincere mind will ask in contemplating this principle. Are we assured of its truth? and Is it practicable as a rule of life?

In the first place, Is it founded in fact? [11] Is there evidence enough to make it reasonable that finite men, atoms as we are in the immensity of being, ignorant as we are of the powers that surround us, should put our trust in an unseen infinite Mind? I say that our constitution answers the question, that we are in our fabric God-believing, God-worshipping creatures, that the common sentiments of men do grope after some great object on which they may rest and depend, and for lack of such object they waste themselves on unworthy substitutes; that if the sentiment of love be analyzed it will be found that it is always necessarily drawn to wisdom and goodness and repelled by sin; that therefore it does point at and prophesy an infinite object, and therein conspires with all the instincts of nature and all the conclusions of reason.

practicality — it works

YOUNG EMERSON SPEAKS

And is it practicable? Is it possible that so vast a thought should be brought down to be the common food of the mind, — should be made familiar enough to be an ever present motive and rule? It is practicable, for it has made thousands good and happy under assaults and suffering. It is practicable; for which of us does not remember in the past years of his life some elevated moments in which this principle did animate him to thoughts and acts of genuine worth? It is practicable, if we seek God in the right place; if, instead of seeking a Thunderer in the sky, we realize that a good man is the clearest manifestation of him, and that therefore Jesus Christ, a poor benevolent Jew, was declared the express image of his person; if we understand the sublime doctrine that the pure in heart shall see him; and so instead of painfully seeking him in extreme miracles, realize that the heart becomes pure by his influence, that the pure heart is united to him, utters his word, beams his glory, is a vehicle through which his spirit passes. Ah, brethren, I fear we are strangers to ourselves. Amid the clamours of our passions, amid the din of this world's affairs, we do not heed the thunder call of a Superior Nature which pleads with and warns us from within. When I say it is practicable, I know I have a witness in every one of your hearts which hath affirmed the same thing many times and put it beyond a doubt. Let me exhort you then to lend an ear to all the good and sacred promptings that hitherto you have withstood, to prefer the good of your whole character to any petty present gratification; to prefer an hour of humble earnest dealing with yourself — humble earnest endeavor at improvement, aiming at the friendship of the Eternal Spirit, to all the praise and advantages which men can confer. For these will pass away with the breath that is in your nostrils. That is eternal.

Find Your Calling

Forgetting those things which are behind and reaching for those things which are before, I press toward the mark for the prize of the high calling of God in Christ Jesus.   Philippians III, *13, 14.*

The Christian doctrine of the immortality of the soul gives the greatest importance to all the events of this life as they in some degree affect the whole being of the soul.

Men in general are so entirely occupied with the particulars, as to give no attention to the general course of their life. But though they consider more the effect of single actions and do not take heed that the course shall be serviceable on the whole, God does. And if men would regard it, it would comfort them to see that all this apparent disorder of innumerable uncontrolled actions resolves itself into a great order and is made by the Divine Wisdom to produce the most beneficent results.

Look at the great throng the city presents. Consider the variety of callings and pursuits. Here is one man toiling with a hod on his shoulder; and another with his saw and tools; a third with his books; a fourth driving bargains at the corners of the streets; another spreads his sail from the wharf toward the sea; another heals the sick; another draws a map; another is hasting to his entertainment and to dangerous pleasures; another is led to the jail between officers; another takes his seat on a bench to judge him. They do not perceive, who make up this sad and cheerful scene, that they are placed in these circumstances to learn the laws of the universe, and that these various implements and callings serve the same use as the child's slate and spelling book, wherewith he also learns his lesson, murmuring all the while at the necessity, and does not yet perceive that for his own good and not for another's it is taught him.

It well deserves attention how fit are the various employments of men not only to occupy their attention and keep them from the misery of idleness but to engage and invigorate their faculties, to form the virtues, in short, to educate the man. It deserves attention how much every one is indebted to his calling for his powers and for his enjoyments. And it is curious to observe how complex is the action and reaction of a man upon his profession and his profession upon the man.

Two purposes are answered by the general distribution of the work of society into various professions and by each man's attention and ability being confined to some one; first, his more efficient action is gained to the common good; and, secondly, his own powers are revealed to him and gradually he is shown what his own peculiar talent is, which is every man's true and eternal calling from God, his Maker.

It is to some remarks upon this last topic that I have to request your attention.

Both propositions contain truth, for the mind is capable of commanding and of being commanded by circumstances. In the fact that the human character is much affected by the accidents of country, parentage and the like we trace the Divine Wisdom operating a progressive education of the race. At the same time it were treachery to our souls to overlook the other fact, the power of man over his condition, which bespeaks the great gift of God in the endowment of the human race with liberty.

On account of the very remarkable effect which particular situations and duties have had on some men a great deal more power has been ascribed to things outward than belongs to them. We hear a great deal of the empire of circumstances over the mind, but not enough of the empire of the mind over circumstances, that the mind is capable of exerting this power.

FIND YOUR CALLING

Circumstances are of the greatest importance as instructors but they suppose a pupil. To say they make the man is to say the air makes the sound which it only conveys or that it is the winds and not the pilot that brought the ship into harbour.

It is not to be denied that all men are much influenced by the fortune of their birth and early associations and many men are passive. A man is born under the shadow of ancient institutions by the side of whose strength his own strength is insignificant. Men are observed to be of their fathers' religion. Men frequently follow, especially in old countries, their fathers' profession. And so it is said, man is formed by these institutions. But observe, on the other hand, how strong is the effect of individual character in each man to change the complexion of the same pursuits in his hands. In a degree he always is affected by the nation, age, family, profession, friendship he falls upon; but he exerts influence as well as receives it. And that, in proportion to the strength of his character.

I submit it to your thoughts whether there be not reason to think that every man is born with a peculiar character or having a peculiar determination to some one pursuit or one sort of usefulness. If he cultivate his powers and affections, this determination will presently appear. If he does not, he will yield to those influences under which he first happens to fall; but as his character opens, there will be this constant effort on the part of his mind to bend his circumstances to his character. Hence we continually see men of strong characters changing the nature of a profession in their hands. What different men have figured under the name of a soldier, from the bloody savage who was brother to the tiger and the wild boar, to the pious and gentle patriot who saved his country. How different has been the profession of ministers of religion as it has fallen upon different men. One is a soldier, one a statesman, one an adviser of the King's conscience, one a dispenser of ceremonies, one an alms giver, one a beggar, one a petty tyrant, one a preacher, one a pastor.

What entirely different professions are contained under the name of merchant or lawyer, each individual pursuing those parts only or chiefly, for which his talents most qualify him. At present, society is serviced by a limited number of professions and each man according to his temper or the temper of his friends is thrown into one of these. But as society advances, no doubt these pursuits will be infinitely multiplied, and instead of a few professions, there will be almost as many callings as individuals. This seems to be provided for in the infinite diversity of human taste and human character. One man loves agriculture, another commerce, another learning, another art; one would live on the mountains; another on the sea; one has skill in speech, another the brain in the hand; one loves the crowd; another to sit and study alone. Even now we occasionally see an individual forsake all the usual paths of life and show men a new one better fitted than any other to his own powers.

And as any man discovers a taste of any new kind, any new combination of powers, he tends toward such places and duties as will give occasion for their exercise. And this because great powers will not sleep in a man's breast. Everything was made for use. Great powers demand to be put in action, the greater they are with the more urgency. Every man is uneasy until every power of his mind is in freedom and in action; whence arises a constant effort to take that attitude which will admit of this action.[1]

Let a man have that profession for which God formed him that he may be useful to mankind to the whole extent of his powers, that he may find delight in the exercise of his powers, and do what he does with the full consent of his own mind. Every one knows well what difference there is in the doing things that we have with all one's heart and the doing them against one's will. If every man were engaged in those innocent things that he best loved, would not the wheels of society move with better speed and surer effect? Would not more be done and

FIND YOUR CALLING

all be done better? And what an increase of happiness! For all labor would be pleasure.

But men exercise their reflexion so little in this matter that you see only rarely in society a man exactly suited to his profession. Often men seem entirely without suitableness to it. Its duties are discharged without love and not only so, but men in that condition are but half themselves. Powers unexerted slumber in them. On the other hand, we sometimes see an individual who seems to have fallen exactly into his right place. And what perfect satisfaction appears in his air and behaviour, how harmoniously all his powers are developed. And with what increased efficiency he works!

These remarks are founded on the doctrine which I believe gains faith in every man's mind as he reflects, that every individual mind has its assigned province of action, a place which it was intended by God to fill, and to which always it is tending.[2] It is that which the greatest cultivation of all his powers will enable him to do best. It is what that particular person was made to do. Every just act, every proper attention bestowed upon his mind makes this aim more distinct to him. It may be hidden from him for years. Unfavorable associations, bad advice, or his own perversity may fight against it but he will never be at ease, he will never act with efficiency, until he finds it. Whatever it be, it is his high calling. This is his mark and prize. This is permanent and infinite; all other callings are temporary, are only means to bring out and present this distinctly before his eyes. Many mistakes may be made in the search but every man who consults himself, the intimations of Divine Wisdom in his own mind, will constantly approach it. It is that state in which all the powers of the man are put in use. And he who steadfastly enlarging his views of what is true, and heroically doing what is right is fast advancing toward this end.[3]

This end, this his high calling — let it be sacred in each man's mind. Let every mind rise to the perception that it was designed by the great Father of all for a peculiar good, — not to be benefitted only in common with nations, or with families, but as an individual. Be content then, humbly and wisely to converse with yourself; to learn what you can do, and what you cannot; to be deterred from attempting nothing out of respect to the judgment of others, if it be not confirmed by your own judgment. Never take for granted a common opinion against the promptings of your heart, considering that another age will reverse all unfounded opinions, and settle them anew. Go forward and accept the gift of the creation and resign yourself to his will by obeying the promptings of the mind. Nor ever consider that your ties in life, your obligations to your family, or to your benefactors or to your creditors, or to your country shut you out of your true field of action, by forbidding you to correct the errors of choice of pursuit into which you have fallen. For you may constantly be tending towards this your use *through* all the common occupations and relations of life, — may constantly, by force of will, be bending them to that. The more distinctly we become acquainted with our powers and destiny, the more effectually do we exert ourselves to give that direction to our common employments; the less do we serve our circumstances, and the more do they serve us.

Furthermore a pious mind will feel assured that God is always giving us freedom as fast as we are fit for it. He who has adopted a great purpose with ardor forsakes everything for it. If his circumstances will admit of it he bends them to his purpose, if not he breaks them to it.[4] It becomes to him father, mother, house and lands. The force of the feeling is his justification. He who does not feel his call with the same force remains where he is. Or if there be any who feel a painful disproportion between their character and their condition and yet labor under a load of embarrassment too great to be removed, in the eternity of their nature and in the omnipotence of God is their hope.[5] The circumstances change, heaven and earth pass but the soul endures. There is no knot which death cannot untie. And Jesus teaches us that death will bring a state

FIND YOUR CALLING

of freedom. Death will presently come and will doubtless bring to all who deserve it much more freedom than they now possess and will permit them to exert their virtues and talents with far more efficiency than they can at present.

Once more, this the high calling of every soul is not in heaven, or over the sea, or existing in a heated imagination or in a remote future, it may be served in this life as well as in the next. It begins to be served whenever a man begins to act according to his conscience and he is leaving it whenever he violates his conscience. (It is your high calling *in Christ*, for the purpose of Christ was to redeem every soul from the bondage of sin to the glorious liberty of the sons of God that each might truly discern his own powers and duties.)

Finally the high calling of every mind is full of infinite glory and joy and sweetness. Every man likes to do what he can do well. But this is to do what God made you to do best. It is no trifling, no easy, no short work. It is a work that demands severe exertion, your head and your heart, and it never will be done. But then it brings the strength it needs for it is embraced with the whole affection of the soul. It makes the day bright. It clothes the world with beauty, the face of God with smiles. It is a path without an end, that beginning in the little pursuits of this world leads up to God's right hand, to pleasures forevermore.[6]

Astronomy

God that made the world and all things therein, seeing that he is Lord of heaven and earth, dwelleth not in temples made with hands; neither is worshipped with men's hands as though he needed anything, seeing he giveth to all life and breath and all things . . . Forasmuch, then, as we are the offspring of God we ought not to think that the Godhead is like to gold or silver or stone graven by art and man's device. And the times of this ignorance God overlooked, but now commandeth all men every where to repent, because he hath appointed a day in which he will judge the world in righteousness by that man whom he hath ordained; whereof he hath given assurance unto all men, in that he hath raised him from the dead.   Acts XVII, 24 ff.

I QUOTE all these memorable words of Saint Paul because they may serve as one out of many passages to show that the Scriptures claim to come from the same Being that made the heavens and the earth; that the God of nature and the God of the Bible are affirmed to be the same;[1] that the Father of Jesus Christ is the Divine Providence in whose wisdom and love all beings are embosomed.[2]

Since this is so, — since the records of the divine dealings with men claim no other origin than the author of nature, we may expect that they are to be read by the light of nature; that

ASTRONOMY

more knowledge of his works will enable us better to understand his word; and that religion will become purer and truer by the progress of science.

This consideration ought to secure our interest in the book of nature. The lover of truth will look at all the facts which every year science is bringing to light with curiosity as the commentary and exposition, say rather, the sequel of the revelation which our Creator is giving us of himself.

With this view I am led to offer you some reflexions that are suggested by the present state of the science of Astronomy, some thoughts upon the influence which the wonderful discoveries men have made of the extent and plan of the universe have had upon religious opinion.

There are many considerations that associate astronomy with the history of religion. It is always at hand as the visible image of every exalted sentiment. Religion in the later ages, suffering from the caprices and errors of men, wanders often far from her object into strange paths; and the attempt is resisted as a sort of violence which strives to reunite Religion with the love of nature. Yet the song of the morning stars was really the first hymn of praise and will be the last; the face of nature, the breath of the hills, the lights of the skies, are to a simple heart the real occasions of devout feeling more than vestries and sermon hearings; and are those natural checks that are ever exerting an insensible influence to hold us back from fanaticism and keep us within sight of the true God.

Then the aspects of the heaven cannot fail to affect all opinion, especially these speculations. These aspects are so prominent. In the beginning of society in mild climates of South Asia, when as yet men had not built magnificent towns, Nature made the riches and the shows of men. What perfection and elegancy in them, — nothing else in nature has the grandeur and influence upon the mind. How delicately at sunset come out these sparks in the vault. The changes which touch us touch not them. From Time which they measure they suffer not. There is the light sphered in the same vessels which contained it (not in Archimedes' or Ptolemy's time) but when the first Syrian shepherd noted down with a savage's imagination the figures he saw nightly sketched in the sky. Yes, and for what inconceivable periods before the human race was. We are new comers into space. Our planet is gray and scarred with wrinkles of immense age, but its inhabitant is a novelty in the cheerful eternity, long ago as bright as now, into which we are born.[3]

And hence it naturally happened that the heavenly bodies were the first objects of idolatry. Symbols of power and beauty, they were readily understood by the perverted to be power and intelligence themselves. And let the proverbial phrases still current in common speech attest how obstinate was the opinion that the stars exercised moral influence upon the lives of men.

If a large class of men are less sensible to impressions of beauty, still to them the heavens were at hand as illustration for all argument. What questions do they not suggest? Let me ask the younger members of this assembly, Have you ever settled it in your mind and do you believe that space is really boundless? You cannot deny the fact without absurdity, and in words you do admit it without hesitation; but I persist in asking, Do you believe it? Dwell a moment on that gigantic thought until you feel the difficulty of the question; until you discern that the first conception which this science presents to man is a space upon whose area all the worlds of God are a mere dot, and the boldest imagination of man or angel can only enter upon its margin. All that exists is lost in the bosom of its great night. Thus impressive and animating are the first aspects of the science.

An important result of the study of astronomy has been to correct and exalt our views of God, and humble our view of ourselves.

In all ancient speculation men were accustomed, of course, to

ASTRONOMY

take man for the type of the highest beings, and suppose whatever is intelligent and good among God's creatures must resemble human nature. Even God himself, the infant religion of all nations has clothed in human form, and idolatry imputed to him the passions as well as the person of man. Astronomy corrects all these boastful dreams, and demonstrates that whatever beings inhabit Saturn, Jupiter, Herschel, and Mercury, even in this little family of social worlds that journey like us around the sun, they must have an organization wholly different from man.[4] The human race could not breathe in the rare atmosphere of the moon; nor the human blood circulate in the climate of Uranus; nor the strength of men suffice to raise his own foot from the ground in the dense gravity of Jupiter.

Each of the eleven globes, therefore, that revolve round the sun must be inhabited by a race of different structure. And to suppose that the constitution of the race of yesterday that now plants the fields of this particular planet, should be the pattern for all the orders that people the huge globes in the heaven is too improbable to be entertained.

Rather believe that the benignant Power which has assigned each creature to its own element, the fish to the sea, the bird to the air, the beast to the field, has not less nicely adjusted elsewhere his creatures to their habitation and has enriched other seats of his love with other and perhaps far more excellent endowments than he has granted to mankind.

In the next place, the science of astronomy has had an irresistible effect in modifying and enlarging the doctrines of theology.[5] It is known to all to whom I speak that until a few hundred years ago it was the settled opinion of all men that the earth was stationary in space, and that the sun and stars actually moved round it every day as they appear to do to the eye. The host of heaven were esteemed so many lanthorns to illuminate and set off the residence of man. It is only since the time of Galileo and Newton it was learned that the little ball on which we live spins upon its own axis to produce this appearance, and that it is at such a dizzy distance from the stars which were supposed thus revolving for its ornament, that it is not visible from them. And not only the earth but the whole system also to which it belongs, with the great sun in the centre, are perhaps too minute for observation from those remote luminaries.

Why need I repeat to you the swelling amount of distances and magnitudes of the stars with which calculation amazes us? They go in the pages of the Almanack into every house and shop. Every mind in the civilized world has caught the general results. Every heart responds to the pious hymn:

> 'Yet not to earth's contracted span
> Thy goodness let me bound;
> Nor think thee Lord alone of man,
> When thousand worlds are round.'

When the solar system had been correctly explained to us we found ourselves journeying in a comparatively small opaque planet around a single star and quite too inconsiderable to be noticed amid the millions of burning suns which the telescope revealed. It was the effect of this new knowledge, to make an equal revolution in religious opinion, as in science, for it was impossible to regard the earth any longer, as the only object in the care of Providence.

It had been the belief of many generations that God from all eternity had foreseen the fall of man and had devised in his councils a method by which man might be saved. The second being in the universe, it was represented, undertook to save them, and in the vain imagination of man the scheme of his redemption, as it was called, occupied the attention of God and of angels, as if there were nothing in being but men. 'The earth,' in the strange language of an old divine, 'was the scaffold of the divine vengeance.'[6] Now this system of theology was every way suited to the ancient system of the heavens. It could not but happen that the telescope should be fatal to both. I regard it as the irresistible effect of the Copernican astronomy to have made the theological scheme of Redemption absolutely incredible.[7] The great geniuses who studied the mechanism of the heavens became unbelievers in the popular doctrine. Newton became a Unitarian.

In spite of the awful exhibition of wisdom and might disclosed to their eyes — the present God, — in spite of the natural expectation which dictated the sentiment, 'The undevout astronomer is mad' — the incongruity between what they beheld and the gross creeds which were called religion and Christianity by their fellow countrymen so revolted them, the profound astronomers of France rejected the hope and consolation of man and in the face of that divine mechanism which they explored denied a cause and adopted the belief of an eternal Necessity, as if that very external necessity were anything else than God, an intelligent cause.

When the student of nature, quitting the simplicity and perfectness of natural laws, came into the churches and colleges to learn the character of God they there found such gross and unworthy views of him as not agreed but contrasted with their own conclusions respecting the cause of Nature, and as with one voice they rejected these creeds. Others finding no congenial faith, rejected all, rejected the hope and consolation of man in the face of the divine.[8]

In the next place, whilst the removing this veil from the creation and enabling man from the little globule in which we are embarked to send his eye so far into the surrounding infinity, has at first had the very natural effect to shake down the systems of opinion which churches and doctors had built and to cast a portion of doubt upon all, this evil was balanced by an opposite beneficial tendency. The investigations of the last two hundred years have brought to light the most wonderful proofs of design — beneficent design — operating far and near in atoms and in systems, reaching to such prodigious extent both of time and space, and so perfectly answering their end, that the mind cannot weigh them without ever increasing surprise and delight. One inquirer ascertains that in a course of years the earth's moon has deviated from her orbit by slow increments that begin to become sensible, and alarms men by showing the future fatal consequence to the earth of these eccentric movements. A more searching observer ascertains by observation and analysis that these irregularities must from the form and relation of the two bodies be periodical, and that when, after a long course of years, they have attained their maximum, a contrary motion takes place and restores the equilibrium. It is the glory of La Grange to have demonstrated that all the irregularities which take place in our system are periodical, an error on one side being compensated by an exactly equal error on the other, and fluctuate between fixed and impassable limits, that there is no ungoverned orb, no loose pin, no lawless particle through all the heights and depths of the city of God.

Cheered by these results we come to feel that planet gravitates to planet and star attracts star, each fulfilling the last mile of its orbit as surely in the round of space as the bee which launches forth for the first time from its dark cell into light, and wandering amidst flowers all day, comes back at eve with unerring wing to the hive. It is the same invisible guide that pilots the bee and pilots the planet, that established the whole and perfected the parts, that giveth to all beauty, and order, and life, and usefulness. And thus I say, my friends, that to the human race the discoveries of astronomy have reconciled the greatness of nature to the greatness of the mind. Once God was understood to be the governor of this world. Now they perceive him to be an Infinite Mind, an awful, an adorable Being, yet as affectionate in his care as he is surpassing in wisdom.

I proceed to say that as this enlargement of our religious views — this correction of error — and this more generous consideration of God's government comes to our minds inevitably by the progress of this science, so it cannot be doubted that it was designed. Though slow, it was the sure result of the divine faculties with which man is endowed. He who made the

ASTRONOMY

eye and the light and clothed the globe with its transparent atmosphere did thereby teach his creature to observe the stars and write their laws. Thereby he opened the heavens to them to reform their religion and to educate the mind. By the mild, affectionate yet thrilling voice of nature he evermore leads them to a higher truth, and rewards every exertion of their faculties by more just knowledge of Himself.

And finally, what is the effect upon the doctrine of the New Testament which these contemplations produce? It is not contradiction but correction. It is not denial but purification. It proves the sublime doctrine of One God, whose offspring we all are and whose care we all are. On the other hand, it throws into the shade all temporary, all indifferent, all local provisions. Here is neither tithe nor priest nor Jerusalem nor Mount Gerizim. Here is no mystic sacrifice, no atoning blood.

But does it take one charm from the lowly grace of Christ? Does it take away any authority from his lips? It abridges what belongs to persons, to places and to times but it does not touch moral truth.[9] We are assured in any speculation we may indulge concerning the tenants of other regions, in the wide commonwealth of God, that if we could carry the New Testament to the inhabitants of other worlds we might need to leave Jewish Christianity and Roman Christianity, Paul and Apollos and Cephas and Luther, and Socinus, but the moral law, justice and mercy would be at home in every climate and world where life is; that we can go nowhere but wisdom will not be valuable and justice, venerable and humility, suitable and diligence, useful and truth, sacred, and charity divine.

The largest consideration the human mind can give to the subject, makes moral distinctions still more important, and positive distinctions less. It will not teach any expiation by Jesus; it will not teach any mysterious relations to him. It will teach that he only is a mediator, as he brings us truth, and we accept it, and live by it; that he only saves us, by inducing us to save ourselves;[10] that God now commands all men, all spirits, every where to repent; and that such principles as Jesus Christ inculcated must forevermore be the standard by which actions shall be judged.

The greatest enlargement that our views of the solar system or of the Creation can attain can never throw the least shade upon the truths, upon moral truth, upon the truths which it was the office of Jesus to unfold. Can never throw a shade upon them! Not only so but they lose all brightness and greatness themselves by the comparison. There is a time when in the human mind, busied before in objects of matter,[11] the voice is heard, Hunger and thirst after righteousness. That word is like another morn risen on midnoon. It is a new heaven and a new earth. The outward Creation, great as it was, pales away and is dull and dim. We feel that millions of suns and systems, new and deeper reaches into the infinite void help us not. They are mere additions of number and magnitude, which, let them reach as far as they will, have no life and can never touch the human heart. We then feel that there is no grandeur like moral grandeur. Before one act of courage, of love, of self devotion, all height and distance are ineffectual and the stars withdraw their shining. This only is real, absolute, independent of all circumstance and all change.[12]

It is, brethren, a glorious confirmation that is brought to our faith, the observation that it agrees well with all the new and astonishing facts in the book of nature. It is good to perceive that the beatitudes of the sermon on the mount will be such to all intelligent creatures. The Scriptures were written by human hands. God intends by giving us access to this original writing of his hand to correct the human errors that have crept into them. Let us yield ourselves with a grateful heart to the instruction that comes from this source and not repine to find that God is a greater, wider and more tender Parent than we were wont to worship. We shall not less distinctly see Jesus to be the gracious instrument of his bounty to instruct men in the character of God and the true nature of spiritual good, the teacher, and, by his teaching, the redeemer of men. But we shall fulfil the intent of Jesus by rendering the praise to God. The hour will already have arrived in our hearts, when means and instruments shall have done their office and when God shall be over all and through all and in all.

The Genuine Man

Stand therefore having your loins girt about with truth.   Ephesians, *VI, 14.*

The new man which after God is created in righteousness and true holiness.   Ephesians, *IV, 24.*

WE HEAR the opinion often expressed that men are in a state of rapid improvement. It is thought that juster views of human nature are gaining ground than have yet prevailed. Men are beginning to see with more distinctness what they ought to be, that is, what true greatness is. What was called greatness, they have discovered to be an imposture. We stand on tiptoe looking for a brighter age, whose signs and forerunners have already appeared. If it be so let us rejoice. Certainly the times past have failed and the welfare of men still is only hoped for.

It seems to be left to us to commence the best of all works. Nations long before us have made desolating wars and gained bloody victories. Others have invented useful and elegant arts. Others have reared grand temples and beautiful palaces. Others have bred great kings — terrible to their enemies and to their subjects; have produced ingenious artists, inspired poets, eloquent orators, wise judges, brave soldiers, rich merchants, benevolent benefactors, learned scholars. Let them all have their due praise. To us has been committed by Providence the higher and holier work of forming *men*, true and entire men.

THE GENUINE MAN

A finished man — who has seen? Men are everywhere, on the land and sea, in mountains and mines; cities and fields swarm with them. They are reckoned by thousands and myriads and millions. Yet where to find one who is that which he should be, that which his Maker designed.[1] There is a man in us, we have not seen executed out of us. Survey the whole circle of your acquaintance, of your neighborhood, of your town and if you can fix upon one complete man, a man independent of his circumstances, a mind which fills and satisfies your idea of the perfection of human nature — one whom you venerate *as a man;* whose value to your eye consists entirely in the richness of his own nature, in the ability and dispositions you suppose him to possess, and not because he belongs to a particular family, or fills a certain office or possesses a large estate, or is preceded by a great reputation. There is nothing for the most part less considered than the essential man. The circumstances are much more attended to. Ordinarily when we speak of great men we mean great circumstances. The man is the least part of himself. We hear the wheels of his carriage. We feel the company that walk with him. We read his name often in the newspapers — but *him,* the soul of him, the praised, the blamed, the enriched, and accompanied, we know not; what matter and quality and color of character he has by which he is that particular person and no other. (Silsbee, Tazewell, Grundy, Barbour — they are mere names — present no specific idea.) You sit in the same room with him and yet *himself* you see not.[2] All are sensible that the eminence which men are acquiring in society every day is of an extremely artificial character and can be gotten and given to almost any man. The error lies in supposing we know those people best whose names or faces we see most frequently.

But not only an inferior man is thus often magnified but men of real ability owe to this noise and pomp the largest part of their eclat. It aids and doubles their greatness. Whichever way the great man turns, whatever he saith or doth, he is never considered on his naked merits. His fame wins for him, argues for him, commands for him. Who can resist this influence and feel that the reason of Caesar is really no more weighty than our own? We meet a prosperous person. The imagination is first excited and the judgment a little shaken by the renown of his name. Then he is announced by all sort of cheerful and respectful attentions. Then every word comes loaded with the weight of his professional character. Then there still is another fence of fine plausible manners, and polished speech, and the men are very few who have the firmness of nerve to go behind all these inclosures, and with an undazzled eye penetrate unto and measure and weigh the man himself; and the men are fewer still who can bear the scrutiny. Behind all this splendid barricade of circumstances is often found a poor, shrunken, distorted, almost imperceptible object who, when exposed, is found helpless and unhappy.

Is it not true in your experience, brethren, that thus the man is the least part of himself? Arts and professions, wealth and office, manners and religion are screens which conceal lameness and imperfection of character. The eye is so entertained with the outward parade that rarely does anybody concern himself with the state of the real person that moves under all. The whole world goes after externals and the soul, God's image and likeness, is overlooked. Is it not true that men do not think highly, reverently of their own nature?[3] To some persons it may sound strange that we say people do not think enough of themselves. Does not the Apostle Paul, they say, teach that a man ought not to think highly of himself? Do we not say of a trifler that he thinks too much of himself? Let us draw the distinction between a right and a wrong estimate of oneself.

There are two ways of speaking of self; one, when we speak of a man's low and partial self, as when he is said to be selfish; and the other when we speak of the whole self, that which comprehends a man's whole being, of that self of which Jesus said, What can a man give in exchange for his soul? And in

THE GENUINE MAN

that sense, when you say of a man that he thinks too much of himself, I say, No, the fault is that he does not think of himself at all. He has not got so far as to know himself. He thinks of his dress, he thinks of his money, he thinks of his comely person, and pleasant voice, he thinks of the pretty things he has got to say and do, but the eternal reason which shines within him, the immortal life that dwells at the bottom of his heart he knows not. He is not great enough — not good enough — not man enough to go in and converse with that celestial scene. Very likely he is so utterly unacquainted with himself, has lived so on the outside of his world, that he does not yet believe in its existence.[4]

It seems to me, brethren, as if we wanted nothing so much as a habit of steadily fixing the eye upon this higher self, the habit of distinguishing between our circumstances and ourselves; the practice of rigorous scrutiny into our own daily life to learn how much there is of our own action and how much is not genuine but imitated or mercenary; the advantage of arriving at a precise notion of a genuine man such as all good and great persons have aimed to be, such as Jesus designed to be and to make many become, such in short, as in the language of the Scripture, is 'the New Man, created after God in righteousness and true holiness.'

And this is my object in the present discourse, to draw the picture of the Genuine Man — I think very few such have ever lived.[5]

But it is essential that he should believe in himself because that is the object in view, to raise up a great counterbalance to the engrossing of riches, of popularity, of the love of life in the man and make him feel that all these ought to be his servants and not his masters, that he is as great, nay much greater, than any of these: to make him feel that whereas the consequence of most men now depends on their wealth or their popularity, he is capable of being sought to become a man so rich and so commanding by the simple force of his character, that wealth or poverty would be an unnoticed accident, that his solitary opinion and his support to any cause whatever would be like the acclamation of the world in its behalf.

This as we shall see is the secret of all true greatness, the development of the inward nature, the raising it to its true place, to absolute sovereignty, hearkening to this voice which to most men sounds so faint and insignificant above the thunder of the laws and the customs of mankind. And it is founded and can only be founded in religion. It can only prefer this self because it esteems it to speak the voice of God.

This example of public life is only a glaring instance of the manner in which we are dazzled by circumstances but you and I in the most private condition are quite as apt to make the same mistake. A failure in trade is called *ruin* though it may only call out the faculties and resources of his character. The death of a parent or relative on whom a family depends is esteemed as irreparable loss. How many women are brought up in the beliefs that an advantageous connection in life is essential to their respectability and comfort and grow up in ignorance of their own resources.

Let me have your attention then (and not that only but your critical judgment. If I speak to any young person engaged in the formation of his character let him compare my account with his own experience) in dwelling on the conspicuous marks of the genuine man.

It is the essence of truth of character that a man should follow his own thought; that he should not be accustomed to adopt his motives or modes of action from any other but should follow the leading of his own mind like a little child.

Vulgar people act from a great variety of motives, sometimes from principle, sometimes from prejudice, sometimes from the expectations other people have of them, sometimes from mean calculation, sometimes from superstition. The genuine man is always consistent for he has but one leader. He acts always in character because he acts always *from* his char-

THE GENUINE MAN

acter. He is accustomed to pay implicit respect to the dictates of his own reason and to obey them without asking why. He therefore speaks what he thinks. He acts his thought. He acts simply and up to the highest motives he knows of.

The excellence of this character will appear by comparing it with the way of the world. In all our intercourse with men we are obliged to make much allowance for what is said out of complaisance and what is said from self interest. What is meant by 'knowledge of the world'? Is it not to be suspicious — not to confide too much in kind words or first impressions?

And sad it is to see how much dissimulation exists. There are some people who never appear to speak from their thought — very well behaved people, too, to whom it never seems to have occurred that they ought to act themselves. They are always plotting. They always have one meaning on their lips and another in their heart; often not so much from a design to deceive, as to make themselves agreeable to their company. It is being agreeable at an immense expense. It cannot deceive any one many times and it cuts up all confidence at the root and undoes the complaisant person. I have seen a person who really never heard with the ear his real intents. He never put off the mask; while every one wondered why one should take so much unnecessary pains he was content to carry that cartload of dishonesty from morning till night, winter and summer for forty years and more.[6]

From such painful folly it is refreshing to come into the pure air and free sunshine of the genuine man. All this imposture seems to him needless and irksome. This duplicity shows that there is no sufficient power of reason within the mind that practises it to counterbalance the temptation of acting from external motives. The person is conscious that his intentions are mean and need concealment. But where the mind has no low ends, and is satisfied of the rectitude of its purpose, it assumes no veil — it needs none, but goes to its object openly, and by the shortest way. He is transparent. His intention shines through all his words and deeds. It was nobly said by an old Roman when the masons offered for a hundred crowns to build him a house such that nobody in the city could look into it: 'I will give you twice so much money,' he said, 'if you will build me a house so that all Rome can see every part of it.' It was well said by George Fox, the Quaker, 'That which I am in words, I am the same in life.'[7] It was to the same purpose that an eminent religious teacher of the last generation, Emanuel Swedenborg, said of his writings that 'they would be found another self.'

But to come a little closer to this matter, to show more particularly how the genuine man speaks and acts, and what is meant by his following implicitly the leading of his own mind. It was happily said of a great man 'that he was content to stand by, and let reason argue for him.' That is precisely the impression left on your mind whenever you talk with a truth speaker, that it is not he who speaks, so much as reason that speaks through him. You are not dealing with a mere man but with something higher and better than any man — with the voice of Reason, common to him and you and all men. It is as if you conversed with Truth and Justice.

This man has the generosity of spirit to give himself up to the guidance of God and lean upon the laws of nature; he parts with his individuality, leaves all thought of private stake, personal feeling, and in compensation he has in some sort the strength of the whole, as each limb of the human system is able to draw to its aid the whole weight of the body. His heart beats pulse for pulse with the heart of the Universe.

To some this may seem a vague expression. There is this supreme universal reason in your mind which is not yours or mine or any man's, but is the Spirit of God in us all. The more it is trusted, the more it proves itself trustworthy.

By the genuine man I understand something more than a man who speaks the literal truth. There are I hope many men who aim to do this, and this, though a commendable, is not the

THE GENUINE MAN

highest virtue, but the genuine man speaks in the spirit of truth. He is one who recognizes his right to examine for himself every opinion, every practice that is received in society and who accepts or rejects it for himself. He is one who though calm and cheerful is in earnest and nothing can make a man calm and cheerful but the belief that he is advancing toward his true ends. Being thus in earnest and examining all things he does what he does and speaks whatever he says with all his heart and soul. And so the effect upon the hearer is that you have his whole being a warrant for every word. So much for *speech*; not less remarkable is the *action* of the genuine man.

He is distinguished by the heartiness with which he gives himself to the affairs that engage his attention, following the advice of the Apostle, himself a high example of this sincerity, 'Whatsoever ye do, do it *heartily*, as unto the Lord, and not as unto men.' And this appears first in the choice of his pursuit.

It is plain to all observers that some men have been formed for public life, for the management of general affairs, of a robust fabric of soul that needs the rough discipline of hot contention, of deep stakes, of great antagonists, and a vast theatre. Others as manifestly are born to benefit men by the advancement of science, by ——.[8] Others embrace the mechanical arts and find no pleasure like that of exercising their own ingenuity to valuable ends. Others delight in the bustle of commerce. Others have quieter yet scarcely less effectual means of serving their fellowmen in gentle offices of compassion or instruction. But to each is his own mode and the genuine man finds his way to that for which he is fitted. Therein he delights and moves with freedom and joy. You shall see others, and this is the great fault of men that in all public business they do not give themselves to the affairs they undertake, they only half act, they speak much, and do much, and yet do not embark themselves fairly and frankly, for better for worse, in the cause but are ever looking around to see what chance there is for their particular advantage. It is only the means to him of a private end. And you never get a perfect confidence in them. Not so the genuine man. He fairly espouses his cause. He grows in its success, he faints in its failure. It is his own cause and his life is in it. All men understand this difference at a glance. I feel who does his work professionally and who does it with the heart.

I am led in connection with these views of genuineness of character to remark upon the stability that belongs to it. 'Be ye steadfast, immoveable' — says Paul, an injunction that cannot be complied with, except by him who possesses truth of character.

By listening to this inward voice, by following this invisible Leader, it is in the power of a man to cast off from himself the responsibility of his words and actions and to make God responsible for him. It is beautiful, it is venerable to see the majesty which belongs to the man who leans directly upon a principle. He has a confidence that it cannot fail him. It is affirmed to him as by oath of God. The conviction that possesses him is equal to the judge. As God liveth it shall be so. Whilst he rests upon it, he has nothing to do with consequences; he is above them, he has nothing to do with the effect of his example; he is following God's finger and cannot go astray. God will take care of the issues. He may walk in the frailty of the flesh with the firm step of an archangel.

[Whilst I follow my conscience I know I shall never be ashamed. When I have followed it, I know my conduct is capable of explanation, though I have wholly forgotten the circumstances. [Webster and Hayne — Adams and Stephenson] Integrity defies the sun to find a flaw in its texture. Scipio burned his African accounts.]⁹

Finally in answer to any (if such there be) who shall say, 'This quality is good, but is there not something better?' I would add one remark, that the conviction must be produced in our minds that *this truth of character is identical with a religious life*; that they are one and the same thing; that this voice of your own mind is the voice of God; that the reason why you are bound to reverence it, is because it is the direct revelation of your Maker's Will, not written in books many ages since nor attested by distant miracles but in the flesh and blood, in the faculties and emotions of your constitution; that Jesus Christ came into the world for this express purpose to teach men to prefer the soul to the body. Until this conviction is wrought and acted on a man can never be said to have fairly set out on his journey of improvement, for this alone can teach him how to blend his religion with his daily labor so that every act shall be done with the full consent of his head and his heart and he shall not regard his business as so much interruption or so much injury to his religious life, and leave his faith at home, when he goes to his store. The Sabbath was made for man not man for the Sabbath and Religion is made for man's benefit not for God's.

And yet who knows not that crowds of men are acting on that error, that their religious character is something separate from their daily actions — quite external — like a dress to wear or a chamber to lodge in, and that trade is to get them money, and prayers and sermons are to get them virtue, but either would be hurt by being joined with the other.

If instead of this, he worked with love in his favorite calling; if he saw in every day's labor, that he was thereby growing more skillful and more wise; that he was cooperating with God in his own education so that every dollar he earned was a medal of so much real power, the fruit and the means of so much real goodness; if neither his working hours nor his rest were lost time, but all was helping him onward, would not his heart sing for joy — would not the day be brighter and even the night light about him — would not company be more pleasant and even solitude be sociable and his life reveal a new heaven and a new earth to his purer eyes?

Were it not an unspeakable blessing to the world the appearance of such men in its affairs, who should show us how much radiance may belong to mere character, who should show us that honour may dwell in a small tenement as well as in a state house, and that there is no place that will not shine under the light of virtues. We do not know how rich we are.

What is the practical end of the views we have taken? This, and this only, — Be genuine. — Be girt with truth. Aim in all things at all times to be that within which you would appear without. Commune with your own heart that you may learn what it means to be true to yourself and follow that guidance steadily. God would have you introduce another standard of success than that which prevails in the world. When you go home at night, and cast your thoughts on your condition, fix them upon your character: instead of asking whether this day has made you richer, or better known, or what compliments have you received, — you shall ask — Am I more just — am I more useful — more patient — more wise — what have I learned — what new truth has been disclosed to me?

Then you will have an interest in yourselves. You will be watching the wonderful opening and growth of a human character, the birth and growth of an angel that has been born, but never will die — who was designed by his Maker to be a growing benefit to the world, and to find his own happiness in forever enlarging the knowledge, multiplying the powers, and exalting the pleasures of others.

Religion and Society

Howbeit when the spirit of truth is come, he will guide you into all truth: for he shall not speak of himself; but what he shall hear, that shall he speak: and he will show you things to come. John XVI, 13.

ONE of the keenest enjoyments of human life is to return home. It has lately been mine. After a short absence spent in continual journeyings among the most interesting monuments of the ancient and the great cities of the modern world God has blessed my eyes with the sight of my own land and my own friends. I cannot tell you, my friends of this religious society, with how much pleasure I see you again and learn of your welfare and of your virtues. I am touched by emotions that are more than pleasant in seeing again this well known company of men and women standing together in the same connexions. I meet you conversing with the same persons with whom I was wont to find you. I am moved with gratitude when I have again found together the husband and wife, the father and children, brothers and sisters, the betrothed, the beloved, — and mark how cunningly these affections of ours root themselves around the heartstrings, and tie the lives, the characters, and the destinies of men together. And I pray God, long to preserve to you the joy and protection of these dear and wholesome associations.

As I have seen you in the streets, and in your dwellings, so now I am permitted by your favor to address you once more in our ancient sanctuary. And as it has been my grateful duty heretofore to provoke you to a good life by suggesting religious sentiments, — let me once more — for one short hour — find my accustomed place in your thoughts; — once more let me invite you to the primal truths, again let us communicate the joy and peace of believing, let the power and love of the Highest overshadow us and, amid the evils we suffer or fear, let us find a respite and sanctuary in those sublime truths which are to be studied rather than comprehended. Brethren, I am one of those who esteem the goodwill of the meanest to be of some importance. I value the friendship of good men as the best gift they can bestow, and so I would cultivate yours by being associated in your minds with those thoughts which are most dear to the best men, and have had the highest worth to each of us in our most virtuous hours.

No topic has seemed to me more suitable than the consideration of the prospects of society in reference to religious instruction. Before I parted from you I anxiously desired an opportunity of speaking to you upon the subject of that change which seems to be taking place under our eyes in the opinions of men on religious questions; of that Teaching which all men are waiting for, and of that Teacher who has been predicted and hath not yet come. The lapse of a few months has in no wise lessened the interest of these questions, and the present condition and prospects of this church may even lend them greater pertinency.[1]

I think I cannot over rate the dignity and interest of this inquiry for it refers to the highest want of the soul. The greatest gift of God is a Teacher and teaching is the perpetual end and office of all things. Teaching, instruction, is the main design that shines through the sky and the earth. It is the end of youth, of growth, of play, of studies, of punishment, of pleasure, of misfortunes, of sickness, of contests, of connexions, of professions — the purpose of all — all teach us something, yes, even sin and death, — and that lesson is the reason of their coming. The end of living is to know; and, if you say, the end of knowledge is action, — why, yes, but the end of that action again, is knowledge. He that has no ambition to be taught, let him creep into his grave. What is he doing among good people? The play is not worth the candle. The laborer is not worthy of his meat. The sun grudges his light, and the air his breath to him who stands with his hands folded in this great school of God, and does not perceive that all are students, all are learning the art of life, the discipline of virtue, how to act, how to suffer, how to be useful, and what their Maker designed them for. It is this persuasion only, that can invest existence with any dignity or hope or raise man above the brutes.

And this will do it. If you believe that every step you take not only enables you to make another, but also brings you within reach of influences before inert, that your life is like the Day which not only shows more objects every moment, but also brings out new properties in every particular object, you will then accept Instruction as the greatest gift of God, and anxiously put yourself in the attitude of preparation.

The language of Jesus Christ himself is sufficiently remarkable. He assured his disciples that he had much more truth to make known to them but that they could not bear it now; but that after he had departed from them, and by his departure, he would send them another Teacher, who would guide them to farther revelations, and that under this guidance, they who believed on him should be able to do greater things than he did.

What is the meaning of all this? He would tell them that God was not yet known in his world, that the divine truth was not opened and could not be opened to the Jewish mind, but that by his death, they would cease from their shallow and fanatical expectation of an Israelitish conqueror, the bandages would be torn from their eyes, and on their despair the light of the true heaven might dawn.

Here are promises whose sense deserves to be more unfolded.

That a Teacher shall come. Who is that Teacher? Let Jesus answer, Even the Spirit of Truth. He would say, that there is a constant effort of the Divine Providence for the instruction of man. Time, the great teacher, is always uttering his lessons — heard or unheard — in the ear of man. Every day is exposing some of the falsehoods that have deceived us. Truth endures and is manifested every moment from day to day, from age to age, ever since the crimson light of the first morning awoke the first man, the Almighty Father accumulates knowledge in the mind of the race; from endless sources — from continual communication — from tradition, from scripture, from comparison of events, from personal experience, from every one of countless occurrences the growing treasure is poured into the world, as the globe itself receives the rays of millions of stars which beam upon it from all the concave firmament around. The Teacher is one, namely, the Spirit of truth; but He speaks by a thousand thousand lips, in all countries, in public and in private places, to mankind. He is never silent. There is no one so remote but he is addressed by him. To drop all personification[2] — the progress of society, the simple occurrences of every day, are always instructing men, undeceiving them, and every event big with what crimes and misfortunes soever, carries with it this beneficent effect, that an experiment has been tried which need not be repeated in the sight and for the sake of the human race. Thus the first Revolution in France was esteemed a great calamity. It is now a page of cheerful wisdom to Europe and to America. And as with one sort of truth so with the highest — the relations, namely, of man to God and the character of God; that is continually being revealed. The rival churches that have risen and disputed, the pious and humble pastors who have labored, the fanatics who have exaggerated doctrines fundamentally true, the infidels and scoffers who have assailed with success the corruptions of Christianity, have all done service to the great cause of truth, which is the Teacher of the human race.

I. Let us inquire in the first place what is the true light in which the life and labors of Jesus should be regarded. The perspective of time, as it sets everything in the right view, does the same by Christianity. We learn to look at it now, as a part of the history of the world; to see how it rests on the broad basis of man's moral nature, but is not itself that basis. I cannot but think that Jesus Christ will be better loved by not being adored. He has had, as we all know, an unnatural, an artificial place for ages in human opinions — a place too high for love. There is a recoil of the affections from all authority and force. To the barbarous state of society it was thought to add to the dignity of Christ to make him king, to make him demigod, to make him God.[3] Now that the Scriptures are read with purged eyes, it is seen that he is only to be loved for so much goodness and wisdom as dwelt in him, which are the only properties for which a sound human mind can love any person. As the world grows wiser, he will be more truly venerated for the splendor of the contrast of his character to the opinions and practices of his age, he will attract the unfeigned love of all to whom moral nature is dear, because he planted himself, in the face of the world, upon that sole ground; showing a noble confidence in the reality and superiority of spiritual truths, that simplicity and at the same time enthusiasm in declaring them, which is itself one of the highest merits and gives confidence to all the lovers of the same truth.

But I ask whether it will not come to be thought the chief value of his teaching — whether it will not come to be thought the greatest value of Christianity — more than any single truth which it inculcated — the general fact that it was a brave stand made for man's spiritual nature against the sensualism, the forms, and the crimes of the age in which he appeared, and those which preceded it? The value of his particular lessons is something less to us than it was to his contemporaries, because like every wise and efficient man he spoke to his times in all their singular peculiarities. His instruction is almost as local, as personal, as would be the teaching in one of our Sunday Schools. He speaks as he thinks, but he is thinking for them. And it is the great mark of the extraordinary force of his mind that notwithstanding this occasional character his sayings have a fulness of meaning, a fitness to human nature and an universality of application which has commended them to the whole world. But in this respect their value is equal to us and to them and to all men, as a great affirmation of the beauty and excellence of moral truth, — a disclosure of that inner world of man whose existence once admitted and beheld, opens an entrance for all the particular doctrines of divine truth.

I say it is the distinction of Christianity that it is the most emphatic affirmation in history, of the existence of the spiritual world. And in this way as Jesus was the apostle of moral nature by word and by act — living and dying — in this way was he the Teacher, the benefactor of mankind, as one who saw, and proved by his actions that he saw clearly and steadfastly an inner world, compared with whose glories the brightness of external nature is mean, and the luxuries of the senses worthless. And this I think is the light in which we are to look at the recorded teaching and example of Jesus.

II. In the second place what has been its subsequent history? A history of growth. A great deal more truth was yet to be made known. Christianity is the most emphatic affirmation of spiritual nature. But it is not the only nor the last affirmation. There shall be a thousand more. Very inconsistent would it be with a soul so possessed with the love of the real and the unseen as Christ's, to set bounds to the discoveries in that illimitable region. None knew better than he that every soul occupies a new position, and that if the stars cannot be counted, nor the sea sands numbered, much less can those moral truths be numbered and ended, of which the material creation is only the shadow. He never said, All truth have I revealed — but that which was committed to me. He plainly affirms the direct contrary. I will send you another Teacher, another Comforter, even the spirit of Truth; he will guide you into all truth. He promised that continual effort of the divine Providence which is always instructing those who are in the attitude of scholars.

Christ tells them that they are not now fit to hear what he is ready to announce, but that they shall hereafter be ready, and the future Teacher shall tell them more and greater things than he. He affirms the fact that the essential condition of teaching is a ripe pupil. The wisest Teacher can impart no more than his disciple can receive. The rapid flashes of celestial thought must wait the tardy expansion of the worldly mind. No teacher can teach without the hearty cooperation of the scholar. This, as I have already intimated, crippled his communications of moral truth. There is much as every one knows of what is called *accommodation* in his discourses; that is, they are clothed in the manner of speaking and in the manner of thinking of the times; otherwise, they would have been altogether rejected by that perverse generation to whom he spoke, and of whom he was obliged to say, that, the very reason why they would not believe him, was that he told them the truth. 'Because I tell you the truth, ye believe me not.' He has always in his mouth expressions of his sense of the littleness of the present and strong assurance of the greatness of the future. His word is a mustard seed — it is a little leaven, — it is a single pearl — but with a prophet's eye he sees that the omnipotence of truth is in it, and beholds already its prolific effects — he sees it quicken in the minds of good men and run like something endued with life from soul to soul, from house to house, from land to land, — searching, agitating, educating society, — touching with sympathy all heroic minds, and preparing hearts to conceive and tongues to utter yet more lofty and significant revelations. 'Greater things than these shall ye do.' We see with our eyes the verification of his promise. We see the enlargement of religious truth in its effects. In the place of the unsupported virtues of solitary individuals that sparkle in the darkness of antiquity, of the little stingy rapacious intercourse of that day — a few Corinthians, a few Romans creeping round the shores of the Mediterranean for piracy and conquest, the nations of the globe are brought together by pacific and equitable commerce; liberal humane Christian associations are correcting the manners and relieving the sufferings of vast masses of men. Bible societies, Temperance societies, Sunday Schools, Peace societies, Seamen's societies, Associations for the Correction of Prison Discipline, for the Diffusion of Useful Knowledge, for the abolition of slavery, and every other benevolent enterprize, [4] — are they not all the fruit of the life and teaching of that lowly Nazarene?

I look upon them all as illustrations of the power of this conviction of which I speak in the human soul. Great and manifold as these institutions are do they not have their origin in the fact that some men (according to the saying of Jesus) have strongly felt that 'it is better to give than to receive' and that they themselves were commanded to seek the welfare of other men.[5] A human mind once persuaded of a simple abstract proposition becomes the servant of that thought and puts the whole material creation as far as its power reaches into subjection to it. And a few men persuaded of the same thing will cooperate and by cooperation make more intense each other's conviction and soon exert a power that multiplies itself in a compound ratio and produces such effects as we behold. I rejoice as others in these effects, yet, brethren, I rejoice with no spirit of noisy exultation. I believe that the truth itself which is thus operative is worth more far more than all its effects. For there is in all moral truth that fruitfulness, that inborn creative force, that ever unfolding power that promises to act upon human society with an energy which nothing can adequately represent.

III. I have said, in the first place, that Christianity was, whilst its author lived, a defence of spiritualism against

RELIGION AND SOCIETY

sensualism; in the second place, that it has been bearing fruit like its seed ever since by producing benevolent institutions and good men. In the third place, I wish to call your attention to the change it is now working.

There is a solemn interest settling upon the future which may well withdraw our interest from what is already around us, were it far more excellent. The dawn is reddening around us, but the day has not come. The Teacher is teaching but has not finished his word. That word never will be finished. It was before the heavens and shall be after them. But a part of this message is spoken this day and every day. There are truths now being revealed. There is a revolution of religious opinion taking effect around us as it seems to me the greatest of all revolutions which have ever occurred that, namely, which has separated the individual from the whole world and made him demand a faith satisfactory to his own proper nature, whose full extent he now for the first time contemplates. A little while ago men were supposed to be saved or lost as one race; Adam was the federal head and, in books of theology, his sin was a federal sin which cut off the hopes of all his posterity. The atoning blood of Christ, again, was a sacrifice for all, by which the divine vengeance was averted from you and me. But now, men have begun to feel and to inquire for their *several stake* in the joy and the suffering of the whole. What is *my* relation to Almighty God? What is *my* relation to my fellow man? What am I designed for? What are my duties? What is my destiny? — The soul peremptorily asks these questions — the Whence and the Why — and refuses to be put off with insufficient answers. It is because so many false answers have been offered that in many earnest well-intentioned men, reason has been so far shaken from her seat, that they have assorted with the infidel and the atheist so called. The questions are now again presented, because the wonder of the surrounding creation begins to press upon the soul with the force of a personal address.

And what is the answer?

Man begins to hear a voice in reply that fills the heavens and the earth, saying, that God is within him, that *there* is the celestial host. I find that this amazing revelation of my immediate relation to God, is a solution to all the doubts that oppressed me. I recognize the distinction of the outer and the inner self — of the double consciousness — as in the familiar example, that I may do things which I do not approve; that is, there are two selfs, one which does or approves that which the other does not and approves not; or within this erring passionate mortal self, sits a supreme calm immortal mind, whose powers I do not know, but it is stronger than I am, it is wiser than I am, it never approved me in any wrong. I seek counsel of it in my doubts; I repair to it in my dangers; I pray to it in my undertakings. It is the door of my access to the Father. It seems to me the face which the Creator uncovers to his child.

It is the perception of this depth in human nature — this infinitude belonging to every man that has been born [6] — which has given new value to the habits of reflexion and solitude. This has caused the virtue of independent judgment to be so much praised. This has given its odour to spiritual interpretations. Many old and almost forgotten maxims have been remembered up from where they lay in the dust of centuries and are seen to beam new light. Such are the old pregnant maxims, 'Know Thyself'; Est deus in nobis, agitante calescimus illo; the Stoical precept, 'The good Man differs from God in nothing but duration,' Bonus Vir nil nisi tempore a deo differt; the inscription on the gate of Athens, 'But know thyself a man and be a God'; 'Revere Thyself.'

And let me add that in this doctrine as deeply felt by him, is the key by which the words that fell from Christ upon the character of God can alone be well and truly explained. Read by the torch of this faith, it seems to me, those discourses shine with heavenly meaning. The Father is in me — I in the Father. Yet the Father is greater than I.

I anticipate auspicious effects from the farther opening of this faith upon the public mind, from the studies and the actings of good men in the course wherein its light will lead them. It will be inspiration to prophets and heroes. It will be day without night. It will be power to the hands and wisdom to the understanding and society to the solitary. In a particular manner will not the increased clearness of the spiritual sight produce a great reform in the tone and character of our public religious teaching? Will it not put an end to all that is technical, allegorical, parabolical in it?

My friends, I shall not now attempt to portray the glory of that latter church which a truly spiritual faith shall have formed and shall enlighten, but I must press earnestly, affectionately upon each of you, my own conviction of its worth. I would urge upon you the cultivation of this religious frame of mind — much meditation upon spiritual truths, especially upon these convictions of the unfathomable depth of the soul and its union with its source. In them only all real strength is found, and all those great traits which we admire in eminently wise and good men, all the supports of magnanimity and trust, all the incentives to a noble daring; in fine the foundations and the frame work in which a solid regular well-balanced character can be reared, which shall be able, if called, to act a part with vigor and success; if otherwise, to look with calm superiority at the disturbances of the political world, at domestic disappointments, or at want and sickness, — which shall be able to go lonely through life, unhonoured, with unappreciated virtues, yet bate no jot of heart or hope, finding sufficient sympathy and applause in God only. I said that Christianity was a brave stand for spiritual truth against the sensualism of ages. A life which it has formed is a miniature of itself. A good life is a brave stand for spiritual truth against sensualism and skepticism, for the simple reason that every good act is a preference of the whole to a part; of the future to the present; of God to men.

It is the same part of our nature, the spiritual faculty, that suggests the belief that death cannot harm you. This soul converses with the past and the distant, and the future, and is conscious that its thoughts have no relation to time or to corruption. A stronger and stronger word of assurance comes from the undeceiving inward Monitor, who speaks as with the voice of the whole creation. I perceive no terrors, no shrinking in that inmost shrine at the approach of death; the fear is external to it, — in the lower faculties, in the senses; — but all is calm within.

May this faith, this expectation of the Teacher, this effort to receive him, this divine spirit of truth, which is at once the prophecy and the fulfilment, animate them who teach and them who hear. Brethren, may it touch with fire the lips that are to speak to you — please God — for many long and happy years. I rejoice in the pleasing prospects of our church. Its peace and prosperity will always be near my heart. And so farewell, my friends, and may the pastor [7] whom God shall send you, find as much indulgence — as much tenderness at your hands, as I have found, even when we have differed upon matters of subordinate importance. May he be a true teacher of the living word. May he do that which I have desired. May he aid in communicating to your minds, that peace which the world cannot give nor take away, by leading you to a nearer knowledge and love of God and habitation in him.[8]

The Miracle of Our Being

I am fearfully and wonderfully made. Marvelous are thy works; and that my soul knoweth right well.   Psalm CXXXIX, 14.

EVERYBODY knows that he is wonderfully made. And yet it will occur sometimes to a thoughtful mind as strange that people do not continually break out into expressions of astonishment at themselves.[1] When an Asiatic prince came to Paris and was asked what seemed to him most surprising in that capital, he replied, 'to find himself there.' With better reason, a man might say that to himself, his own existence in the world, was more amazing than any other fact. I believe few persons perceive the marvel of their own constitution; and yet it is more wondrous than any fiction that was ever conceived. 'Truth is strange — stranger than fiction.'[2]

The fine contrivance in every part of our frame, the perfect fitting of the members and the admirable working of the whole machine transcend all praise; then the fitness of man to the earth; and his peaceful dwelling among the cattle, the birds, and the fish, turning the earth into his garden and pleasure ground; the round of the seasons and the universal order — is all set down in the books. This external fitness is wonderful, but I doubt if to those who saw this only, it would ever have occurred to remark upon the marvel. It has been said with some ingenuity of conjecture, that without the phenomenon of sleep we should be Atheists; because if we had no experience of the interruption of the activity of the Will, 'we could never be brought to a sense and acknowledgment of its dependence on the Divine Will.' ³ With more assurance it may be said of the things apprehended by the senses, that they are so nicely grooved into one another that the sight of one suggests the next preceding, and this the next before, so that the understanding in the study of the things themselves would run forever in the round of second causes, did not the soul at its own instance sometimes demand tidings of the First Cause. Were there not graver considerations to be remembered there is something almost comic in seeing such a creature as is a man growing up with perfect senses and faculties, and going in and out for seventy years, amid the shows of nature and humanity, making up his mouth every day to express all degrees of surprize at every impertinent trifle, and never suspecting all the time that it is even singular that he should exist.

But superficial views will not always satisfy us. It will not always suffice us to ask why this bone is thus terminated, and be answered that it may fit that socket; or why is this animal thus configured, and be answered that the residence and the food of the animal requires such frame — but the question starts up and almost with terror within us, why the animal or any animal exists? to what farther end its being has regard beyond this nice tissue of neighboring facts? Why organization — why order exist? Nay, why the interrogator exists, and what he is?

The bare fact of your existence as a man is one of such bewildering astonishment that it seems as if it were the part of reason to spend one's lifetime in a trance of Wonder, — altogether more rational to lift one's hands in blank amazement, than to assume the least shadow of dogmatism, of pride.

I say these things because I think that man's mind has not yet arrived at a just perception of his own position and duties in the creation, who is not yet alive to the miracle that surrounds him.⁴ 'Let others wrangle,' said the pious St. Augustin, 'I will wonder.' ⁵ It is related of the wisest man in the ancient

THE MIRACLE OF OUR BEING

world, the Athenian Socrates, that on one occasion, he stopped short in his walk, and stood stock still in a rapture of amazement from sunset to sunrise.

But we may be conscious of the mystery, without always saying so. Certainly; and a man might be well forgiven his omission to express his admiration of that which *is*, if his way of living indicated any sense of his powers and relations.

But see the oddity of his demeanor. This little creature set down — he knows not how — amid all the sublimities of the moving Universe, sharpsighted enough to find out the movement of the sphere he inhabits and of the spheres in the depths around him; and not only so, but capable by intellect and affection, of acting upon remote men as upon himself: Yes, and from his little hour, extending the arms of his influence through thousands of years and to millions of millions of rational men: Nay, by means of Virtue, of entering instantly upon a life that makes the whole grandeur of the Creation pale and visionary. Yet this little creature quite unmindful of these vast prerogatives, struts about with immense activity to procure various meats to eat and stuffs to wear, and most of all, salutations and marks of respect from his fellows. He seems to think it quite natural he should be here, and things should be as they are; — so natural as not to deserve a second thought: and the moment he has got a neat house to sit down, and to eat, and to sleep in, he is so possessed with a sense of his importance that he not only thinks it more excellent than if he knew the whole order of the creation, but he expects impatiently great deference from his fellow men.

We go so gravely about our ordinary trifling employment that we are apt to lose the sense of the absurdity of much that we do. We allow, by our acquiescence, a man that has more houses and ships and farms than his neighbors to assume consequence in his manners on that ground; although we know very well when we ponder the matter that if instead of a few thousand acres of land or a score of ships or houses he owned

205

the entire property of the world, he would be as much in the dark, as mortal, and as insufficient to himself as he is now. He could not then solve not so much as one word of the vast mystery that envelopes us; he would not have a particle more of real power. In the great All, he would be the insect he is now. Yet the extent and consistency of the world's farce keeps each particular puppet in countenance, and we go on in the universal hunt for station and land and horses and ships and stocks and attentions and compliments,—hiding the inanity of the whole thing in the multitude of the particulars. Is it not as if one should have a nest of a hundred boxes, and nothing in the last box?

And hence the wise laughter of the ancient philosopher Democritus, who made a jest of all human society and pursuits. No wise man, he said, could keep his countenance in view of such folly.

But why call it ludicrous? Is it not necessary that we should acquire property?—Yes. We have animal wants, which must be supplied. Commerce—a net woven round every man—grows out of them. Every man should do his part, one should sow the field, and one weave the cloth, and one draw the contracts, and one build the ship, and one plough the sea, and one throw the harpoon. There is much that is wonderful, but nothing that is ludicrous in this, simply considered. The ludicrous part of it, is in the acting as if it were just that for which we lived, and the entire oversight of the end, for which this is the means. The proud man, the sensualist, the denier of divine power, the avaricious, the selfish,—by such earthworms the wonder of our being is not perceived: they are merely the highest class of animals, and like ants and horses and elephants they do not perceive anything extraordinary in their life.

And what remedy? What can save us from this capital error, or repair it?—The exercise of reason, the act of reflexion redeems a man at once out of this brutishness. The man who

THE MIRACLE OF OUR BEING

reflects, is a man, and not an animal.⁶ By the act of reflexion man perceives 'that he is wonderfully made.' Moreover, as we shall presently have occasion to notice, the chief distinctions of his condition begin with that act. The ox knoweth his owner and the ass his master's crib but my people doth not know nor consider. I take it to be a main object of that education which this world administers to each soul to touch the springs of wonder in us, and make us alive to the marvel of our condition. That done, all is done. Before, he was so wrongheaded, so at discord with things around him, that he was ridiculous: now, he is at one with all. He accepts his lot: he perceives the great astonishment. He adores. Awaked to truth and virtue — which is the two fold office of Reason, he passes out of the local and finite, he inspires and expires immortal breath.

Let me for more accurate consideration separate a few of the particulars that amaze the contemplative spirit.

1. See how cunningly constructed are all things in such a manner as to make each being the centre of the Creation.⁷ You seem to be a point or focus upon which all objects, all ages concentrate their influence. Nothing past but affects *you*. Nothing remote but through some means reaches *you*. Every superficial grain of sand may be considered as the fixed point round which all things revolve, so intimately is it allied to all and so truly do all turn as if for it alone. This is true in the lowest natures to the least leaf or moss. Look at the summer blackberry lifting its polished surface a few inches from the ground. How did that little chemist extract from the sandbank the spices and sweetness it has concocted in its cells? By any cheap or accidental means? Not so; but the whole creation has been at the cost of its birth and nurture. A globe of fire near a hundred millions of miles distant in the great space, has been flooding it with light and heat as if it shone for no other. It is six or seven months that the sun has made the tour of the heavens every day over this tiny sprout, before it could bear its

207

fruit. The sea has evaporated its countless tons of water that the rain of heaven might wet the roots of this little vine. The elastic air exhaled from all live creatures and all minerals, yielded this small pensioner the gaseous aliment it required. The earth by the attraction of its mass determined its form and size; and when we consider how the earth's attraction is fixed at this moment on equilibrium by innumerable attractions, on every side, of distant bodies, — we shall see that the berry's form and history is determined by causes and agents the most prodigious and remote.

What then shall we say of the manner in which one man is made the center round which all things roll, and upon which all things scatter gifts. Let us take one from the crowd — not one of the children of prosperity, but a poor solitary virtuous man — the humblest who is capable of reflexion.

He stands upon the top of the world; he is the centre of the horizon.[8] Morning and evening lavish their sweetness and their solemnity upon his senses. Summer and winter bring to him the instruction of their harvests and their storms. All that he sees and hears gives him a lesson. Do not the ages that are past report their experience for his tuition and millions of millions of rational spirits epitomize their fate for his behoof? Is he not continually moved to joy or grief by things said a thousand years ago? He understands them. His soul embraces the act or the sentiment as if it were done or said for him only. Is not his condition different for every one of the men that has acted upon the world? See how much Luther — see how much Columbus, Newton, Grotius, Jefferson, Franklin, have affected his condition; and all the inventors of arts. Do they not give him the unshared total benefit of their wisdom? Does not Socrates, and Solomon, and Bacon, and Shakespear counsel him alone? Jesus lives as for him only? God exists for him only? And Right and Wrong, and Wisdom and Folly? the whole of Pleasure; and of Pain; and all the heaven of thought? Are they not all poured into his bosom as if the world had no other child?

THE MIRACLE OF OUR BEING

The perfect world exists to every man, — to the poorest drover in the mountains, the poorest laborer in his ditch. Quite independent of his work are his endowments. There is enough in him (grant him capable of thought and virtue) to puzzle and outwit all our philosophy. The history of one man, inasmuch as it is searching and profound, is as valuable as the history of a nation. Thoroughly acquaint me with the heart of one living man, — though the humblest, and what can Italy or England teach me more with all their wars and all their laws? Sharpen these obtuse perceptions of ours and show us the motives, the fancy, the affection, the distorting and colouring lenses that pauper makes use of, and the redeeming power that still sets him right after countless errors, and that promises him a kingdom of heaven whilst he shuffles about in his barnyard, and we shall be able to do without Tacitus and Clarendon.

2. Thus is each man placed at the heart of the world. But that is only half of his advantage. That is to receive influence. There is more in him. He is not designed to be an idle eye before which nature passes in review, but is by his action enabled to learn the irresistible properties of moral nature, perceived dimly by the mind as laws difficult to be grasped or defined, yet everywhere working out their inevitable results in human affairs. Whereupon if a man fall they will grind him to powder. There is nothing in material nature (certainly nothing in fiction) so splendid and perfect as the law of compensations — the law according to which an act done by any moral being draws after it its inevitable fruit which no chance and no art can elude. The nature of these laws, their extent, their omnipotence he can learn only by *acting*, and observing how they determine and reward every action. The Creation is so magically woven that nothing can do him any mischief but himself. An invisible immortal fence surrounds his being which defends him from all harm he wills to resist; the whole creation cannot bend him whilst he stands upright;

but, on the other hand, every act of his, is instantaneously judged and rewarded: the lightning loiters by the speed of retribution; every generous effort of his is compensated by the instant enlargement of his soul; his patience disarms calamity; his love brightens the sun; his purity destroys temptation; whilst falsehood is a foolish suicide and destroys belief; selfishness separates itself from the happy human family; idleness whips itself with discontent; malice multiplies its foes, so that ever it seems that each individual is solicited by good and by evil spirits and he gives himself up to them whose bidding he does, and they labor to make him more entirely their own, and to induce him to confirm his last action by repetition, and by fresh energy of the same kind.

To open to ourselves — to open to others these laws — is it not worth living for? — to make the soul, aforetime the servant of the senses, acquainted with the secret of its own power; to teach man that by self-renouncement a heaven of which he had no conception, begins at once in his heart; — by the high act of yielding his will, that little individual heart becomes dilated as with the presence and inhabitation of the Spirit of God.

3. Shall I select as a third trait wherein the miracle of our being is specially manifested, and one which only begins with reflexion, this, that the exercise of reason turns all our evil to good? Thus the moment Reason assumes its empire over a man, he finds that he has nothing low and injurious in him but it is, under this dominion, the root of power and beauty. His animal nature is ennobled by serving the soul: that which was debasing him will now prove the sinews of his character; his petulance is the love of order; out of his necessities grows the glorious structure of civilization. Nay, what trait he blushes for and reckons his weakness because it is different from other men whom he admires, is probably what he should throw himself on his knees and thank God for, as his crowning gift. For there is somewhat peculiar in every man which is on that

> Every misfortune can be turned to benefit

THE MIRACLE OF OUR BEING

account apt to be neglected but which must be let grow and suffered to give direction to the other faculties if he would attain his acme and be dear and honorable to his brethren. He finds that whatever disadvantages he has labored under; whatever uncommon exertion he has been called to make; whatever poverty; what sickness; what unpopularity; what mistake; yes, even what deep sin he has been given up to commit; when once he is awakened to truth and virtue; penetrated with penitence, touched with the veneration of the Almighty Father and stung with the insatiable desire of making every day his soul more perfect, then, all these, the worst calamities, the sorest sorrow, are changed, are glorified.[9] He owns his deep debt to them, and acknowledges in them the omnipresent energy of the God who transforms all things into the divine.

And what is this admiration to which we would excite the soul? What is it but a perception of a man's true position in the Universe and his consequent obligations. This is the whole moral and end of such views as I present. I desire a man to consider faithfully in solitude and silence the unknown nature within him that he may not sink into his own contempt, and be a spectacle of folly to the wise. I would have him open his eyes to true wonder, that he may never more be agitated by trifles. I would have him convinced that by the act of his own will alone, can that which is most worth his study be disclosed to him. I would have him perceive that the unreflecting laborer is but a superior brute; that the reflecting laborer only is a man. Let him consider that all riches, though convenient to the senses, cannot profit *himself*, but that a true thought, a worthy deed, puts him at once in harmony with the real and eternal. Let him consider that, if he loves respect, he must seek it in what really belongs to a man, and not in anything accidental such as fortune or appearance. Instead of making it his pride to be announced as a person of consideration in the state, or in his profession, or in the fashionable world, or as a rich, or a travelled, or a powerful man, let him delight rather to make himself known in all companies by his action, and by his discourse as one who has attained unto self-command; one who has thought in earnest upon the questions of human duty; one who carries with his presence the terrors and the beauty of justice; and who, even in a moment when his friends ignorantly censure him, is privy to the virtuous action he has performed, and those he has in hand.

What is this admiration? Is it not the fountain of religion in the soul? What is it but an acknowledgment of the Incomprehensible — a response to the Wisdom and Love which breathe through the creation into the heart! What does the world suggest but a lofty faith that all will be, that all is well: that the Father who thus vouchsafes to reveal himself in all that is great, and all that is lovely, will not forsake the child for whom he provideth such costly instruction — whom every hour and every event of memory and hope educate. What does it intimate but presages of an infinite and perfect life? What but an assured trust through all evil and danger and death?

Notes

Notes

PRAY WITHOUT CEASING
(No. 1)

IN A SCRAP of autobiography Emerson tells of meeting some farm laborers while he was recuperating from an illness at his uncle's farm in Newton during the summer of 1825. One of them, an uneducated but thoughtful Methodist, said to him that men were always praying and that all prayers were granted. 'I meditated much on this saying and wrote my first sermon therefrom, of which the divisions were: (1) Men are always praying; (2) All their prayers are granted; (3) We must beware, then, what we ask.'

Emerson's references to this farmhand in the later Journals indicate the lasting significance of the insight celebrated by this sermon. The recollection of his indebtedness to this Methodist explains in part Emerson's life-long disregard of sectarian differences. About the same time that he was writing the sermon he tried to express in poetry its central thoughts. (See *Poems*, p. 380.)

The sermon itself was written July 25, 1826. It was preached for the first time on October 15, 1826 in Waltham where Emerson's uncle, Samuel Ripley, was minister. Only the week before he had presented the sermon before the Middlesex Association of Ministers when he requested and received a licensure to preach.

He preached this sermon thereafter eleven times, for he was frequently invited to supply vacant pulpits before he was called to the Second Church of Boston in 1829: Waltham, Oct. 15, 1826; First Church, Boston, Nov. 12, 1826; Charleston, S.C., Dec., 1826; St. Augustine, Fla., March, 1827; Washington, D.C., May, 1827; Philadelphia, May, 1827; New York City, June, 1827; New Bedford, Mass., Nov. 20, 1827; Concord, N.H., Jan. 6, 1828; Lexington, Mass., April 3, 1828; Concord, Mass., April 20, 1828; North (Second) Church, Boston, Nov. 9, 1828.

This sermon and another, on 'The Uses of Unhappiness' (No. 2) Emerson carried with him on the trip he took for the sake of his health during the winter of 1826–27.

Like many a first sermon this discourse covers a good deal of ground. But the young preacher sticks close to his outline and does no more than mention ideas which were to characterize both his sermons and his essays: 'We stand in the midst of two worlds, the world of matter and the world of spirit'; 'your reason is God, your virtue is God and nothing but your liberty can you call securely and absolutely your own'; there is 'a pre-existent harmony be-

NOTES

tween thoughts and things'; nature 'helps the purposes of man'; a man 'is the architect of his own fortunes'; 'after death there is life'; 'conscience, God's vice-regent'; 'what is the past? It is nothing worth.'

He sent the sermon to his mentor, Aunt Mary Moody Emerson, who wrote him it lacked 'unction and authority and allusion to a venerable name.'

When Emerson used this discourse as a Fast Day Sermon at Lexington, April 3, 1828, he substituted for the original cumbersome introduction the following brief and succinct paragraphs:

'The duty of prayer is one of those most insisted on in the enumeration of our duties. It is always appropriate. I shall need no apology for inviting your attention to the consideration of prayer; of prayer, as it is a state of mind, a state of continued preparation for the duties of life.

'There is a previous consideration of great importance to which we must attend. It is this, that though we have no faculties by which we can see the thoughts of men, and are always obliged to judge of men's thoughts by their words and actions, yet it would be foolish in us to suppose that no beings have such faculties. On the contrary — as God sees the soul — so it is probable that the thoughts which are now passing in our minds are perceived by some beings, as properly as the sounds of the voice or the motions of the hand are by us. Now this is very little remembered by us. We give heed to the body and not to the mind. We are absorbed in the contemplation and the pursuits of outward things, of bread and wine and dress, of houses and furniture. This is the great error which the strong feeling....' (See p. 2.)

Although he preached only one other sermon on prayer (No. 86), the subject receives frequent incidental treatment.

This first sermon has both a title and a number. Most of the later sermons have merely a number.

Page 4, note 1. These two sentences are reproduced almost verbatim in Sermon 150. In his lectures and essays Emerson frequently used passages from earlier addresses. He does so rarely in his sermons.

Page 11, note 2. The two preceding paragraphs appear to have been added to the sermon some time after its original composition.

ON SHOWING PIETY AT HOME
(No. 10)

This is Emerson's most-preached sermon. He used it on a journey to the Connecticut River valley, preaching at Northampton and elsewhere as a missionary of the American Unitarian Association; and at Concord, New Hampshire, on the trip on which he met and fell in love with Ellen Tucker, his future wife.

Emerson preached this sermon twenty-seven times: First Church, Boston, Aug. 12, 1827; Federal St., Boston, Aug. 19, 1827; Northampton, Sept. 9, 1827; Deerfield, Sept. 23, 1827; Greenfield, Sept. 30, 1827; New Bedford, Nov.

NOTES

6, 1827; Harvard, Nov. 27, 1827; Watertown, Dec. 9, 1827; Concord, N.H., Dec. 23, 1827; Waltham, Feb. 10, 1828; Carlisle, Feb. 17, 1828; Concord, Mass., Feb. 24, 1828; Dedham, Mr. White, March 2, 1828; Lexington, March 16, 1828; Medford, March 23, 1828; Lechmere Point, March 30, 1828; Shirley, June 8, 1828; Charlestown, Second Church, June 29, 1828; North (Second) Church, Boston, (A.M.) July 13, 1828; Second Church, Waltham, Aug. 31, 1828; West Cambridge, Sept. 21, 1828; Dover, N.H., Oct. 19, 1828; Groton, Jan. 4, 1829; Stow, Feb. 8, 1829; Second Church, (P.M.) Boston, Dec. 29, 1829; Friend St. Chapel, Boston, Nov. 28, 1830; Burlington, Vt., June 5, 1831.

In 1858 Emerson makes the following reference to this sermon in his Journal: 'I remember that when I preached my first sermon in Concord, "On Showing Piety at Home," Dr. Ripley remarked on the frequent occurrence of the word *Virtue* in it, and said his people would not understand it, for the largest part of them, when Virtue was spoken of, understood *Chastity*. I do not imagine, however, that the people thought any such thing. It was an old-school preacher's contractedness.' (Vol. V, p. 142 f.)

Like most of the other sermons this manuscript is without a title. The title has been borrowed from Emerson's later reference to it.

Page 15, note 1. He repeats his text in this sermon to a degree unusual with him. Frequently his texts are used as points of departure rather than as subjects for exposition.

Page 17, note 2. This phrase is reminiscent of a sentence in a letter to his Aunt Mary, written four months before from Charleston. (*Journals*, Vol. II, p. 184.)

Page 20, note 3. The passage from here to the end of the paragraph Emerson deleted from the sermon probably at some time after its initial delivery.

Page 20, note 4. A few weeks after the composition of this sermon, Emerson jotted down in his Journal these words, probably with this passage of his sermon freshly in mind: "'Tis an old and vulgar maxim, Take care of the minutes and the hours will take care of themselves; but like many old and vulgar things 'tis better than gold of Ophir, wisely used.'

THE CHRISTIAN MINISTER — PART I
(No. 28)

In four sermons Emerson expounds his conception of the task of the minister. This sermon and the following (No. 29) he preached on Sunday, March 15, 1829, four days after his ordination.

Page 22, note 1. There is here scratched out in the original manuscript the following: '"Odio humani generis" is the expression of Tacitus upon the Christians in speaking of the occasion when St. Paul is supposed to have suffered martyrdom.'

NOTES

Page 25, note 2. In later life Emerson's private experience of the power of public prayer was not altogether happy. (See the Divinity School Address, 1838.)

Page 25, note 3. Emerson later abandoned this interpretation of the function of the minister in public prayer as that of the spokesman of the congregation. As long as he was minister of the Second Church he continued to lead in prayer. Thereafter he declined to perform the act in public unless he felt inspired to do so. He had had his doubts about the propriety and effectiveness of public prayer before he entered the ministry. (See *Journals*, Vol. II, p. 94.)

Page 25, note 4. 'Quotations from Scripture' appear with considerable frequency in the sermons. The texts, however, serve to introduce the theme rather than to control the thought. In fact the young preacher several times changes his texts, without modifying the sermon itself. He seems to have thought first of his subject and second of a text to fit it. Is the subject of cultivating the mind 'to be abandoned for lack of a text?', he enquires rhetorically of his congregation. (No. 36.) With one exception, — and that a sermon written after he quit the church, — he has a text for all his discourses. This accorded with contemporary homiletical practice. Oliver Wendell Holmes made the happy suggestion that the mottoes which Emerson loved to place at the head of the chapters of his books are an equivalent of the texts that preceded the sermons.

Page 25, note 5. These comments on contemporary preaching raised questions in the minds of some of the congregation, which finally made their roundabout way to the young preacher's ear and caused him to write to Dr. Ware assuring him of his genuine regard for the Bible. (From an unpublished letter. See page vi.)

Page 26, note 6. All his life Emerson found the subject of eloquence fascinating. 'The highest platform of eloquence,' he said, 'is the moral sentiment.' In his preaching he mounted that platform again and again.

Page 28, note 7. That Emerson felt himself to be blazing trails in regard to the style of pulpit discourse, undoubtedly in the face of criticism, is apparent from several other references in the sermons to unconventionality in choice of theme and manner of treatment. His later characterization of sermons as being insulated from life did not apply to his own.

Page 28, note 8. Later in life when he sat in the pew, he spoke in a different vein. (See *Journals*, Vol. IV, p. 244.)

Page 29, note 9. Like the subsequent essays the thought of the sermons is frequently illustrated by anecdotes and apothegms derived from the literature of Greece and Rome. Emerson also used for illustration such 'homely facts' and objects as weeds, berries, rainbows, magnets, coal and spider webs.

Page 29, note 10. 'We have raised this house,' says Emerson in an address at the Dedication of the new Vestry, 'for the worship of God as he is *revealed*, for the study of his Revelation, for the study of the New Testament. In the belief that abundant light shall break forth from that book to guide us,

NOTES

we come here to find it, to hear the voice of truth, to receive the impulses of good.

'In the explanation of the New Testament, very different sense is put upon its text by different Christians. As long as it belongs to me to aid you in the examination of that book, I shall with God's help, speak what I think. I know this is easily said, but hardly to be done. The more it is considered the more the difficulty will appear... Please God that this room may never be dishonoured by dissimulation, or the truth hindered by the love or the fear of man!' (No. 108 A.)

He selects two and one half times as many texts from the New Testament as from the Old Testament. The Gospel of Matthew supplies him with the largest number taken from a single book, sixteen, but texts from the Epistles of Paul outnumber those from the first three gospels, forty-five to thirty-one. The fourth Gospel and the Epistles of John are drawn upon nine times. 'I wish to study the Scriptures in a part of every day,' Emerson confides to his Journal, 'that I may be able to explain them to others, and that their light may flow into my life.' (Vol. II, p. 309.)

Page 30, note 11. With the following passage may be compared an equally moving section of the Journals, written three months earlier when he was considering the call to the church. (Vol. II, p. 262.) Emerson sought to fulfill the office of the ministry according to these terms even after he ceased professionally to be a minister.

THE CHRISTIAN MINISTER — PART II
(No. 29)

This second discourse on the office of the ministry was preached at the afternoon service, following that of the morning sermon on the same subject.

Page 32, note 1. In none of the many references to the Lord's Supper does Emerson give any indication to his congregation of the view of the rite he sets forth in his final sermon on the Communion, which brought about the break between himself and the church. (Published in *Miscellanies*, p. 3 ff.)

Page 33, note 2. The following sentence is scratched out in the manuscript: 'Nor is it less injurious to his character when he degrades his office to be a spy in the families of his flock; nor less when he flatters your vices and condescends to scandal in servility to you.'

Page 34, note 3. Often for Emerson another day means another mood. It is a far cry from this declaration to a later derogatory characterization of the minister as 'a warming pan, a night-chair at sickbeds and rheumatic souls.' (*Journals*, Vol. IV, p. 420.)

Page 35, note 4. Emerson wrote twelve sermons on the subjects of death and immortality and preached them fifty-six times, fourteen times in his own church and twenty-five times after his resignation. It was a theme that constantly occupied him. Death was a familiar visitor to his, as to most of the

NOTES

large families of his time. Severe illness in his youth had turned his thoughts in that direction. In one of his sermons he makes the comment that 'fifteen or sixteen persons die in this parish every year.'

In an early sermon at the Second Church he tells his congregation that he reserves the discussion of the grounds of the hope of immortality a little longer, 'for one would not enter lightly upon the great topic to which all the energies of the greatest minds have ever been directed and whose leading evidences are familiar to you.' (No. 34.)

Page 36, note 5. A sentence in the 'Preacher' (1880) echoes this remark: 'When there is any difference felt between the foot board of the pulpit and the floor of the parlor you have not yet said that which you should say.' Other material for that discourse Emerson drew from these earlier observations and writings; among them, perhaps: 'a vivid thought brings the power to paint it.'

Page 37, note 6. There is scratched out in the manuscript the following clause: 'because in the past week those duties were plainly and feelingly opened by one who is no stranger to the pastoral work.'

Page 37, note 7. Emerson refers to the Reverend Henry Ware, Jr., 1794-1843, his predecessor and colleague. In a letter written in 1817 Mr. Ware spoke of 'the duty of commemorating our Lord in the Supper' as being like the duty of prayer and social life, a requirement for Christian people.

Page 37, note 8. The minister was expected to visit each of the families in his parish at least once a year. Immediately after his ordination Emerson plunged into a strenuous round of routine pastoral activities — weddings, baptisms and pastoral calls — the last, according to an unpublished letter, seeming both endless in number and fatiguing. But he tried, as the same source indicates, to keep his mornings free for study and writing. (See p. vi.)

SUMMER
(No. 39)

This carefully constructed and pregnant sermon anticipates several of the major themes of Emerson's first book *Nature*, published seven years after the composition of this discourse.

Page 39, note 1. When philosophers and scientists in the eighteenth century formulated the theory of a world-machine, Christian thinkers like William Paley proceeded to adjust the doctrine of Creation to it. God, they said, is the Designer and Creator of the world. With ideas of this sort the young Emerson was thoroughly familiar and he embraced them eagerly. He quotes Paley's Natural Theology 'with pleasure.' 'The discoveries of science, not the instructions of revealed religion but the discoveries of science, have compelled men to believe that nothing is made without a purpose; no limb, no bone, no antennae, no hair, no feather, without a distinct purpose that is disclosed as our knowledge is increased.' (No. 66.)

NOTES

But the science of the day tended to weaken as well as to strengthen belief in God. The very perfection and immutability of the creation appeared to negative the possibility of any present divine activity in the world. Emerson is one of the first of his generation in this country to reinterpret the doctrine of Creation in dynamic terms, in order to rationalize such perennially precious religious needs as those of immediate communion with God and assurance of his providential care. Creation indeed is an act of God which occurred sixty centuries ago. But Creation is likewise a continuous activity on God's part. 'The same power is needed this moment as was needed the first moment to produce the same effect. To him it is the same to uphold as to establish. It is a creation of each instant. I look then at my present being as now received, as now sustained by the Omnipresent Father.'

This theory of the immanent relation of God to the world, which constitutes the major theological doctrine of the Romantic movement of thought in Europe at the turn of the century, Emerson preached to a congregation brought up as he himself had been brought up, on a theory of an original Creation with occasional subsequent divine miraculous intervention. He and his people belonged to two different worlds of thought.

Page 40, note 2. This theory of Omnipresence tends to minimize the importance of evil and to lessen the significance of religious institutions: if God is 'the substratum and basis of every one of his works,' — and 'this is the meaning of his omnipresence,' (No. 96) — then nothing is absolutely evil; if God be present everywhere the church loses its uniqueness as the place of his abode. The sacredness of every place destroys the sacredness of all special holy places. To distinguish cause and effect in Emerson's attachment to the doctrine of Omnipresence is futile. Omnipresence made evil seems less significant to him; the relative insignificance of evil made Omnipresence palatable to him. His attempt to make an adjustment between the localization and the omnipresence of God finds expression in a curious statement in one of the sermons: 'A truly devout man at church would not see the walls nor the passing multitude. He needs no aid from company. Sufficient to him would be the presence of the Omnipresent.' (No. 106.)

Page 41, note 3. Emerson's first essay on 'Art' (*Essays, First Series*) echoes this idea. His poem, 'The Problem' also comes at once to mind.

Page 41, note 4. This is one of the unconventional illustrations he warned his congregation in his ordination sermon that he might use. In another sermon he devotes almost a page to a different berry. Strawberries begin to ripen in Eastern Massachusetts at the time of year the sermon was delivered.

Page 43, note 5. The humanist trend of Emerson's thinking comes to expression in this striking departure from the Calvinistic tradition. Emerson speaks for the liberal religious movement of his time when he states that 'God is the servant of the universe'; he acts to 'benefit us.' (No. 141.)

Page 43, note 6. Compare the following extract from a sermon on a wholly different theme, 'Thinking Well of Human Nature': 'The shell which the sea casts up on the beach, cannot admire its form or the splendor of its colors.

NOTES

Man can. And why was the cup of the lily so exquisitely carved, and the petals of the tulip so richly dyed? Why all this divine *taste* (let me so speak) displayed in the architecture and the decoration of the world? Was it for the eye of horses, and eagles, and bats, or for the discerning, measuring, educated eye of man?' (No. 155.)

Nature re-echoes this sentiment: 'The world thus exists to the soul to satisfy the desire of beauty.' (*Nature, Addresses and Lectures*, p. 24.)

Page 43, note 7. All his life Emerson enjoyed the 'unpretending company of the fine race of flowers,' and formed many friendships with them. (*Journals*, Vol. II, p. 200.) But the sermons do not smell of sweet-fern as much as do the essays.

Page 44, note 8. The idea of nature as metaphor, which finds its first expression here, recurs in *Nature* and thereafter frequently in Emerson's writings.

Page 44, note 9. Compare 'Works and Days,' first delivered in 1859: 'An everlasting Now reigns in Nature, which hangs the same roses on our bushes which charmed the Roman and the Chaldean in their hanging-gardens.' (*Society and Solitude*, p. 174.)

Page 45, note 10. On the blank last page of the manuscript is written, perhaps with another sermon in view: 'Addenda. All students of natural science simple and amiable men; not petulant like men of letters. Effect of some facts upon the mind — as the angles of the cell of the beehive.'

TRIFLES
(No. 44)

This sermon, like that on 'Solitude and Society' (No. 55) anticipates a theme that continued to engross Emerson long after he gave up his pastorate. 'Scorn Trifles' seems to have been a common saying in the Emerson household, for which Mary Moody Emerson was responsible. The manuscript has pencilled on its first page 'Juvenes,' though when this annotation was made cannot be ascertained. Originally the sermon had a text from First Corinthians VI, 2.

Page 46, note 1. A similar notion is expressed in 'Culture.' (*Conduct of Life*, p. 150.)

Page 46, note 2. The brackets are Emerson's. Perhaps they indicate that this sentence was omitted on the second delivery of the discourse.

Page 47, note 3. 'Cities degrade us by magnifying trifles.' (*Conduct of Life*, p. 153.)

Page 47, note 4. See Note 2 above.

NOTES

A FEAST OF REMEMBRANCE
(No. 50)

This is the only sermon, aside from one three years later in which Emerson set forth his objections to the rite (No. 162; see *Miscellanies*, p. 3 ff.), which is devoted entirely to the subject of the Lord's Supper. The sermon contains no indication of any 'want of sympathy with it' which Emerson later came to feel so strongly. The same is true of the occasional references to it in the other sermons. In 'God's Wrath and Man's Sin' (No. 89) he refers to it as 'one of the Gospel kindnesses.'

There is wanting from this sermon the elaborate exegesis of Scripture which is found in the later sermon on the same theme. As a rule, the young minister did not preach expository sermons, although in a discourse on the Holy Spirit (No. 110) he devotes two pages to a discussion of the 'eighteen different senses' of the use of 'the word signifying Spirit in the Scriptures.' The suggestion which has been made in connection with the later sermon on the Communion that 'it seems quite unlike his usual method' needs modification in the light of the sermons as a whole. One reason why Emerson did not more frequently expound Scripture in his sermons was that he was including such exposition in the weekly exegetical lectures which his colleague had established and which he gave from time to time on such subjects as the origin, authorship and genuineness of the Gospels, as well as detailed studies of passages from the gospels, such as the Beatitudes. (Unpublished Vestry Lectures.) His abandonment of the traditional view of the authority of the Bible undoubtedly tended to diminish his use of it. It may well be that the desire to be freed from the recurring responsibility of preparing these exegetical lectures entered into his final decision to leave the profession of the ministry. Such would seem to be the significance of the comment in the Journals for January 4, 1832: 'It is the unsaid part of every lecture that does the most good. If my poor Tuesday evening lectures (*horresco referens*) were to any auditor the total of his exposition of Christianity, what a beggarly faith were it.' (Vol. II, p. 444.)

The Second Church celebrated the Lord's Supper monthly. A pre-communion service was held on the preceding Friday evening, the so-called Monthly Lecture.

Page 56, note 1. This diversity of views regarding the Lord's Supper Emerson again pointed out in his later sermon on the subject.

Page 57, note 2. Emerson at this time appears to have thought that Jesus established the rite as a permanent memorial. His later views stand in direct contradiction: 'Jesus did not intend to establish an institution for perpetual observance.' (No. 162.)

Page 58, note 3. In the early eighteenth century Solomon Stoddard had startled the churches of New England by asserting that the Lord's Supper was a 'converting ordinance' rather than the special privilege of church members who were in good and regular standing. He admitted to the Communion table not only those who could give assurance of having been converted but also those who had not yet had such an experience, but who nevertheless were respectable members of the community and who desired to associate themselves with the church. He hoped the Communion service might prove a means of religious education. Stoddard's practise carried one stage further the secularization of the New England established churches which the Half-Way Covenant initiated. According to the latter arrangement the Lord's Supper had still remained the special privilege of the church member.

Emerson in denying that a 'line runs through the world dividing men into saints and sinners' sides with Stoddard and indeed with the Catholic emphasis in the church as over against the primitive church and orthodox Protestantism. His words, 'the aim of this ordinance is nothing but this, to make those who partake of it better,' might almost be quoted from Stoddard. To Emerson character was not so much a matter of achievement as of direction of life.

Page 58, note 4. In the early days in New England the established Congregational Church was identical in membership with the civil parish. With the loss of the initial religious fervor and the influx of immigrants who did not share the interpretation of religion of the original settlers there began to develop in the civil-religious parish an outer circle of persons for whom the Christian religion was less a matter of living reality than a formal social obligation. The disestablishment of the church in the early nineteenth century did away with the civil control and support of the church. But the rôle formerly played by the civil parish was continued, still under the name of the Parish (or Society, or Congregation) by men and women who were interested in religion but who were unable to meet the special qualifications which were laid down for church membership. In such institutions the Parish continued to control the property, raise the budget and call the minister. The Church, a smaller group than the Society, customarily took charge of cases of discipline, of the benevolences and of the Lord's Supper. Many persons were members both of the Society and the Church. The anomalous division between church and congregation, to which Emerson refers, still obtains in many churches of the Congregational order in the United States, although a large number of them have coalesced parish and church in one institution. The ancient difference between the inner and outer circle is often taken care of in such cases by providing an associate membership as well as a full and regular membership.

Page 58, note 5. 'It is the custom to invite members of other churches of every denomination, who may be present, to unite with us in celebrating the death of our common Lord. This invitation is given just previous to the reading of the last hymn of the public service.' (From the Records of the Second Church.) Emerson's suggestion that the invitation be extended even to those who are not Christians was in line with the trend of liberal religious thought

NOTES

of his day, which was becoming increasingly concerned to find the common religious denominator underlying all the historic religions.

Page 58, note 6. Emerson shows no hesitation about recognizing the fact of sin, but he is inclined to deal with it in its ethical rather than its religious aspects: 'There are some whose souls are spotted with sins, who have abused this departing period [the year just ending] to the devising and ripening and practice of schemes of fraud; others, who have sinned against the law of Truth; have injured the reputation of good men; have spoken falsely to gain safety, or favour, or money; others, who have drunk deeply of the cup of sensual excess, who have sinned, and lie in wait to sin again.... Are there any such amongst us, brethren? Does any part of this guilt sit heavy on the souls of any of us? To such I say, Beware of yourselves; there is terror in your nature, if Revelation will not reach you. It has been the opinion of wisest men on a survey of the human mind that God had lodged a Judgment Seat therein, when he formed the Memory.' (No. 61.)

CONVERSATION
(No. 52)

This sermon presents an unconventional application of Emerson's familiar principle of the value of common blessings and the obligations of common duties. His later writings are studded with comments on the art of conversation, although he did not devote a whole essay to this fascinating theme.

Page 62, note 1. Emerson bracketed this sentence probably when he gave the sermon the second time.

Page 63, note 2. 'Every one will remember how often he heard in youth without heed the common proverbs that pass from mouth to mouth, and the lively satisfaction he derived from the perception of their truth the first time that his own experience led him to express the same fact in similar language.' (No. 76.)

Page 64, note 3. In his sermon, 'Words are Things,' Emerson considers in sadly-learned detail, this 'sore side' of conversation, as he calls it.

'It was said of one of the Roman emperors that at nineteen he put on the cloke of dissimulation, which he never put off. And we meet people for whom simple truth never seems enough. If you talk to them they afflict you with an excess of interest in all that you say and add to their exclamations of surprise, grimace and gesticulation. You wonder that the fatigue of acting a part does not become intolerable to them.

'This remark may be extended to much of that profusion of words in which in writing or in speech we express civility. I know that here many persons would find the chief difficulty lie. It was petulantly said of the French language which is most copious in forms of civility that one could not speak twenty words in it without lying. And many well meaning persons who speak the honest English tongue do yet surrender their integrity to what they think

225

NOTES

good nature demands, a compliance with deceitful forms of speech. I believe there is more courtesy in words of truth than in words without it. I believe that neither justice nor benevolence ever require flattery.' (No. 134.)

Page 64, note 4. This idea finds amplification in the essay on the Over-Soul. (*Essays, First Series,* 277 f.)

Page 65, note 5. This is the earliest public utterance of a principle that governed Emerson all his life. He avoided controversy, confident that truth could take care of itself. 'It needs a Saint to dispute.'

Page 65, note 6. In the essay on 'Culture' this idea reappears: 'As soon as he sides with his critic against himself, with joy, he is a cultivated man.' (*Conduct of Life,* p. 158.)

Page 65, note 7. Elsewhere Emerson remarks that, though religion is bound to chasten the levities of conversation, taking away not only its malice but its exaggeration and folly and so being a great help to the peace and the instruction of the world, nevertheless conversation need lose none of its wit and brilliancy. 'All that virtue demands is the intention of truth and it may choose what forms of fiction or gaiety it will.' (No. 49.)

Page 66, note 8. Another sermon makes application of this judgment:
'The nearer anything is to the heart the more impatient we are of insincerity. We can bear that people should exercise their loquacity upon things indifferent to us but they might forbear idle prating about that which is sacred to us. I speak of the mourner. When men are afflicted they want truth. Only truth is tolerable to the petulance of grief. He that does not speak it insults you with every word. He is not seeking truth and therefore what you say and feel has no interest to him and you will not molest yourself by uttering it. He is thinking only of himself, and how he shall come off. Let him be silent. We learn from him the sad difference between words that are things and words that are words. The mourner is suffering now under a privation of the affections and this insincerity adds a privation of the whole spiritual world.' (No. 134.)

THE MINISTRY: A YEAR'S RETROSPECT
(No. 69)

This sermon, preached on the first anniversary of his ordination, contains more than one hint that Emerson had not had an altogether happy time as minister of the church.

Page 67, note 1. Early in March, 1830, Emerson had taken his young wife south in search of health. During his absence from the Second Church he preached at Hartford, and at Philadelphia.

Page 69, note 2. Several times in his journals Emerson refers to himself as a spectator rather than a doer or a participant. 'I was born a seeing eye, not a helping hand.' The pastoral office has need of both.

Page 71, note 3. 'Almost every man when he sits alone in his chamber with his book, hath sometimes had those searching glances at life that penetrated beneath the outward shows of things and gave him for a moment the truest estimate of wealth and fame and sensual pleasure, that for the moment he regarded them from the height from which angels and God regard them, and saw precisely how far they were objects of legitimate desire. By much sitting alone and the custom of thinking, these views will become habitual.' (No. 55.)

Page 71, note 4. With this remark may be compared a rueful entry in the Journals three years later: 'In this world, if a man sits down to think, he is immediately asked if he has the headache.' (Vol. III, p. 207.)

A loose leaf of manuscript has the following note: 'Facts. That an hour of systematic research is worth years of heedless opportunity and observation. Better go up against the wall in blank inefficiency when you pursue a thought than give up the search for a more attractive object.'

This whole paragraph seems to have been intended to meet criticism of his failure to pay sufficient attention to parish calling. It may be surmised that in Emerson's case inclination coincided with duty at this point. He doubtless welcomed every legitimate excuse to refrain from making pastoral calls, for he was uneasy in casual personal contacts.

Emerson's temperament needs to be taken into account in connection with his preferences for abstractions above personalities, with his theory that persons are nothing. A minister, however, who loves the race in general but not in particular, will not easily satisfy either his parishioners or himself that he is doing what is expected of him as a pastor. Emerson ultimately found no way to solve the conflict between the required duties of his pastoral office and the free development of his thinking and his disposition, save by freeing himself from the pastoral relationship altogether.

Page 72, note 5. Just how much variety his sermons exhibited may be seen by consulting the list of sermon topics on page 263. Of approximately sixty sermons he delivered during this period Emerson devoted almost half of them to a discussion of the improvement of character; and a quarter to the meaning of religion. 'Our connexion with society' is another familiar subject 'to which we have already repeatedly directed our meditations.' (No. 55.)

Page 72, note 6. Emerson wrote three sermons on the observance of the Sabbath, which he delivered thirteen times. The most important way to keep the Sabbath holy, he said, is to attend the two services of worship, which requires about three hours of the day.

A few years after leaving the pastorate he writes of the young preacher's discouragement at learning the motives that bring his great congregation to church. (*Journals*, Vol. III, p. 475.) Whether he had himself been discouraged or not by such knowledge he does not say but he was clear-sighted enough to perceive the operation of a variety of motives and frankly to mention them to his congregation. Some come 'for decency, not from devotion,' in order to maintain their 'reputation for decorum.' They 'bring up their bodies to church to make a bed of their pew.' They are the people who 'come up to church and go away unchanged, untouched.... Who does not know that a

227

mere toy, a little noise, a new face, or a new dress, will catch the eye of many a person of mature age, and occupy his attention to the exclusion of all serious thought in the house of God?' For others who go to church 'forms which once were expressions of their fervent soul are now relied upon as marks of what they have done, and as anchors by which they seem to hold fast to the shore now that the waters ebb.' But 'indolent worship is none,' nor is reminiscent worship anything.

Yet Emerson believes in the social institutions of religion. 'I am not so unreasonable as to undervalue the privilege of truly social worship. I know well that our religious feelings are wonderfully assisted by our love for each other; that among friends we worship more joyfully than among strangers.' (No. 106.) But he holds that no one should be driven to worship by violence. Show him, he declares, 'the loveliness of obedience, the reasonableness and truth and advantage of religion. Any other course is like the insane persecutions of former days when men were dragged to the stake and there offered the alternative of the mass or the fagot.' (No. 142.) From this view of the young preacher it is a far cry to the vote cast by Emerson, the sixty-five-year-old member of the board of Overseers of Harvard University in favor of compulsory chapel attendance.

Page 72, note 7. In a sermon a few months earlier he had said: 'We go to church and suffer ourselves to depend for the profit we get there upon the accident whether the services shall be administered with ability or not. The taste of the times is grown fastidious, and if the preacher does not gratify the imagination or enlarge our conceptions of God, we go away unedified, unsatisfied, and possibly chagrined. My brethren, if the preacher was in fault so is the hearer. The mind that is in a religious frame, in a highly excited state — welcomes with delight every new truth which the reason or learning of the pulpit can bring to the cause of religion but it does not depend on them for its devotion. It hath fire on its own altar. It brings to church such cogent arguments of God's providence, such warm love to Him, that it fills the house with fragrant piety, it gives fervor to prayer, enthusiasm to praise and sense to sermons.' (No. 55.)

A few years later, after his experience of sitting again in a pew on Sundays he reflected that 'it were no bad topic for the preacher to urge the talent of hearing good sermons upon their congregations.' (*Journals*, Vol. III, p. 278.)

THE INDIVIDUAL AND THE STATE
(No. 70)

This is one of four sermons specially prepared by Emerson to be delivered on Fast-day, the first or second Thursday in April. (Nos. 17, 70, 113, 150.) Fast-day was instituted in 1694 as a day for public penance. It was not officially abolished in the Commonwealth of Massachusetts until 1894; but already in Emerson's time it had begun to lose its original religious character.

In one of these sermons Emerson deals with the private religious obligation

NOTES

to prayer, humility and fasting. In the other three, however, he follows a common practise both among his predecessors and contemporaries of passing judgment upon social trends and political issues.

Page 76, note 1. In later life Emerson himself continued with rare exceptions to observe the principle laid down in the sermon. 'I do not often speak to public questions,' he observed in his lecture in New York City on the Fugitive Slave Law, 'they are odious and hurtful, and it seems like meddling or leaving your work. I have my own spirits in prison; — spirits in deeper prisons, whom no man visits if I do not. And then I see what havoc it makes with any good mind, a dissipated philanthropy. The one thing not to be forgiven to intellectual persons is, not to know their own task.' (*Miscellanies*, p. 217.) And at about the same time he notes in the Journals: 'It is becoming in the scholar to insist on central soundness rather than on superficial applications.' (Vol. VIII, p. 531.)

Page 76, note 2. When Emerson preached this discourse the first time as a Fast-day sermon he used the following brief introduction instead of the preceding paragraphs:

'We are summoned on this occasion to consider in a peculiar manner the general offences of the people and to pray for the community in which we live.'

Page 77, note 3. Emerson repeats this political maxim of Thomas Jefferson in his essay on 'Politics.' (*Essays, Second Series*, p. 215.)

Page 77, note 4. 'I have lived all my life in this state, and never had any experience of personal inconvenience from the laws, until now.' [Fugitive Slave Law, 1851.] (*Miscellanies*, p. 179.) The sermons contain no hint that there might be laws which cannot be obeyed 'without loss of self-respect and forfeiture of the name of gentleman.'

Page 78, note 5. In his Fast-day sermon the next year Emerson devotes more attention to this tendency to disunion. He analyzes the signs of potential civil war thus: 'Our treatment of the Indian in one portion of the country, a barefaced trespass of power upon weakness and the vindication of that wrong by the law of the land and the general indifference with which this outrage passes before the eyes of the whole nation is a most alarming symptom of how obtuse is the moral sense of the people... The ferocity of party spirit... The low esteem in which the Union of this country stands, ready to be sacrificed to any momentary pique or trivial interest... The increasing habit of regarding power as a prize instead of a trust... The absence of stern uncompromising men of principles from the helm of power in its ordinary administration... The desperation of our trade... A madness or avarice in the young... The love of display, of fine houses, fine clothes, fine furniture; the ambition of the young to begin their housekeeping at the same rate of expense where their fathers left off.' (No. 113.)

Page 79, note 6. Twenty-five years later Emerson elaborates this indictment. (*Society and Solitude*, p. 165.)

Page 80, note 7. 'Most presidents are merely clerks of some real power

NOTES

which stands erect at their side and does its will by them,' Emerson remarks in another sermon.

Page 81, note 8. The early American theocratic principle of direct action of the church upon the state gave place in the eighteenth century to the theory which Emerson here states, that Christianity is to make itself felt by the pressure of individuals rather than by the pressure of the organized church. In this view he agrees with the orthodox evangelicalism of his day.

Page 81, note 9. Emerson had expounded this other worldly Christian theory of dual citizenship in a Thanksgiving Day sermon, which, however, he had not preached in the Second Church: 'The country we now love with the fondest affection, may flourish or may fall, — but to us it cannot long be a country. It must grow cold — this warm thrill of patriotism — before more deep and solemn feelings. It is really to us of trifling importance what events await it; for we are citizens of another country.' ('Gratitude.' No. 12.)

In the present sermon he endeavors to combine other worldliness and this worldliness by the theory that God has 'joined together the good of this temporal and of that eternal world.'

RELIGIOUS LIBERALISM AND RIGIDITY
(No. 75)

Emerson deals with sectarianism in several discourses but this is the only sermon devoted exclusively to that theme. The sermon illustrates both Emerson's temper of mind and the contemporary religious stage on which he played his part.

Page 82, note 1. In a later sermon he suggests a different basis of sectarian division: 'Christendom is filled with churches of different creeds, each of which meets the wants of some one class of minds, from the most gross and sensual, to the most spiritual worship, and every mind falls into that which is best for him.' ('The Living Christ,' No. 142.)

Page 82, note 2. A sentence follows in the manuscript which Emerson enclosed with a parenthesis, as though he had not used it on one of the occasions of the delivery of the discourse as a whole. 'I avoid for obvious reasons the use of the word *orthodox*, which is always used arrogantly when applied to a man's self and ironically when applied to another.'

Emerson's frequently expressed distaste for doctrine and doctrinal preaching should be considered in the light of his own preference for principles and necessary truths rather than for practical counsels or homiletical entertainment. The young preacher agrees with the 'received opinion that whenever a doctrine is received by large numbers of men and is observed to reappear in different ages and countries, that doctrine is founded in truth.' (No. 110.) 'There never was a dogma that has been received by multitudes, but it could be traced down to its eternal foundations in this moral nature (of man).' (No. 111.) He tells his congregation that he believes there is in nature the

NOTES

firmest foundation, even for the doctrine of Election, though not 'in the absurd way in which that doctrine has been taught.' (No. 35.)

Page 83, note 3. William Ellery Channing, who did more than anyone else to make the liberal movement of his time conscious of itself and its mission, declared in like manner of his own body of published writings: 'A respect for the human soul breathes through them.' Every system of theology has, as Emerson points out, some single fundamental insight or principle on which its whole structure is reared.

The inability of the young preacher to look at one side only of the truth makes it difficult for him to side with any party. In his theory of human nature he shares with the liberal party the 'principle of man's capacity for virtue.' 'I think well of mankind.' (No. 155.) He assumes that his congregation contains no grossly immoral people. But his views on human nature are not biased by sentimentality. Although virtue *is* natural and fundamental and vice is unnatural and superficial (No. 59), depravity, nevertheless, is real. It is 'planted wherever the seed of man was sown.' (No. 57.) Emerson recognizes the existence of torpidity and apathy. The central principle of all sin is self-love. And self-love will turn the world into a hell of slavery, exploitation and instability of credit and trade. (No. 96.)

But Emerson cannot believe that anyone is wholly depraved. 'God,' he declares, 'has so far protected this his minister in the soul [Conscience] that though as we sin, it points to lower and lower degrees of right, — yet its divine instinct is never wholly subdued. It always points *from* Hell.' (No. 54.)

Page 83, note 4. In a later lecture on 'Society' (1836) Emerson reiterates this distinction, using the popular labels: 'The Orthodox Christian builds his system on the fear of sin, the Liberal builds his on the love of goodness.' (Cabot's *Memoir*, Vol. II, p. 729.)

Page 85, note 5. Now and again Emerson puts in a sermon a compact and succinct summary of the main points of his own message. Each of the phrases expands into a sermon.

Page 86, note 6. Emerson frequently applies to religious controversy the touchstone of its effect upon character.

Page 86, note 7. In a later sermon Emerson applies this principle to an enterprise that had divided the American churches for almost a hundred years, and which the liberals had consistently attacked, namely religious revivals:

'If you love truth more than you love party go and converse with a pious man who believes in the divine efficacy of these occasions [revivals of religion] and you will find that whatever dislike you may have to the manner in which these meetings are managed the whole design can be defended on principles which you cannot reject. Thus the more exalted are your views of God the more reasonable it will appear to you that when the attention of any young person wholly intent on the pleasures of the senses is for the first time by good arts secured, and that suddenly, to the idea of God and to an efficient faith in his own immortality, he must be startled, he must feel strongly....

'Then it is [the object of these meetings to make a] confession of sin and of

E — defends revivals

NOTES

suffering under the sense of wickedness. And will any humble believer of God speak with contempt or hostility of this feeling? No, never. However alien from your habits the exterior of them may be, the principles on which Revivals are sought for, are perfectly sound. My only want of sympathy with them is that in their history the reason of man has not been addressed. Such representations of God have been made as keep down and hurt the mind and do not exalt it. Such representations of God as could be received only by feeble and slothful minds, but must forever keep aloof from the assembly of an enlarged intellect. Among that portion of the community whose frame of mind makes them more open to this influence than to any other, why should not these seasons of excitement have the happiest effect? If it save one soul from sin, towns and counties may well assemble for such a purpose. This faith which they first receive, though erroneous, is only the first stage of their education. The truth that is concealed in this impure food will nourish them to a strength that requires an appetite that selects a better aliment. The religious mind is always in the right road to truth. But let not knowledge be proud, look on without feeling the admonition of this fervor. In view of other's devotion let conscience do its office....

'Do you think because you do not receive the doctrines of Total Depravity and the Vicarious Suffering of Christ, that therefore you may unblamed indulge in any practice which a stricter brother would condemn? Do you think you may neglect a trust or forget a favor or lie later in bed, because you do not believe in Plenary Inspiration?' [The last paragraph is from a second manuscript of the same sermon, No. 111.]

Emerson was one of the few liberal ministers to speak in behalf of revivals at a time when the antagonism of the liberal churches had been aroused by the avowal of the orthodox Lyman Beecher to drive Unitarians out of Boston.

Page 86, note 8. Although Emerson used the word 'Unitarian' infrequently he was explicit in his expressions of adherence to the liberal religious movement. He speaks approvingly of 'the simplicity and beauty of that purified Christianity, which a better understanding of the Scriptures and of the character of God have taught us, over some of the dark superstitions which our fathers received.' (No. 14.)

'The blessed position,' he remarks elsewhere, 'into which the course of things has thrown me and those of my brethren who are called Liberal Christians in this vicinity is that we have no ties of opinion to each other. The theory we hold is the true one, that every man is a sect himself, and only unites for social worship with such as are nearest him in faith and feeling, without entering into any compact of opinion with his brethren or imposing any upon them. And it is hence more in our power than it ever was, in the history of the Church, or any class of teachers, to say exactly what we think. Please God this liberty may be a substance not a name. Please God that this room may never be dishonored by dissimulation, or the truth hindered by the love or the fear of man!' (No. 108A.) It was only later that he complained of Unitarianism's 'pale negations,' but in Blotting Book II he notes

NOTES

for his private enjoyment that 'Doctor Bradford thinks that the difference between the Orthodox and the Unitarian is that those have the liver complaint and those have it not' (p. 24).

Page 87, note 9. 'A sect or party is an elegant incognito devised to save a man from the vexation of thinking.' (Journals, June 20, 1831.)

Page 87, note 10. Like other liberal religious leaders of the day Emerson was deeply concerned lest the abandonment of orthodox doctrine should result in the loss of controlling convictions of any kind. He saw more clearly the problem of the transference of emotions from one set of doctrines to another than he did its solution.

Page 88, note 11. To Emerson liberalism did not connote indifference or compromise. He knew which was his side of the line and took it, though reluctantly and in no pugnacious spirit. 'I suppose it is not wise' he writes in his Journal within the following year 'to belong to any party.' Eventually he followed this leading.

THE AUTHORITY OF JESUS
(No. 76)

This is one of eight sermons devoted primarily to an exposition of the person and work of Christ. He preached these sermons a total of fifty-one times. This particular sermon was preached eight times, twice in the Second Church and six times after the resignation from the church. It exists in manuscript in three versions.

Page 90, note 1. Jesus is 'a perfect pattern of obedience to God.' (No. 5.) References to Jesus as an example are frequent in the sermons.

Page 91, note 2. Summarily put Emerson's Christology is the characteristic Arianism of the religious liberals of the day, like William Ellery Channing. Jesus is the incarnation of the pre-existent Logos, or Word: the 'Word made flesh.' God, Emerson says, 'sent Christ out into the light of worldly life.' (No. 60.) Yet he considers the Word subordinate to God the Father, the religion Absolute. Emerson does not account this doctrine any more fundamental to Christianity than that of the Trinity or the Atonement, which are also speculations secondary in importance to the relation of the moral nature of man to God. (No. 43.)

Page 92, note 3. Emerson's commonest interpretation of the office of Christ is that of Teacher. At times he identifies the teacher with the teaching. 'Jesus frequently uses... his own name for the truth which he taught, Christ for Christianity. "I am the way and the truth and the life"; "no man cometh unto the Father but by *me*," that is, by that holiness or Godlikeness which I inculcate.' (No. 142.) As a young preacher Emerson was already troubled by the 'absurd and mistaken manner' in which the human race in welcoming 'their moral Saviour has added to him titles of esteem and veneration till succeeding generations have been led, in the extravagance of love, in dis-

233

NOTES

regard of his own caution, to confound the dignity of him that was sent, with that of him who sent him.' Nevertheless he also can say, 'It should not be thought strange that if we value infinitely this gospel and him who brought it in his hand and in his heart from God; if our trust and joy in him should sometimes overgo the limits of a cold respect and rise to exultation.' (Nos. 60 and 62.)

His later strictures on preaching and Christianity often seem to serve him as a kind of general confession and penance for his own ways of thinking as a young preacher.

Page 93, note 4. Emerson elsewhere gives another interpretation of the living truth which is in Jesus. In a Christmas sermon he says 'the interest created by Jesus is of a *personal kind*.... An interest such as only attaches to *persons* was created in the truth which he taught. The more this is considered, the more important it will appear; and this in two ways; namely, that, thus only can it become the object of the *affections*, and thus only can truth and virtue come to have the solidity of fact. How vague and cold is our regard for patriotism, courage, purity, honesty, compared with our attachment to these qualities in the person of a friend. They are dead possibilities till they live in a soul. As no man would care for an empty ship foundering in a tempest; but it is the presence of breathing, thinking men therein, that tortures us with interest in their danger. And as they say in the arts, that a landscape is imperfect, without animals and men, — so, the infinite field of moral truth is but a wearisome and barren immensity till it is *peopled* with examples.... It is only a fact that puts skepticism at an end.' (No. 60.) The young preacher feels that the landscape of ethical precepts needs the humanizing figure of Jesus in it to give it vitality.

Page 93, note 5. Emerson indicates that the quotation is from Butler. When making his decision to study for the ministry, Emerson, then twenty years old, wrote in this Journal, 'My reasoning faculty is proportionately weak, nor can I ever hope to write a Butler's *Analogy*....'

As a college student Emerson had recited in this book as well as in Paley's *Evidences of Christianity* and *Moral Philosophy* which he elsewhere quotes.

Page 94, note 6. Emerson refers frequently to Jesus as the image of the perfect man, who has no taint or mortality. The innocence of the sinless martyr is perfect, radiant, and as such refreshing, invigorating. (No. 5.) What distinguishes his life from that of other good men is the 'presence of a Superior Will to his own or to that of any created being in every one of his actions.' (No. 96.) His divinity lies in the majesty of his character. He is the 'express image of God only inasmuch as he was a better man than any other.' (No. 89.)

Page 95, note 7. Emerson accepts the miracles of Jesus without question, though here, as in his subsequent sermon on 'Miracles' (No. 103) he subordinates their importance. Elsewhere he refers to other miraculous aspects of Jesus' career. Jesus received 'a miraculous influx of light into the soul which superseded the necessity of painful progress from the elements of knowledge.' (No. 30.) Jesus could also foresee the future.

NOTES

Page 97, note 8. Both in an early and in a late sermon Emerson puts forward for consideration the opinion that Christians have contact with the living Christ, not only as they remember him and his teaching but as they become aware of his immediate personal presence. His hesitancy in so speaking is due to no lack of conviction on his part but to his realization that he may be speaking to those 'to whom the love of Christ has an unamiable sound.' (No. 111.) He shares the 'opinion entertained in all ages by the wise and good, that when death has interrupted our communion with our friends, that communion is not wholly broken... they are still permitted to observe our actions... perchance they sometimes suggest to our secret souls motives of encouragement or reasons of consolation.' (No. 5.) In particular, 'the holy child Jesus, the benevolent, the perfect son of man, dwells with us alway, composing more of our strength and peace and purposes than we have powers to discern.' (No. 142.) The young preacher is not sure that his congregation will share this view with him and he does not consider it fundamental.

Page 97, note 9. A later Christmas sermon on 'The Universal Empire' strikes the same note: 'It is still at this day as it was at the first, the Word made Flesh, the Word of truth made Flesh or realised in the actions of good men that reconciles men to God.' (No. 138.)

Page 98, note 10. Emerson has two sermons on the love of the Christian for 'the Great Founder of the Christian Religion,' Jesus, 'the soul's personal Friend.' It appears to him that his congregation hesitates to give utterance to the exalted affection they secretly must cherish, as though such a sentiment were unbecoming or presumptuous. 'I think that we cannot help (if any goodness is in us) loving our religion and as we love it imbibing a sacred attachment to its author. Christianity is not something to be defended and respected but something to be panted after and gloried in.' (No. 62.)

SELF-CULTURE
(No. 87)

'Ever since I was a boy,' Emerson begins his essay on 'Compensation,' 'I have wished to write a discourse on Compensation.' His congregation at the Second Church heard his remarks on this subject more than once. His fourth sermon was largely devoted to it, where he treats the theme in connection with the gaining of wealth, a collocation of themes that anticipates his poem on 'Compensation.' The subject occupies an important place in this discourse, in which he deals with it as a motive for conduct. No sermon does he devote entirely to the subject. He used this sermon nine times. It is one of the few preached three times at the Second Church and twice at East Lexington.

Page 101, note 1. That the self can be improved and that its improvement is a natural desire of human beings is characteristic of the young preacher's view of human nature. He devotes four sermons to the subject. Our bodies

235

NOTES

'grow to the height of but a few feet; we can walk but a step at a time; we can lift but a small weight. But our intellectual and moral powers are a very striking contrast to this pinched ability. Who ever knew so much that he could learn no more? ... Did ever a man come to the end of virtue, grow so good that he could not be better?' (No. 67.) His sermons are frequently counsels of perfection: 'Man is Improvable,' (No. 49), 'Spiritual Improvement is Unlimitable,' (No. 83), 'Self-Improvement.' (No. 144.)

Page 101, note 2. The possession of freedom is the central proposition in Emerson's theory of human nature. 'There is nothing but your free power to choose that you can call your own.' (No. 118.) Freedom is God's gift and distinguishes us from all his other creatures. It is because of his freedom that man is naturally lonely and solitary and accountable. But he 'can part with it. It is a very delicate and evanescent property. It will not belong to you without you use it.'

To reconcile the free agency of man and our dependence on God is beyond the competence of the human intellect, Emerson confesses, and yet both are facts. 'When we say that we are free we rest on a conviction that is too mighty for reason and must stand whether reason can sanction or no.' (No. 53.)

Page 101, note 3. Written in pencil at the bottom of the manuscript page: 'When do you think they will begin, after a thousand years or a hundred or ten? or when you enter?'

Page 101, note 4. In pencil: 'Make the same impression and eat the same fruits.'

Page 102, note 5. This and the following sentence occur in the essay on 'Compensation.' That essay contains other excerpts from the sermons.

Page 103, note 6. Disease and death were all too familiar to Emerson as a youth, right within the home circle. His father died when he was eight; a sister when he was eleven; his brother, Edward, was broken in health. He himself had suffered severely. This section of the sermon is no mere sop to homiletical conventionality.

Page 104, note 7. This line from Milton's sonnet is not marked by quotation marks. Milton had almost become Emerson's literary second nature.

TRUST YOURSELF
(No. 90)

Much of Emerson's later thinking is amplification rather than addition or revision of his earlier thought, and this particular sermon represents one of his first full length studies of a familiar theme. The essay on Self-Reliance surpasses the sermon in richness of reference and incisiveness of phrase; but the thought of the sermon is as forceful as that of the essay. The two treatments offer a valuable basis for a comparison of the youthful and the mature Emerson.

Page 105, note 1. In his concern for the individual soul Emerson stands in

NOTES

line with the individualistic strand in Christian tradition, which lays primary emphasis upon personal salvation.

Page 105, note 2. Emerson turns his text to good account in characterizing the enhancement of self-respect as one of the major effects of Christianity. All his principles he found rooted in the Bible, though in later years he inclined less and less to indicate their source or to illustrate them by the texts he so cherished in his earlier days.

Page 106, note 3. Emerson valued self-respect more highly than he did social recognition. He felt that a vice of his own constitution was 'an excessive desire of sympathy.' (*Journals*, Vol. III, p. 221.)

Page 106, note 4. In an incompleted sermon manuscript Emerson applies this doctrine of self-reliance to religious faith and points out the sorry effects upon the church of the failure to rely upon one's own faith:

'Men allow the Church to regulate their faith... Calvin thinks for thousands; and Wesley for thousands.... Every falsehood which one of these leaders received is transmitted from church to church for ages. If each soul had been instructed that its first duty as a moral being was to reflect, to go alone before God with its prayer and its obedience, no errors would have been transmitted with authority.

'And see the consequences in the distracted, bleeding, I had almost said, — the hating church of Christ; the church of Christ where only the *name* is found, and *he* is much a stranger....

'I am not so unreasonable as to undervalue the privilege of truly social worship. I know that our religious feelings are wonderfully assisted by our love for each other; that among friends we worship more joyfully than among strangers; and that all strong affection leads as it were directly to religion. All I urge upon you from the text, is, that your faith must have an independant connexion with God in the first instance. Else it is not faith but a parrot's talk. But once having that union formed, all your friendships, all your affections for your brethren will increase it and be increased themselves.' ('Independence in Faith,' No. 106.)

Page 107, note 5. The substance of the following passage will be found in the *Journals*, Vol. II, p. 301, 309 f.

Page 108, note 6. Compare the sentence in 'The Sovereignty of Ethics': 'Jesus... refused to listen to others and listened at home.'

Page 109, note 7. Two years later Emerson practised what here he preaches.

Page 110, note 8. This doctrine of a divine principle within the soul justifying self-trust, raises Emerson's thought above the meagre humanist level. Self-trust has cosmic significance because it means essentially trust in the God within. This is the doctrine of the Over-Soul, though Emerson did not originate that term until later. Emerson was speaking in violent reaction against a philosophy of religion that interpreted the difference or separation between God and man in such an extreme way as to make contact or union between them almost impossible.

Page 110, note 9. In a sermon on a complementary theme Emerson guards

237

NOTES

himself even more explicitly against the excesses of individualism which are latent in his doctrine of self-reliance: 'Whilst you trust in self, *the origin of self must be perceived*. The moment a man loses sight of the truth that he did not make himself, — that he is not a cause, but a mere effect of some other cause, and so a mere manifestation of power and wisdom not his own — the moment he lets this truth go, he becomes a bundle of errors and sins.... This distinction once seen [that a man is not his own] is the perfect check, entire security.... To a man who does not perceive this fact the same doctrine [reliance upon himself] is welcome but it inflames his pride and darkens his knowledge.' 'It is the observation of this fact that has made good men fear trust in self.' (No. 123.)

Page 111, note 10. Another conclusion is pencilled on the manuscript, probably as a substitute for the above paragraph when Emerson delivered the sermon a second time. As a rule these new conclusions, of which there are several, exhibit greater succinctness and directness than the originals:

'The sense of the worth of a human soul may well be urged on the consciences of those to whom is committed the charge of instructing you. We may well tremble at the greatness of the office we assume. But it is little that we can do for you. The minister passes away to the world of spirits or to other duties on earth and the care of your soul must always rest on yourself. Let me then exhort you in the word of the apostle, Let every man prove his own work, then shall he have rejoicing in himself alone.'

HOW OLD ART THOU?
(No. 101)

Emerson read this sermon as a lecture at an annual Watchnight service, which Henry Ware, Jr. had instituted some years before. 'The Year's End' (No. 61) and 'The Record of Time' (No. 139) he used on similar occasions.

Page 113, note 1. Emerson declares again and again that the chief significance of Christianity is its revelation of immortality. 'The doctrine of the immortality of the human soul is the main doctrine that makes all the value of Christianity... I do not know why any man who weighs his profession should call himself a Christian except out of gratitude to Christianity for this doctrine.' ('Christianity, the Medicine of Immortality.' No. 34.) It is the teaching of Jesus rather than his resurrection on which he counts, although references to the latter, which historically is the basis of the Christian hope, are not wholly wanting.

Page 114, note 2. Emerson uses traditional theological terms infrequently; either favorably, as in this instance, or unfavorably. Again and again, however, he reproduces the substance of doctrines without the terms themselves. Doctrines, he said, have been 'strained a great way, yea, out of all shape, but they are originally solemn verities.' (*Journals*, Vol. II, p. 356.) He states the significance of this fundamental doctrine of evangelical Christianity again

NOTES

in a sermon on 'The Common Basis of Truth': 'Let the doctrine be simply stated that we must be born again and all will admit it. That is to say, every good man admits the doctrine that in the worldly man the whole arrangement of his thoughts and purposes is from self as the principle; and in the good man the whole arrangement of the thoughts and purposes is from God, as the principle; and that this arrangement in every man from self-love must be changed and all his soul transformed to have the love of God for its principle, or he cannot be saved, because the love of God *is* salvation.' (No. 111.)

If rebirth is possible so also is spiritual death. 'The seed of the second death is selfishness' (No. 65) and a man can do much to 'unredeem, to uncreate himself.' (No. 115.) But though a man can descend far toward a second death, Emerson believes no one can quite destroy the principle of virtue within himself. In a man's own hands are the issues of his life.

Page 114, note 3. As in many other sermons Emerson distinguishes between time and eternity in quantitative rather than qualitative terms. Elsewhere he speaks of space and time as problems we ponder all our lives. Like most people, however, he found one of these problems more fascinating than the other. His world was a world of time (and timelessness) rather than of space. Perhaps that is why he had so little use for travel.

Over the fire-place in his later study at Concord hung a copy by his friend Wall of a painting in the Pitti Palace, Florence, then attributed to Michael Angelo, of the Three Fates, symbolic of Emerson's interest in Time. In 1824 he had concluded an analysis of himself with a prophetic flourish: 'Spin on, ye of the adamantine spindle, spin on, my fragile thread.' (*Journals*, Vol. I, p. 367.)

Page 115, note 4. The essay on the 'Over-Soul' has a faint echo of this passage; otherwise he appears not to have used this striking metaphor again.

Page 117, note 5. Pencilled on a blank page of the manuscript opposite this passage are the lines:
> Can crowd eternities into an hour
> Or stretch an hour into eternity.

This couplet reappears in 'Over-Soul.'

Page 119, note 6. In an early discourse Emerson remarks that 'thoughts never lose their immortal youth. Moral truth does not grow old' (No. 6), a view he corroborated when he was past sixty, 'Within I do not find wrinkles and a used heart, but unspent youth.'

MIRACLES
(No. 103)

The manuscript of this sermon contains more passages scratched out and rewritten than any of the others. Emerson had trouble in putting his thoughts in just the order to suit him; the thought itself he had firmly in mind before he began the composition of the sermon. That Emerson as a young preacher did not abandon belief in miracles arises in part from the transitional character

NOTES

of his thinking. The mind of the young preacher was the stage on which struggled for supremacy two theories of the universe. The cultural crisis of his day came to a focus in his thinking. His decision to abandon the profession of the ministry was his vote in favor of the new age. To its major premises he committed himself, though at the time he could not foresee all the implications. For further comment on his views of Miracles, see Introduction, p. xxvii f.

Page 120, note 1. Emerson raises no question as to the possibility of communication from God to men. This is a fundamental and unquestioned axiom in his philosophy of religion, both as a preacher and a lecturer.

Page 121, note 2. An early entry in the Journals shows that Emerson probably had Hume in mind.

Page 121, note 3. The mature Emerson denies that 'God causes a miracle to make men stare and then says, Here is truth.' (*Journals*, Vol. IV, p. 427.)

Page 122, note 4. So Emerson had declared in a letter to his Aunt Mary some months before.

Page 122, note 5. This suggests the theory of occasionalism elaborated by the seventeenth century philosophers, Geulincx and Malebranche, although it is not known whether Emerson was directly familiar with their writings.

Page 124, note 6. Not often in the sermons does Emerson make a contrast between popular Christianity and the Christianity of the educated man. This is more characteristic of the mature Emerson.

Page 125, note 7. In the above passage, reproduced almost verbatim from the Journals (Vol. II, p. 325) Emerson names the skeptic: Hume. He studied Hume carefully and sympathetically.

SELF AND OTHERS
(No. 104)

This is one of four sermons on Charity. Emerson preached them seven times in behalf of three different charitable societies, and eight times as general sermons.

The benevolent agency of the Second Church, known as the Evangelical Treasury, was organized in 1824, as an independent body within the church. Each member contributed one dollar a year. An annual collection was taken at a church service at which the minister preached a sermon giving an account of the Treasury's activities. The budget during his pastorate never exceeded two hundred dollars. The money was allocated to a pastor's committee in charge of relief of the poor and sick of the parish (fuel, rent and the like), the Sunday School, the city Missionary Society, the instruction of the poor in the city, the Church Library. 'It is the interest and the duty of every family and every individual to give the greatest activity of circulation to good books of every kind, those seeds of civilization, those silent benefactors, those modest missionaries that carry light and truth and virtue from one generation

NOTES

to another.' (No. 40.) According to Emerson's statistics in the sermons, there were thirteen thousand families in Boston in 1829, and between three and four thousand families were left without the reach of religious instruction.

The Boston Quarterly Charity Lecture, a second of these philanthropies, was organized by Boston churches in 1700. The income from the collection at the close of the lectures (and from private contributions after 1783) was used for the support of two hundred and sixty-four pensioners (in 1818). Since 1860 this Lecture has been given once a year.

The Howard Benevolent Society was an early Unitarian philanthropy whose endowments are still operative in Boston. The present sermon was first preached at the annual meeting of this society.

An unpublished portion of the Journals indicates that there were questions about the efficacy of indiscriminate charity in the young minister's mind, which must have increased his respect for the investigatory work of these Societies, such as it was:

'All powers are trusts for greatest possible use. This is the reason why it is not becoming for a good man to squander his property in alms. One of the poorest uses to which you could put a thousand dollars would be to give it away in indiscriminate alms. It would probably occasion a good deal of momentary luxury and leave the receivers speedily as poor as it found them. Meantime it would have taken from you the power to pay the wages of honest industry, which in your hands it had been wont to pay when it supported the families of laborious tradesmen.' (*Blotting Book*, No. III, 1829.)

Emerson did not preach this sermon at the Second Church but he incorporated in it portions of several sermons he had already preached there. Later as a lecturer he frequently combined sheets of manuscript from former lectures to make a new address or essay. But a patch-work sermon of this character is rare.

As in many other sermons dealing with a practical theme Emerson here seeks to discover and set forth the principles that underlie the practice he commends.

Page 127, note 1. Emerson uses this paragraph again in a sermon on 'Friendship,' No. 140.

Page 128, note 2. This paragraph with its reference, — one of several — to 'the present despondency' was omitted on subsequent deliveries of the discourse.

Page 128, note 3. Jonathan Edwards had dealt with the pros and cons of this theme in a posthumously published dissertation on 'The Nature of True Virtue.' His most prominent follower, Samuel Hopkins, carried on the discussion in 'The Nature of True Holiness.' Thereafter it continued to occupy the thoughtful attention of New England pulpits. Emerson takes a position similar to Edwards, who, for all his Calvinism, was also a philosophical idealist and a profound student of ethical theory, with views similar to Emer-

NOTES

son's. The most notable thinker of the eighteenth century and the most notable thinker of the nineteenth century both stand in the Platonic tradition within the Christian movement.

Page 128, note 4. This and the preceding sentence are taken from an earlier sermon on 'Self-Denial,' No. 65. Emerson mentions this doctrine of Political Economy more than once.

Page 130, note 5. The persons for whom this motive is appropriate are described in another sermon:

'As thus in seeking our own advantage we are promoting the good of others, I believe in the next place that the converse of this proposition is demonstrably true, that when we aim at others' good we are really obtaining our own. But far be it from me to offer this fact in the light of a motive to Benevolence. It can only be presented as a motive to those hardened self-seekers who are incapable as yet of being reached by any higher one. The only way in which this fact ... becomes interesting to the lovers of God, is as an evidence of the perfect harmony of the laws of their Father's kingdom. Thus are the intentions of God plainly shown that his creatures should serve another.' (No. 65.)

Page 130, note 6. The Second Church numbered a few indigent persons in its membership. It was perhaps in the course of calling on these parishioners that Emerson made the observation which he records in a sermon: 'We live in a fair city. It is full of commodious and spacious mansions. But the eye that sees the morning sun shine on long streets of decorated dwellings is apt to forget how many obscure garrets, how many damp basements are here and there found amid this magnificence, that contain victims of great suffering, poor men and women reduced by consumptions or bedridden with rheumatisms, or worn with fruitless labors to meet demands the quarter day.' ('Charity,' No. 40.)

Page 131, note 7. Omitted on subsequent delivery of the discourse was the following phrase: 'as the Committee of this Society have abundant occasion to observe.' The Society referred to is the Howard Benevolent Society.

Page 131, note 8. The sentiments put on the lips of the selfish man are to be found also in an earlier sermon to raise funds for the Evangelical Treasury of the Second Church. (No. 40.)

Page 131, note 9. The first draught of this paragraph is printed in the *Journals*, Vol. II, p. 353.

Elsewhere in the sermons Emerson uses a traditional Christian motivation for charity: give alms for the sake of your own salvation, whether now or in the life to come.

Emerson later had in mind perhaps this sermon and another on 'Right for Right's Sake' when he wrote in his Journal: 'Naples, March 13, 1833. When I was at home and felt vaunty, I pestered the good folks with insisting on discarding every motive but the highest. I said you need never act for example's sake; never give pledges, etc. But I think now that we need all the advantage we can get, that our virtue wants all the crutches.' His trip abroad, wrenching him free as it did from his accustomed and re-enforcing environment, proved

NOTES

to be an education for the young minister in human nature (including his own) in ways he had not expected.

Page 134, note 10. Emerson had written in his Journal a month before: 'God is the substratum of all souls. Is not that the solution of the riddle of sympathy?' (Vol. II, p. 323.) In another sermon he says, 'That we think so differently is in great part because we sin so much.' But 'who ever doubted as he reasoned with his fellow-man in an earnest desire for truth that the hour would come when both would think alike?'

The young preacher makes a great deal of this principle of 'likeness.' It is because men have a common nature that we can know others by our knowing ourself. 'Every man knows every other man by himself.' (No. 51.)

Page 135, note 11. The above paragraph in the manuscript is scratched out with a pencilled line.

CONSOLATION FOR THE MOURNER
(No. 107)

Ellen Tucker Emerson, Emerson's first wife, died on February 8, 1831. They were married six months after Emerson became the minister of the Second Church. This sermon was preached less than two weeks after her death. It shows the young minister's concern not to obtrude his private affairs into the pulpit, — he was always restrained at this point. Yet he seeks to make his personal experience a bridge by which to cross over to the thoughts and emotions of his listeners.

Emerson's opinion about immortality remains almost unchanged throughout the years of his ministry and for some time thereafter and to that same opinion he returned after a middle period of exploring alternative possibilities. Occasionally to be sure, the young preacher expresses doubt. 'There are times when every man takes the gloomy view, feels the sentiment of Saint James, What is our life but a vapor that appeareth for a little time?' ('A Future Life.') But though the beam of the balance trembles, as he writes to his Aunt Mary, and as the sermons indicate, 'it settles always on the right side, for otherwise all things look so silly.' (*Journals*, Vol. II, p. 211.)

Page 139, note 1. Thus briefly but adequately Emerson identifies himself with his congregation in the experience of grief.

Page 139, note 2. Pencilled on the opposite blank page of the manuscript is this sentence: 'And feels even then that God is good.'

Page 140, note 3. The reference is doubtless to Mrs. Emerson, whose words the published *Journals* record in part. (Vol. II, p. 357.)

Page 141, note 4. Emerson criticizes Calvinism for its vice of picturing heaven 'from the senses' although he acknowledges that even the most literal of the Christian ideas of heaven are superior to the views of Greeks, Romans and Turks.

The complaint against Christianity because of its failure to give more dis-

NOTES

immortality

tinct information about the future life he counters with several suggestions. Specific knowledge would unfit us for our duties here by distracting our attention from its just objects. A greater knowledge of the future would also tend to destroy our freedom and so make us incapable of virtue. We should no longer choose virtue for its own sake. The principle of disinterested love would have no opportunity to develop: no risk, no liberty, no virtue.

Nevertheless, 'our entire ignorance of what the mode shall be is no more an argument against the future state than the apparent deadness of the egg is a proof that it shall not be a bird, or the want of intelligence in the human embryo a proof that it shall not be a speaking, reasoning man.' (No. 163.)

The young preacher, however, finds it impossible to restrain his curiosity and to remain true to his ignorance about the mode of the future life. 'What shall hinder me now,' he enquires, 'from forming some idea, though faint, of the feelings of an hour I shall spend when a thousand years are come and gone?' (No. 34.) He thinks of eternal life in terms of duration, an idea he was later to abandon. His principle of continuity comes into play here. 'The wiser sort of men have always inclined to the belief that it was a continuance not a contrast of this life. In the language of the noblest of Christian poets,

> "What if earth
> Be but the shadow of heaven, and things therein
> Each to the other like, more than on earth is thought."'
>
> (No. 126.)

Page 141, note 5. Emerson adheres to the Platonic theory of disembodied spirit rather than to the Hebraic and Aristotelian theory of some form of corporeality in the future life, although he occasionally uses the term resurrection rather than immortality. He does not seem, however, to mean resurrection of the body.

The nature of the soul provides him with his major argument for immortality. One of his profoundest insights he considers to be the existence of spiritual things as 'really and distinctly as brass or stone, and which are moreover eternal as brass or stone are not; because they are what time cannot change, cannot touch.' (No. 34.) Frequently he enumerates the things that are unaffected by time and place. He has observed also that 'anyone accustomed to much meditation upon moral and religious questions may notice that after he has been occupied with vigor for any length of time upon such subjects as upon human liberty, upon the perfectness of the retributions that take place, or upon the analysis of the affections, — or upon any question of simple right, — if from the midst of these thoughts, he glances at the question of the separate being of the soul, he will have a far deeper conviction of his immortality than at other times.' (No. 94.)

Page 141, note 6. The young preacher takes personal immortality for granted. In two different sermons he includes the following statement: 'Jesus, armed with miracles, teaches distinctly and with authority the immortality of the soul, — not a mystical existence of the soul absorbed into God, as some philoso-

NOTES

phers said, nor of resurrection after an interval of death, but a continuance of the individual being. God is the God of Abraham, he saith, and of Isaac and of Jacob; and to Him they live, that is, Abraham as Abraham and Isaac as Isaac. This is plain. This is what we want.' (No. 94; No. 126.) One of these sermons (No. 94) he preached three times as late as 1836. It might seem that he had these passages from the sermons in mind when he entered in his Journals his later doubts about personal immortality: 'There is no promise to Aaron and Abner that Aaron and Abner shall live' (Vol. V, p. 241); 'Jesus never preaches the personal immortality.' (*Letters and Social Aims*, p. 348.)

Even as a young minister Emerson begins to speculate about alternative views of the nature of the life to come. On one of the blank pages of a sermon manuscript he writes, 'Note. What use was meant by that ancient theory that the human soul was an emanation from the soul of the world, but at death returned into it, which was illustrated by the figure of a phial of water broken in the ocean? Every view of the relation of man to God that ever had currency is valuable.' (No. 35.)

Page 141, note 7. 'Though I think the argument from nature is strong, we must depend on Revelation for our chief evidence.' (No. 34.)

Page 142, note 8. Emerson wistfully dismisses the spiritualist's claim of 'intercourse with a disembodied man.' (No. 34.)

Page 142, note 9. A passage has been omitted here, which Emerson ran a pencil through: 'And the spirits have not forgot any good work, any upward effort of their brother on earth. For there is joy in heaven over one sinner that repenteth.' Several times he expresses his belief that the souls of departed friends continue to observe and love us.

Elsewhere Emerson calls attention to the incentive which a belief in one's own immortality provides. Without that hope 'all effort at virtuous desire would be taken away.' Undoubtedly he had such exaggerations of his own earlier sermons as well as those of other preachers in mind when he later inveighed against the use of the doctrine of immortality as a motive for virtue.

Even within the period covered by the sermons he shows signs of abandoning this position. In the next to the last sermon he preached as minister of the Second Church he declares with emphasis that it seems to him 'grossly defective to urge people to a good life because their future well-being depends upon it. That is not the right reason.' And in the same discourse he modifies his earlier interpretation of Christianity as the medicine of immortality. 'Jesus did not go through the world with his finger on his lips, telling men they must prepare to die.... The language that is heard in the world is, "Remember thou must die." I do not like this language. I say, What have I to do with death?... A great man [Goethe] wrote upon a tomb, "Think on living."' (No. 163.)

NOTES

HYMN BOOKS
(No. 131)

Very few of Emerson's lyrics have found their way into hymn-books. *Hymns for the Church of Christ*, edited by his friend, F. H. Hedge, and F. D. Huntington in 1853, is the first hymnal to include a hymn by him.

Still in use also in many hymnals is the hymn Emerson wrote for the ordination of Chandler Robbins, his successor at the Second Church in 1833, which begins

> 'We love the venerable house,
> Our fathers built to God.'
>
> (*Poems*, p. 223.)

Page 145, note 1. The young preacher found that the same thing was true of his prose. He often corrected his sentences, indeed in this particular sentence he originally wrote 'made' but scratched it out in favor of 'tried.'

Page 146, note 2. In the manuscript Emerson has inadvertently, as the context shows, transposed the words 'first' and 'last' in this sentence and the next.

During his ministry the Second Church had an organist and choir which sang in the singers' gallery. It consisted of two professional singers, a man and a woman, and a volunteer men's chorus, and was under the direction of the Singing Committee. The expense for the yearly salary of these three musicians was $487.00. Once a year they gave a sacred concert in the church.

Page 147, note 3. Originally Emerson wrote 'Milton' but scratched it out.

Page 148, note 4. Jeremy Belknap, (1744–1798), minister of the Church in Long Lane, later known as the Federal Street Church and now as the Arlington Street Church, Boston, was a notable patriot and literary figure. In 1795 he edited his hymn-book entitled, *Sacred Poetry, Consisting of Psalms and Hymns, adapted to Christian Devotion, in Public and Private, Selected from the Best Authors, with Variations and Additions*. Emerson's father helped Belknap arrange some of the music for the accompanying tune-book. William Emerson himself published a hymn-book in 1808: 'A Selection of Psalms and Hymns, Embracing all the Varieties of Subject and Metre Suitable for Private Devotion and the Worship of the Churches.'

The first page of the manuscript of each of Emerson's sermons ordinarily bears in the upper left-hand corner a list of numbers indicating the hymns or psalms to be sung in connection with the sermon, from one of three books: Belknap's, Dabney's, or Greenwood's.

Page 148, note 5. Space is left in the manuscript for Psalm 95, but it was not copied out. The same is true of the next hymn referred to.

Page 149, note 6. New England inherited the traditional Calvinistic opposition to modern hymns. For the praise of God, it was held, 'inspired' words should be used. The first hymn-book published in this country, the *Bay Psalm Book*, was a metrical psalter, which maintained its place for over a

NOTES

century. No tunes for it were published until 1690, and then only for unison singing. The first hymn-book to break with this tradition by including original compositions as well as imitations of the psalms of David, appeared in 1719. In successive hymn-books the proportion of hymns to psalms has increased until at the present time few of the latter find a place.

Page 149, note 7. On a blank page of the manuscript at this point Emerson has pencilled the 'frame of his kite,' as his brother Charles called the skeleton of a sermon:

Faults of Belknap

1. False views of God
2. False views of Christ
3. Loose notions about immortality
4. Unchristian sentiment
5. Material imagery, gross notions of spiritual things; and low and flat expression
6. Bad method of Psalms and Hymns

Page 150, note 8. The *Collection of Psalms and Hymns for Christian Worship*, edited by Francis William Pitt Greenwood, (1797–1843), minister of King's Chapel, (the Stone Chapel), in 1830, ran to over fifty editions, and was well known by older members of the present generation in their youth. In 1846 Emerson still thought it the best collection in the English language.

Page 150, note 9. Emerson preached this sermon at the afternoon service on October 2, 1831. He notes in his Preaching Record that on October 16 the Proprietors adopted the hymn-book. The treasurer's books indicate that the cost was $154.53.

THE CHOICE OF THEISMS
(No. 137)

A letter from Emerson's Aunt Mary Moody Emerson, written two years earlier appears to have been the germ of this sermon. The title is taken from an outline of the sermon which is pasted on the last sheet of the manuscript:

> 'There is no such thing as atheism
> But only choice of theisms
> The whole structure of man is theistical
> Witness the universality of Admiration
>
> Consider particularly the sentiments of
> 1. Love: 2. Loyalty: 3. Honour
> These are deifications
> But are these sufficient principles? No
> They prefigure and point at the true
> principle which is the love of God. Carry

NOTES

    either of them out ad infinitum and it
    becomes that.
    Describe the greatness and application
    of this sentiment'

Pencilled below this outline are the words, 'plurima nix.' What they may mean is possibly suggested by a pencilled addendum to another sermon (No. 120): 'I am tired of talking now the lust of talking is over and only want to excite the rest of the body and so quiet the lungs.' See also Notes to No. 143.

This is one of a score of sermons devoted explicitly to an exposition of the nature of God and man's relationship to him. (See Introduction, p. xxii f.)

With the exception of the sermon preached at the Second Church immediately after his return from his first European trip (No. 165), and a funeral discourse after the death of his friend George Sampson, a member of the church, this is the only regular sermon Emerson preached in his former pulpit after his resignation. He had first delivered it there two years earlier. On the fifteenth anniversary of his ordination he made an address to the Second Church, the manuscript of which is incomplete.

The prospect of preaching again in his former pulpit appears to have prompted his comment in the Journals on the contrast between his earlier situation as minister and his present position as a guest-preacher: 'I please myself with contemplating the felicity of my present situation. May it last. It seems to me singularly free, and invites me to every virtue and to great improvement.' (*Journals*, Vol. III, p. 233.)

During the summer of 1836 when he supplied the pulpit in Concord for several Sundays, he used this sermon among others. The experience led him to note, 'I know not why, but I hate to preach here in Concord.' (*Ibid.*, Vol. IV, p. 66.) His feelings did not prevent him from continuing to preach occasionally in the village church for several more years, the last recorded date being January 20, 1839. In the Preaching Record he has listed in a special column the sermons he preached there, 'fifty in all.'

Page 151, note 1. The Journals contain a passage on Admiration, written a few months before, which, however, covers ground altogether different from the sermon.

Page 151, note 2. In his introduction to a volume of Plutarch's *Morals*, published in 1871, Emerson again expresses this opinion: 'It is fatal to spiritual health to lose your admiration.'

Page 153, note 3. A couple of months earlier Emerson had jotted down in his Journal this quotation from Schlegel's *Guesses at Truth*. The quotation immediately following is from *Sense of an Honest and Experienced Courtier* by Charles Saint Évremond, (1610–1703).

As a young preacher Emerson had already begun his practice of spicing his writings with quotations. This particular sermon contains a larger number of quotations than most of the others. In approximately half of the sermons Emerson quotes the prose of some author ancient or modern, among them Xenophon, Socrates, Epicurus, Epictetus, Chilo, Plutarch, Phocion, Galen,

NOTES

Clement of Rome, Justin Martyr, Augustine, Eusebius, Chrysostom, Bernard (the church fathers at second hand); Luther, Newton, Saint Philip Neri, Jeremy Taylor, Milton, Montaigne (twice), Shakespear (once); Berkeley, Young, Marivaux, Butler, Hartley, Fénelon, Lord Shaftesbury, Doctor Johnson, Walter Scott, Goethe (once), Bacon (twice), Paley, Penn, Fox, Coleridge, Fichte, Pestalozzi and others.

Many of the quotations are anonymous, and are often given with no indication, save quotation-marks, that they are quotations. The longer ones ordinarily have an introductory phrase, e.g. 'I rejoice to add from the most popular writer of our times a pleasing testimony to the same truth.' Here follows a quotation from *Ivanhoe*, on character. Some of the quotations in the sermons reappear in the Essays.

Page 154, note 4. 'Men are loyal.' (*Conduct of Life*, p. 204.)

Page 154, note 5. According to an annotation on the manuscript, the incident is taken from Segur's account of Napoleon's Russian Campaign.

Page 155, note 6. In about fifteen percent of the sermons Emerson quotes poetry, single lines, couplets and once, four stanzas. As in the present case the majority of the quotations are anonymous.

He appears never to have introduced his own poetry into the sermons but on at least two occasions he has scribbled some verses of his own on the blank pages of a manuscript:

> The little child may sing for joy.
> Who shall rob him of his toy?
> It is an empire to him.
> By its side king's crowns are dim. (No. 72.)

Pencilled on another blank sheet are the following lines, which constitute the first draught or raw material of a poem he seems never to have polished and published:

> I love the golden day,
> I love the starry night.
> The one is grand and gay,
> The other hath its own delight;
> Each hath its own delight.
> God hath made nothing poor.
> Every sense is a treasury door.
> And the whole world is running o'er
> Into the infinite universe. (No. 38.)

Lower on the same page is a sketch similar to those that decorated many a page of the Journals.

Page 157, note 7. This paragraph has been pencilled on the blank left page of the manuscript.

Page 159, note 8. Emerson devotes at least three sermons wholly to this

NOTES

theme: 'Belief in God Innate' (No. 23); 'The Oracle Within' (No. 88); 'God in the Soul' (No. 109). In later years this theory of the immanence of God in human personality was characterized by the essayist's critics as 'egotheism.' The young preacher had already endeavored to meet the objection in a sermon on 'Love for Christ'; holding that there is no danger of identifying our imperfections with God's cause. 'A man may wish to impose on others the belief that he is a good man, but he cannot impose on himself. For there is always this simple test of any true advancement in religious life, namely, that every step increases the extent of our prospect, so that with every acquisition, we more clearly perceive our own deficiencies.... If we have made progress in goodness we shall want more and if we have not we shall not be able to persuade ourselves that we love him in whom the goodness of heaven dwelt.' (No. 62.)

Page 159, note 9. The young preacher never questions the view that God is personal, though he also gives expression to ideas which later tend to engross his thought, — God as law, as activity.

Page 160, note 10. Emerson had used for his scripture reading on the day he preached this sermon Acts XVII, from which this sentence is taken. Customarily he notes on the manuscript the passage from the Bible to be used in the service of worship at which the particular sermon is delivered.

Quotations from the Bible appear on many pages of his sermons; often with an indication of their source, — 'Solomon says,' 'Jesus says,' — more commonly without reference of any kind and even without quotation marks. Quotations from the New Testament predominate. Very occasionally Emerson uses by way of illustration a long passage from the Bible which has nothing to do with his text or his Scripture reading. Thus in a sermon on 'Uneasy Yokes and Light Burdens' he gives two pages to Naaman, the leper.

Page 161, note 11. 'It seems sometimes to be thought that there is something of the imagination in faith, as if men converted their wishes into beliefs. On the contrary, I suppose what we are taught by faith, to be the most real and certain part of knowledge. Faith in the Gospel sense, is, the perception of spiritual things.... It is not hope, it is sight.' (No. 121.)

FIND YOUR CALLING
(No. 143)

To present-day readers, as to the six congregations who heard this discourse after Emerson resigned from the Second Church, the illustration of the principle by Emerson's own vocational decision, cannot but be obvious. Sentiments like these, expressed in the later essays, have unshackled life for countless young readers. Emerson preached this first in his own church four months before he decided to change his vocation. Looking back upon his decision a year later he writes with double assurance: 'The call of our calling is the loudest call.' (*Journals*, Vol. III, p. 232.)

NOTES

Page 166, note 1. The following passage has been scratched out in the original manuscript:

'The practical consequence of this is, that when a man's profession has been chosen for him against his inclination, or when he has chosen it for himself before he was acquainted with the character of his own mind, if it admit of being bent to his character, it will be; if not, he will grow impatient of it and change it.'

Page 167, note 2. The traditional Christian doctrine of divine calling has been radically modified by Emerson but traces of it still remain. He believes God has a place for every man to fill but it is up to the man to find and fill it.

Page 167, note 3. A passage in 'Spiritual Laws' is reminiscent of this and the next paragraph.

Page 168, note 4. The original form of these sentiments, penned in the Journals a week before, has a sequel which discloses even more distinctly than the sermon the autobiographical significance of this discourse. (See Introduction, p. xxxiii.)

Page 168, note 5. Emerson repeats this idea of another opportunity in the next life, in a lecture given many years later. (*Natural History of the Intellect*, p. 83.)

Page 169, note 6. At the end of the manuscript is pencilled the enigmatic phrase, 'plurima nix.' (See also notes to No. 137.) Its meaning may perhaps be surmised from the young preacher's mood a few days before he wrote this sermon. (*Journals*, Vol. II, p. 448, and p. 457.) (See above, Note 4.)

On the next page Emerson wrote: 'P.M. Callings of men in vulgar life useful to educe their powers and teach each man what is his "high calling" or the use for which God made him. As a man discovers that let him sacredly follow it. It is different to every man. To one, poetry; to another, agriculture; to another, trade; to another, learning; to another, ethics; to another, the brain in the hand; to another, the state; to another, philosophy. Whatever it be, follow it. It is that state in which every power of a man is in full exercise and no power is demanded which he has not. Every right exertion tends to show a man more distinctly what this is. According to the force of this call, i.e. according to the distinctness with which he sees his use, will be his efforts to bend his circumstances to it. If his profession cannot be bent he will exchange it for others more congenial to him. But the effect of the improvement of society and of individuals will be to multiply indefinitely the professions and instead of compelling each individual to bend himself to some unsuitable work, to do that work he can. Blessed time and blessed men when each does that and only that for which he was made.'

NOTES

ASTRONOMY
(No. 157)

In a youthful entry in the Journals Emerson tells how the pulpit Orator may expand his hearers' views of the sublime doctrines of religion. Let him 'embrace the universe and bring down the stars in their courses to do homage to their Creator.' Twelve years afterwards he himself fulfils this forecast in the present sermon. But what he calls in his essay on *Friendship* 'spiritual astronomy' proved to be his special science. When he hitches his wagon to a star of principle, of moral sentiment, he too shines.

His essay on 'Nature' is reminiscent of some of the views here expressed: 'Man carries the world in his head, the whole astronomy... suspended in a thought.' (*Essays, Second Series*, p. 183.)

The very week after he first delivered this discourse he communicated to the church his views on Communion which three months later led to his resignation.

Page 170, note 1. Rationalistic critics of Christian theology in Emerson's time and earlier denied this equivalence of the God of nature and the God of the Bible. Emerson declines to subordinate the revelation of the Bible to that of nature. Yet in the next paragraph but one he goes so far as to say that the Bible is to be interpreted in the light of our knowledge of the natural world. He holds that scientific knowledge clarifies, purifies and enlarges the knowledge which is gained from divine revelation. In an earlier sermon he had declared 'this preaching distrust of human reason that cries out so loud upon *infidelity* calls its own name; it is based on infidelity. It fears the light. It believes that free discussion, fair examination, will show falsehoods in its religious system. Are men afraid that their reason will outsee God?' (No. 123.)

Page 170, note 2. Emerson preached this sermon a second time 'on the day of the solar eclipse at Waltham, November 30, 1834.' On that occasion he wrote a special introduction.

Page 172, note 3. According to the calculations of orthodox Christians in Emerson's time and later the creation of the world and of man occurred about six thousand years ago. (4004 B.C.) Emerson holds to this chronology in part. The sermons contain several passing references to the creation of man at that time. But under the influence of more recent theories of the geologists he abandons this date for the creation of the world itself.

Page 173, note 4. The speculations of Bernard Fontenelle concerning the inhabitability of other stars, in his *Conversation on the Plurality of Worlds* (1686) had reached the popular mind of America a generation or two before Emerson's time. Emerson's library contained a copy of a new edition in French issued in 1814.

Page 173, note 5. In 1867 Emerson repeats this idea in his 'Progress of Culture.' (*Letters and Social Aims*, p. 211.) He is one of the earliest American

NOTES

religious thinkers to recognize 'modern science as the paramount source of the religious revolution' of his time. His own philosophy of religion was such as to leave his faith and the faith of those who followed him untouched by the advance of science.

Page 174, note 6. This quotation from Jacques Le Saurin, Emerson uses again in his *Life and Letters in New England*. The latter repeats one or two other points from this sermon.

Page 175, note 7. In the Journals for 1852 Emerson similarly declares, 'The most important effect of modern astronomy has been the tapping our theological conceit, and upsetting Calvinism.' (Vol. IX, p. 16.)

Page 175, note 8. This paragraph in the manuscript is scratched out by a pencilled line, probably for one of the three subsequent deliveries of the sermon.

Page 177, note 9. This anticipates the opinion about Jesus in the Divinity School Address: 'The soul knows no persons ... By his holy thoughts Jesus serves us, and thus alone.'

Page 178, note 10. As a young preacher Emerson placed little emphasis upon the doctrine of Grace. The word and the idea it expresses seldom appear in his sermons. He is intent upon stressing the importance of a truth which Calvinism, in its concern to magnify the sovereignty and initiative of God, had suppressed. He insists that human beings can and must take the initiative. 'To your weak hands God has given the keys of heaven and hell ... He will work for us whilst we work, he will stop when we stop ... God helps them that help themselves.' ('Spiritual Influences Reciprocal,' No. 118.) Notwithstanding this emphasis upon human freedom and responsibility Emerson does not overlook the fact of man's dependence. Indeed unless men recognize their dependence upon God their whole life will be a bundle of errors, for we neither create our selves nor our circumstances. Humility is the proper attitude for a human being to assume toward God. Later in life, when it seemed to him no longer necessary to rehabilitate the principle of human initiative, he began to lay more emphasis upon the grace of God. The young minister was, at this point, farther from the Christian tradition than was the older lecturer and essayist.

Page 178, note 11. 'Astronomy is thought and harmony in masses of matter.' ('The Method of Nature,' *Nature, Addresses, Lectures*, p. 219.)

Page 178, note 12. This paragraph is written on a loose sheet of manuscript and apparently should be inserted here.

THE GENUINE MAN
(No. 164)

This proved to be the last sermon Emerson preached as minister of the Second Church. On the following Sunday the Proprietors (i.e. the pew owners) voted to accept the resignation he had sent them five weeks before. Emerson is here preaching to himself as well as to his congregation. In this as in several other sermons he formulates his doctrine of self-reliance.

NOTES

The following December Emerson, twenty-nine years old, a widower, and cut adrift from his vocational moorings, sailed for Europe. Letters to friends at home indicate his continued interest and affection for the church. After his return he preached this sermon a number of times, thirteen in all: Second Church, Boston, Oct. 21, 1832; New Bedford, Nov. 16, 1833; Hollis Street, Boston, Feb. 23, 1834; Federal Street, Boston, April 13, 1834; Watertown, May 11, 1834; Fall River, May 18, 1834; Second Church, Waltham, June 1, 1834; Bangor, July 6, 1834; Second Church, New York, Oct. 26, 1834; Lowell, Jan. 18, 1835; Lexington, Lower Village, May 10, 1835; East Lexington, April 15, 1835; West Lexington, March 16, 1837.

There are two manuscripts of this sermon. The inferior and incomplete version has only the second text. A blank sheet of the manuscript here used has the following outline:

> 'All partial excellences have been shown
> To us remains the work of forming *entire men*
> The man less considered than the circumstances
> Importance of the distinction to us.
>
> > Marks of the genuine man.
> > 1. He believes in himself.
> > 2. He speaks the truth.
> > 3. He thinks the truth.
> > 4. He acts the truth.
>
> Grandeur of this character and its identity with religious life.'

It was after preaching this sermon at Waltham 'to deaf and hearing' that he wrote in his Journal some remarks on the church and preaching that found their way into his essay on 'The Preacher,' published in 1880. (Vol. III, p. 302.) His later criticisms of preachers and preaching Emerson based only in part on his experience as an attendant at the Concord Church. He was also thinking in large measure of his own preaching. His later self criticized his earlier self.

Page 181, note 1. In his essays more than in his sermons Emerson qualified his high evaluation of human nature. The young preacher could not bring himself to believe that the divine image is entirely obliterated in any human being.

Page 181, note 2. Two sentences originally in both manuscripts have been run through with a pencil: 'Everybody is sensible of the absolute ignorance in which we stand of the real character of persons. There are persons who seem to live in the statehouse, to move in processions and whose names are always in the newspaper, and yet of whose real character we are in total ignorance.'

Page 182, note 3. Two sentences originally in the manuscript have been pencilled out: 'It is counted a small thing to injure the truth or to sacrifice a scruple of conscience to the opinion and practice of all society or to the obvious

NOTES

need of getting a decent livelihood. Yet it is to sacrifice the substance for the shadow, it is to sacrifice themselves for pottage.'

Page 183, note 4. The paragraph originally concluded with the following sentences which have been scratched out: 'Long and weary road that lies before him! Painful, perhaps frightful convulsions that he must suffer before the twilight of that inner day can dawn upon his understanding!'

The young minister recognized in his thinking the need for the religious experience of conversion.

Page 183, note 5. The next three paragraphs have been added in pencil.

Page 185, note 6. 'Some people who live only for appearance. Apicius sold his house but kept the balcony to see and be seen.' This is a pencilled addition.

Page 186, note 7. The reference to George Fox made this a particularly appropriate sermon for New Bedford. The struggle which had taken place there between orthodox and liberal (Hicksite) Quakers ended in the latter connecting themselves with the Unitarian Church. The Unitarians were prepared to give up the method of celebrating the Lord's Supper to which Emerson and the Quakers objected, but were unwilling to dispense with public prayer. Emerson therefore declined to accept the call to become minister of the church.

Emerson had preached in the New Bedford Church on three Sundays in November, 1827, after his return from his trip to the South. Orville Dewey, a relative of his, the minister at the time, had been given leave of absence on account of his health. Emerson also preached there once while he was minister of the Second Church. After his return from Europe, during another leave of absence granted to Dr. Dewey on account of his health, Emerson occupied the pulpit on thirteen different Sundays and once on Thanksgiving day. (November 1833 to March 1834.) According to the records of the Church for December 8, 1833, the clerk was instructed to 'express to Ralph Waldo Emerson its grateful approval of his recent ministerial labors amongst us and to invite him on behalf of the Society to continue with us until Dr. Dewey returns.' ... And again, on June 30, 1834, after continued ill-health forced Dr. Dewey to resign, a committee was appointed to supply the pulpit and was instructed 'to extend an invitation first to Reverend Ralph Waldo Emerson.'

Page 187, note 8. The sentence is left incompleted with a space of three or four more lines for its amplification.

Page 188, note 9. The brackets here and just above are Emerson's.

RELIGION AND SOCIETY
(No. 165)

After his return from Europe Emerson preached three times in his former pulpit: Oct. 27, 1833, No. 165; Dec. 15, No. 137, a sermon he had used in the church two years before; Aug. 3, 1834, No. 168, a funeral sermon for his friend and former parishioner, George Sampson. The present discourse is one of

NOTES

the five regular sermons he wrote after leaving the church. Of these five the manuscript of one is missing; one is incomplete; one, brief and very simple was delivered at the Seamen's Bethel, Father Taylor's Chapel where Emerson preached several times; the other two are included in this volume: Nos. 165 and 169.

Page 192, note 1. For the above informal paragraphs Emerson substituted an introduction briefer and more suitable for a general audience when he preached the sermon a second time:

'I wish to invite your attention to a consideration of the prospects of society in reference to religious instruction; of that change which seems to be taking place under our eyes in the opinions of men on religious questions; of that Teaching which all men are waiting for and of that Teacher who has been predicted and hath not yet come.'

Page 194, note 2. In two other sermons Emerson deals with the propensity to personification in the streams of religious culture which combined to form the Christian movement:

'The custom of all Eastern writers to *personify* abstract ideas, that is, to speak of love as a person, of wisdom as a person, may be seen in every page of the Scriptures. Mercy and truth have met together. Righteousness and peace have kissed each other. Poverty shall come as an armed man; want as one that travelleth.' (No. 110.)

Page 195, note 3. The Divinity School Address echoes these sentiments about certain Christian attitudes toward Jesus, as do many of the sermons.

Page 198, note 4. These humanitarian activities were generously and courageously supported and in some cases originated by a minority among the liberal Christians of Emerson's day.

According to the records of the Second Church the Society for the Abolition of Slavery held its annual meeting at the church in December, 1832. Perhaps it was at this meeting that the anti-slavery speaker, referred to by Emerson's son (*Journals*, Vol. VI, p. 536) appeared in Emerson's pulpit. The sermons contain several references to slavery, about which, as Emerson remarks, there is 'much complaint.' (No. 96.) 'Nothing,' he declares, 'is more respectable than the entire self-devotion of Wilberforce to the cause of African slavery.' (No. 7.) Until fifty years ago, he points out, slavery passed as an innocent institution, but now it has been judged by Christ 'and must be cut off root and branch. It is now threatening those who are engaged in it and us, for our share of the guilt, with accumulated evil.' (No. 95.) Therefore, 'let every man say to himself, — the cause of the slave, it is mine.' (No. 150.)

Page 198, note 5. The passage from here to the end of the paragraph was bracketed by Emerson at some subsequent delivery of the discourse.

Page 200, note 6. In his theory of human nature Emerson definitely broke with orthodox Christian conceptions. But he parted company also with older Unitarians like Ware and Channing. He is here heralding a new era in

NOTES

the philosophy of religion, which emphasized the immanence of God in man, or in Emerson's terminology, the infinitude of man.

Page 202, note 7. The reference is to Chandler Robbins, who was ordained as Emerson's successor shortly after this sermon was preached and remained for forty-one years. During his pastorate the church, seeking to adjust itself to the changing city, occupied five successive edifices.

Page 202, note 8. A different conclusion was at some time substituted for the above paragraph:

'Be assured, brethren, that a disposition to use the light we have, to serve God according to our best knowledge, is the certain way of acquiring new truth. *If ye will do the will of my Father, ye shall know of the doctrines.* This spirit is the spirit of Truth. This is he that when he comes, shall guide you into all truth. For he shall not speak of man, — of anything finite or mortal. He shall speak of that which is within and above man, — that which he heareth from God, the Source of truth. And whatsoever he heareth from God, that shall he speak. And he shall show you things to come.'

THE MIRACLE OF OUR BEING
(No. 169)

Emerson wrote this sermon in 1834, two years after his resignation from the Second Church. On the last Sunday mentioned in the Preaching Record he used this sermon. Like many of the others this sermon has two manuscripts. One of them, which is transcribed in this volume, is a cleaner copy and written on a better grade of paper than the other.

Page 203, note 1. The first two sentences have been run through with a line different in color from the ink with which the page as a whole is written.

Page 203, note 2. At this point the manuscript contains a paragraph which has been scratched out: 'The proposition that we are wonderfully made, is applied by people generally to the external constitution of men and admitted without debate, and without afterthought. And undoubtedly our physical constitution is ingenious enough to warrant the remark.'

Page 204, note 3. The quotation is from an article in the *New Jerusalem Magazine*, November 1832.

Page 204, note 4. This sentence has been scratched out in the manuscript.

Page 204, note 5. The *Journals* (August 28, 1830) contain Emerson's first reference to this quotation: '*Alii disputent, ego mirabor,* said Augustine. It shall be my speech to the Calvinist and the Unitarian.'

Page 207, note 6. Man's superiority to the animal world Emerson takes occasion to note in several of his sermons.

Page 207, note 7. This idea Emerson later expresses with succinct perfection in his poem, 'May Day.'

Page 208, note 8. In a sermon on 'Solitude and Society,' preached five years before, Emerson writes, 'When I look at the rainbow I find myself the center of its arch. But so are you, and so is the man that beholds it a mile from both of us, and so is every beholder though they be hundreds of thousands.' (No. 55.) This passage in its first form is published in the Journal, November 7, 1829. In both these places Emerson uses the illustration to show that a man, though influenced by others, is 'imperially free.' On other occasions also Emerson employs the same anecdote or saying to point more than one moral.

Page 211, note 9. Emerson deals with the subject of evil at length in two sermons, and accords incidental treatment to it in many other discourses. His relative indifference to the problem anticipates his later attitude.

In neither the earlier nor later period of his life did he fail to encounter evil. He felt its knife in protracted personal illness, bereavement and vocational frustration, although he never had to face long periods of pain, hunger, and economic insecurity, nor a social situation which made his ideals seem utterly impossible of realization. According to his own description, he was born tranquil, never a keen sufferer, and 'he would not affect to suffer.'

He deprecates the exaggerated emphasis people often lay upon evil. 'It is often said there is no rose without its thorn. Would it not be more becoming and more just to say, there is no thorn without its rose?' (No. 151.) The young preacher holds that 'our sufferings are small and momentary compared to the enjoyments to which we have access.' He is determined not to overlook the enjoyments. Nevertheless, idealist though he is in his philosophy, and so inclined to minimize the importance of the phenomenal world, he never denies the reality and bitterness of evil. He names pain and death as 'our ghastly enemies.' (No. 6.) Temptations, 'our evil angels,' as well as mutation, loneliness, injustice and the lack of appreciation also find mention in his sermons. 'Each of us has his own cross to bear.' (No. 117.) But for himself he 'never could give much reality to evil and pain.'

The explanation on which Emerson counts most is the educative value of evil. 'Pains are teachers.' 'Want, Difficulty and Affliction, are the rough but needful masters which God has provided for the teaching of man.' (No. 109.) Emerson considers the formation of character to be the main reason for our human existence: 'not that we should make a fortune; not that we should get a recipe for comfort; not that our assistance is anywise necessary to [God] in carrying on his glorious beneficence, but simply that he has placed us here for our discipline.' (No. 117.) This moral discipline has in mind 'the pursuits and events of our after existence.' (No. 7.)

It takes a religiously-minded person, however, to perceive that there is no evil without its use. The irreligious mind, according to Emerson, cannot think straight on this problem. Many people are nothing more than grown-up children, whose hearts are vexed all day by the petty disaster of a wound or a slight denial. They are like the young seabird, unskillful to withstand the blast and unacquainted with the art of balancing itself, which becomes the sport of the winds of fortune. (No. 56.) The religious man may not know the speculative solution of the problem of evil but he knows practically how to handle it. First he acknowledges its actuality and its universality. 'Evil floats in the air and grows in the grain and impregnates the waters of the world.' (No. 117.) A man must not expect to be the only exception to the invariable order of human life. Calamities will befall him. When they are unavoidable he will have sufficient imagination to realize that they are widely shared and the thought will help alleviate the affliction.

The mainstay of the religious person in his experience of evil is his confidence that a Providence rules the world, so that even the 'seeming exceptions and violations of the general order are made to contribute to ultimate good.' His belief in divine superintendence assures him also that 'what men call the disorders of nature, as earthquakes and floods, are yet contained in a high order and are ministering to good remote yet certain.' (No. 66.) He is reconciled to evil because our good is comprehended in God's great operation for all. He will therefore neither fret nor be guilty of the 'absurdity and presumption of an inexcusable railing at the order God has established.' (No. 2.)

In this aspect of his philosophy of religion as in so many other points, Emerson stands firmly in the main line of Christian tradition. In later life he inclines increasingly to phrase his conviction in terms unfamiliar to that tradition (although he never abandons 'Providence') but he does not give up the fundamental insight of his fathers, that all things work together for good to them that love God. 'All is for the best, is the creed of simple nature. Thy will be done, is the sentiment of the gospel.' (No. 96.)

The Preaching Record

Among the unpublished manuscripts which throw light upon Emerson as a young preacher is a small note book, of forty-two pages, four by six and one-half inches, which served first as a School Record and then as a Preaching Record. In it Emerson has recorded the date, place and number of each sermon, beginning with Number 1 on October 15, 1826, at Waltham and concluding with Number 169 on Jan. 20, 1839, at Concord. It contains also certain other memoranda. According to this Record Emerson preached eight hundred and eighty-five times. But the Record itself is not quite complete. Several of the manuscripts have on them a pencilled 'Salem' or 'S' or 'NYC,' indicating that they were used in Salem or New York City, although these engagements are not noted in the Preaching Record. The Journals likewise mention occasional preaching engagements not referred to in the Record. It should also be recalled that Emerson is reported by his biographer to have preached a sermon as late as 1846 — but no annotation has been discovered by the editor of a date after 1839. The Preaching Record, then, is not absolutely complete but it furnishes evidence of meticulous care on Emerson's part to keep a memorandum of his preaching engagements. From it we learn that he preached several of his sermons fifteen or sixteen times, and one of them twenty-seven times. (No. 10.)

The manuscripts of the sermons are doubled sheets of paper, approximately eight inches by ten inches, stitched together. Occasionally Emerson attached an extra half-sheet by a seal or placed a loose paper within the folded sheets.

During the first nine months at the Second Church Emerson preached in other churches ten times in the morning and fifteen times in the afternoon, — in Concord, New Hampshire, and Concord, Massachusetts; Lynn, Watertown, Salem, Springfield, Waltham, Cambridge, and Boston. He also spoke once in the Harvard College Chapel. On four Sundays he did not preach at all. The second year (1830) he was absent from his own pulpit over forty times, seventeen times in the morning, and twenty-nine in the afternoon. On two Sundays he did not preach at all. The larger number of absences from the Second Church this year is partly accounted for by the trip he took to the South to enable his wife, who was suffering from tuberculosis, to escape the harshness of the Spring climate in Boston. During his three weeks' absence

THE PREACHING RECORD

in March he preached at Hartford and Philadelphia. In the course of the year he also preached for William Ellery Channing, the 'star of the American pulpit' as Emerson later called him. But in none of the Boston churches did he preach oftener, outside the Second Church, than in the neighboring New North Church, of which Francis Parkman, father of the historian of New France and New England, was minister.

During the year 1831 Emerson occupied other pulpits other than his own thirty-nine times, fifteen times in the morning, and twenty-four times in the afternoon, not including the extra evening services at which he occasionally preached in the Friend Street Chapel. On two Sundays only, in February at the time of his wife's death, he did not preach at all. The record for one Sunday the month before reads: 'Severe snowstorm no sermon A.M.' During the last nine months of his pastorate the ratio of absence from his own pulpit continued about the same, though the closing of the church for repairs for six weeks in the early summer increased the number of his absences. This was at the very time when he was making up his mind to resign his office of minister. During part of that critical period he secured other men to preach for him.

Emerson records the writing of one hundred and seventy-one sermons, in addition to a few extra miscellaneous discourses. With two exceptions (Nos. 64, 167) all these manuscripts are in existence. Less than twenty of this total he preached only once, some of them being appropriate only to the occasion for which they were written, such as his ordination sermons, and some, perhaps seeming to him insufficiently meritorious to warrant repetition. But at least fifty of his sermons he preached twice in the Second Church, ordinarily with an interval of at least a year between the two deliveries. In repeating a sermon in his own church he usually gave in the afternoon a discourse he had previously given in the morning. In Blotting Book II (p. 22) he reports an anecdote that deals with the question of repeating sermons. 'How soon will it do to repeat a sermon?' asked a clergyman of McLeod, the Scotch Presbyterian in Charleston. 'Why, I dinna ken, but if ye put a new beginning, and a new ending it will do the same afternoon.'

A List of the Sermons

IN THE following list of sermons the titles placed in quotation marks are Emerson's own. For the most part he merely numbered his sermons. For the other titles the editor has endeavored to choose a key phrase from the body or the text of each sermon. An asterisk indicates that the sermon is included in the present selection. The three sermons listed under Miscellaneous Discourses have been numbered by the editor to indicate their chronological position in the list as a whole.

The dates of the first and last time and the total number of times each sermon was preached are taken from Emerson's Preaching Record.

No.	Title	First and Last Times Preached	No. of Times Preached
1	*Pray Without Ceasing	October 15, 1826 November 9, 1828	12
2	Uses of Unhappiness	October 15, 1826 March 29, 1829	8
3	Setting A Good Example	June, 1827 August 24, 1828	13
4	Wealth and the Law of Compensation	June 17, 1827 February 25, 1838	3
5	Christ Crucified	June 24, 1827 July 27, 1828	12
6	Change and Permanence	July 8, 1827 April 11, 1830	13
7	Sabbath Observance	July 15, 1827 March 22, 1829	9
8	God to be Loved not Feared	July 29, 1827 November 22, 1829	8
9	What Is Man?	August 5, 1827 May 3, 1829	3
10	*'On Showing Piety at Home'	August 12, 1827 June 5, 1831	27
11	Wisdom	August 5, 1827 May 16, 1830	3

A LIST OF THE SERMONS

No.	Title	First and Last Times Preached	No. of Times Preached
12	Gratitude	November 29, 1827 December 1, 1836	3
13	The Nativity	December 25, 1827 December 28, 1828	4
14	Progress of Religious Opinion	June 1, 1828 May 20, 1832	6
15	Improvement of Time	April 13, 1828 December 25, 1836	13
16	Pride and Humility	April 13, 1828 September 6, 1829	6
17	The Duty of Penitence	April 3, 1828 April 9, 1829	3
18	Uneasy Yokes and Light Burdens	April 27, 1828 March 20, 1831	15
19	Actions derived from Principles	May 11, 1828 September 18, 1836	16
20	Calumny	June 22, 1828 September 20, 1829	10
21	Conscience, A Proof of God	August 17, 1828 January 8, 1837	13
22	Truth	September 14, 1828 October 11, 1829	5
23	Belief in God Innate	September 28, 1828 March 5, 1837	5
24	Self-Direction and Self-Command	October 12, 1828 January 31, 1830	5
25	The Rights of Others	November 2, 1828 July 16, 1837	6
26	Affections for God can be Cultivated, I.	November 16, 1828 November 1, 1835	10
27	Self-Knowledge and Self-Mastery	November 23, 1828 August 6, 1837	6
28	*The Christian Minister, I.	March 15, 1829	1
29	*The Christian Minister, II.	March 15, 1829	1
30	The Best Part of Life Unseen	March 22, 1829 May 30, 1830	2
31	Religion Is Doing One's Duty	March 29, 1829 June 20, 1830	11
32	Forgiveness	April 5, 1829 June 21, 1829	2
33	Gentleness	April 19, 1829 March 13, 1835	12

A LIST OF THE SERMONS

No.	Title	First and Last Times Preached	No. of Times Preached
34	Christianity, the Medicine of Immortality	April 26, 1829 June 20, 1830	4
35	Affections for God can be Cultivated, II.	May 3, 1829 August 28, 1836	7
36	Cultivating the Mind	May 10, 1829 January 8, 1832	2
37	The Heaven of a Common Life	May 24, 1829 April 29, 1838	8
38	The Christian Is Free and Solitary	May 31, 1829 June 27, 1829	2
39	*Summer	June 14, 1829 July 16, 1837	3
40	Charity	June 14, 1829	1
41	Death Levels Varieties	July 5, 1829 July 30, 1837	3
42	True Freedom	July 5, 1829	1
43	Christianity Confirms Natural Religion	July 12, 1829 February 11, 1838	10
44	*Trifles	July 26, 1829 December 11, 1831	2
45	The Love of Virtue Is Innate	August 2, 1829 March 12, 1837	6
46	Inextinguishable Expectations	August 23, 1829 March 12, 1837	2
47	Self-Command	August 30, 1829 October 16, 1836	4
48	Faith and Works	September 6, 1829 April 9, 1837	3
49	Man Is Improvable	August 20, 1829 October 29, 1837	10
50	*A Feast of Remembrance	September 27, 1829	1
51	Atheism and Ignorance	October 11, 1829	1
52	*Conversation	October 18, 1829 April 2, 1837	2
53	Freedom and Dependence	October 25, 1829 October 29, 1837	3
54	'Habit'	November 8, 1829 July 3, 1836	5
55	Solitude and Society	November 15, 1829 April 9, 1837	2
56	A True Account of the Soul	November 22, 1829 February 12, 1837	3

A LIST OF THE SERMONS

No.	Title	First and Last Times Preached	No. of Times Preached
57	Thanksgiving	November 26, 1829	1
58	A Man's Treasure Is His Soul	November 29, 1829 May 1, 1831	2
59	Perseverance	December 13, 1829 July 3, 1836	6
60	The Significance of Christ	December 27, 1829 December 25, 1836	3
61	The Year's End	December 31, 1829	1
62	Love to Christ	January 10, 1830 February 5, 1837	5
63	Non-Conformity	January 24, 1830 September 4, 1831	2
64	(Missing)	January 31, 1830 September 18, 1836	14
65	Benevolence and Selfishness	February 7, 1830 November 5, 1837	7
66	Providence	February 14, 1830 March 18, 1832	2
67	The Power of the Soul	February 28, 1830 December 11, 1831	3
68	Improvement by Small Degrees	March 7, 1830 November 5, 1837	3
69	*The Ministry: A Year's Retrospect	April 4, 1830	1
70	*The Individual and the State	April 8, 1830 November 13, 1836	3
71	The Good Heart	April 11, 1830 February 12, 1837	3
72	The Childlike Character	April 25, 1830 December 25, 1836	3
73	Through a Glass Darkly	May 2, 1830 October 23, 1836	4
74	Death	May 9, 1830 January 15, 1832	3
75	*Religious Liberalism and Rigidity	May 16, 1830 June 30, 1831	3
76	*The Authority of Jesus	May 30, 1830 August 21, 1836	8
77	Christian Charity	June 6, 1830 July 3, 1831	2
78	Salvation, Now	June 13, 1830 March 26, 1837	10

A LIST OF THE SERMONS

No.	Title	First and Last Times Preached	No. of Times Preached
79	Doing Good	June 27, 1830 / November 8, 1835	5
80	Patriotism	July 4, 1830	1
81	The Fruits of Religion	July 4, 1830 / August 7, 1836	10
82	The Virtue of Humility	July 18, 1830 / January 8, 1837	3
83	Spiritual Improvement Unlimitable	July 25, 1830	1
84	Acquiring True Knowledge	August 1, 1830	1
85	God and Speculation	August 15, 1830 / August 20, 1837	8
86	Prayer, the First Christian Duty	August 29, 1830 / December 18, 1836	3
87	*Self-Culture	September 5, 1830 / January 13, 1839	9
88	The Oracle Within	September 12, 1830 / March 5, 1837	3
89	God's Wrath and Man's Sin	September 26, 1830 / December 4, 1836	6
90	*Trust Yourself	December 3, 1830 / November 12, 1837	4
91	Consolation In Trouble	October 10, 1830 / February 26, 1832	2
92	Reason and Revelation	October 24, 1830 / February 18, 1838	3
93	The Kingdom of Heaven Is Within	October 31, 1830 / September 4, 1836	10
94	The Fear of Death	November 21, 1830 / November 20, 1836	11
95	The Judgment of Christ	November 14, 1830 / March 26, 1837	14
96	Doing The Will of God	November 28, 1830 / February 14, 1836	4
97	Reasons for Thanksgiving	December 2, 1830 / December 1, 1836	2
98	Perfect Love Casteth Out Fear	December 5, 1830 / November 6, 1836	3
99	Temptation	December 12, 1830 / January 31, 1836	4
100	Why Christianity Advances	December 26, 1830 / November 6, 1836	3

A LIST OF THE SERMONS

No.	Title	First and Last Times Preached	No. of Times Preached
101	*How Old Art Thou?	December 31, 1830 January 13, 1839	3
102	Strength for the Burden	January 2, 1831 January 3, 1836	3
103	*Miracles	January 23, 1831 January 31, 1831	2
104	*Self and Others	January 12, 1831 July 24, 1836	6
105	The Imperfections of Good Men	January 23, 1831 August 14, 1836	3
106	Independence in Faith	January 30, 1831	1
107	*Consolation for the Mourner	February 20, 1831	
108	Grief	January 27, 1831 March 13, 1836	4
109	God in the Soul	March 6, 1831 August 14, 1836	5
110	The Holy Spirit	March 20, 1831 August 6, 1837	5
111	The Common Basis of Truth	March 27, 1831 November 26, 1837	8
112	Peace in Solitude	April 3, 1831 April 17, 1836	2
113	Fasting, Humiliation and Prayer	April 7, 1831 April 6, 1837	3
114	Trust in the Lord	April 24, 1831 June 5, 1836	3
115	The Marks of a Christian	May 1, 1831 February 5, 1837	4
116	Keeping the Sabbath, Parts I and II	May 15, 1831 October 22, 1837	4
117	Calamities	May 29, 1831 June 19, 1836	7
118	Spiritual Influence Reciprocal	June 19, 1831 November 1, 1835	15
119	The Love of Christ	June 26, 1831 October 12, 1837	3
120	Religious Books	July 3, 1831	1
121	Spiritual Discernment	July 17, 1831 April 3, 1836	16
122	We are Not Our Own	July 24, 1831 April 9, 1835	3
123	The Limits of Self-Reliance	July 31, 1831 July 30, 1837	2

A LIST OF THE SERMONS

No.	Title	First and Last Times Preached	No. of Times Preached
124	Freedom	August 14, 1831 / November 15, 1835	11
125	No Harm can Befall a Good Man	August 28, 1831 / November 27, 1836	2
126	A Future Life	September 11, 1831 / February 2, 1834	2
127	All Truth Is Related	September 18, 1831 / July 24, 1836	6
128	The Objects of Education	September 23, 1831 / October 31, 1831	2
129	Enduring Temptation	September 25, 1831	1
130	Love Thy Neighbor	October 2, 1831 / September 24, 1837	2
131	*Hymn-books	October 2, 1831	1
132	Obeying the Commandments	October 16, 1831	1
133	The Reality and Blessedness of Religion	October 30, 1831 / June 19, 1836	3
134	Words Are Things	November 6, 1831 / June 26, 1836	9
135	Right for Right's Sake	November 20, 1831 / February 18, 1838	2
136	The Occasion for Praise	December 1, 1831 / January 15, 1837	7
137	*The Choice of Theisms	December 4, 1831 / October 15, 1837	11
138	The Universal Empire	December 25, 1831 / December 27, 1835	3
139	The Record of Time	December 31, 1831 / January 3, 1836	2
140	'Friendship'	January 8, 1832 / January 29, 1832	2
141	The Sum of Religion: Do Thyself No Harm	January 15, 1832 / September 25, 1836	13
142	The Living Christ	January 29, 1832 / May 29, 1836	2
143	*Find Your Calling	February 5, 1832 / January 10, 1836	7
144	Self-Improvement	February 12, 1832 / June 5, 1836	14
145	Judging Right for Ourselves	February 26, 1832 / February 4, 1838	4
146	The Education of the Soul	March 4, 1832 / July 12, 1835	2

A LIST OF THE SERMONS

No.	Title	First and Last Times Preached	No. of Times Preached
147	The Christian Venture	March 18, 1832 December 18, 1836	3
148	'Sunday Schools'	March 25, 1832 December 20, 1835	3
149	The Virtues Near at Hand	April 1, 1832 May 17, 1835	14
150	'Fast Day'	April 5, 1832 April 7, 1836	4
151	The Pleasures Near at Hand	April 8, 1832 August 20, 1837	3
152	The God of the Living	April 22, 1832 July 23, 1837	8
⟩ 153	The Satisfaction of Religion	April 29, 1832 March 27, 1837	7
154	Duty	May 6, 1832 August 15, 1838	7
? 155	Thinking Well of Human Nature	May 13, 1832 February 4, 1838	8
156	Envy	May 20, 1832 March 19, 1837	4
157	*'Astronomy'	May 27, 1832 November 19, 1837	4
158	A Living Religion	June 10, 1832 February 25, 1838	2
159	Truth	June 17, 1832 November 19, 1837	4
160	The Increasing Knowledge of God	September 2, 1832 September 25, 1836	18
161	Work	September 2, 1832 February 19, 1837	8
162	The Lord's Supper	September 9, 1832	1
163	Indifference to Death	September 16, 1832 March 30, 1837	10
⟩ 164	*The Genuine Man	October 21, 1832 March 16, 1837	13
165	*Religion and Society	October 27, 1833 June 4, 1837	3
166	Dependence and Independence	March 30, 1834 March 6, 1836	6
167	(Missing)	May 25, 1834	1
168	Death	August 3, 1834	1
169	*The Miracle of Our Being	September 7, 1834 January 20, 1839	9

270

A LIST OF THE SERMONS

No.	Title	First and Last Times Preached	No. of Times Preached
170	Duty, Our Salvation	April 26, 1835	1
171	The True Priesthood	July 17, 1836 July 17, 1836	2

MISCELLANEOUS DISCOURSES

[66A] 'The Right Hand of Fellowship'	February 17, 1830
[108A] The Dedication of the Vestry	February 28, 1831
The Evidences of Christianity	Undated.

Index

No references are made to the titles of the sermons listed on pages 263 ff.

Addison, Joseph, 147
Almanack, 115, 174
America, xi, 107, 194
Analogies, 44
Aristotle, Aristotelianism, xl, 244
Art, 41
Augustine, 133, 204, 249, 257
Authority, xxi, xxvii, 57, 79, 89 ff., 94 f., 97, 136

Bacon, Francis, 62, 208, 249
Baptism, xvi, 31
Barbauld, Anna Letitia, 147
Beauty, 4, 10, 16, 39, 108, 121, 172, 210, 222
Beecher, Lyman, 232
Belknap, Jeremy, 148 f., 246
Benevolence, 123, 128 ff., 242
Bible, xvi, xxv, 25, 29, 44, 68, 70, 84 f., 101, 105, 111, 113 ff., 124, 144, 170, 178, 218 f., 223, 232, 237, 250, 252
Browne, Thomas, 159
Bushnell, Horace, xxix
Butler, Bishop Joseph, 95, 234, 249

Calvin, Calvinism, xii f., xxxviii, 87, 102, 133, 148, 221, 237, 241, 243, 246, 252 f., 257
Catholicism, Roman, 102, 133, 146, 177
Channing, W. E., v, xi f., xxi, xxviii ff., 231, 233, 256, 262
Character, 4 f., 9, 15, 81, 86, 94, 106 f., 141, 183 f., 201, 227, 231, 234, 251, 254, 259
Charity, xv, 130, 134, 229, 240 f.
Chesterfield, xx
Christianity (*see also* Religion), xix, xxv ff., xxx, xxxiv, 1, 23, 27 f., 55, 70, 88, 90 f., 105, 115, 133, 139, 149, 175, 194 ff., 201, 223 f., 230, 235, 238 f., 245, 256, 259
Christianity, liberal, v, xii, xv, xxiii, xxvii f., 82 ff., 149, 224, 230 ff., 234, 256

Christianity, orthodox, xii, xxviii, 82 ff., 87, 230 ff., 252, 256
Church, xxvi, xxx, xxxiii, 3, 20, 32, 58, 71, 86, 113, 201, 224, 227 f., 230, 237
Church, Second of Boston, vi, xiii f., xv f., xvii, xxxi, xxxiii, xxxvi f., xxxviii, xxxix, 191, 202, 218, 223 f., 240, 242, 246, 253, 256, 257, 261
Civilization, 46
Clarendon, 209
Coleridge, S. T., xii, xxix, 126, 249
Collins, Anthony, 156
Columbus, 49, 208
Compensation, 10, 106, 209, 235
Congregationalism, xii, 224
Conscience, xxv, 9, 11, 17, 20, 64, 67, 75, 188, 216, 254
Conversation, 16, 60 ff., 70, 91, 106, 108, 134, 225 f.
Covenants, 58
Cowper, 147
Creeds, 86, 230
Culture, xi

Death, 9, 12, 33 f., 103, 113, 127, 138, 216, 219 f., 235 f., 239, 259
Design, 44, 85, 203
Dewey, Orville, 255
Doddridge, Philip, 147
Duty, xxxviii, 7, 14, 36, 70, 75, 109, 147

Economy, Political (*see also* Politics), 54, 128, 242
Education, xvi, 82, 85, 99, 164, 189, 197, 207
Edwards, Jonathan, xxx, 241
Election, 117, 160
Eliot, S. A., vii
Eloquence, xix, 26, 146, 218
Emerson, Charles, 247
Emerson, Edward, 236

273

INDEX

Emerson, Ellen Tucker, xiv, 216, 226, 243, 261 f.
Emerson, Mary Moody, xiii, xxxvi, 216, 222, 240, 243, 247
Emerson, R. W., references to other writings of:
   'Compensation,' 235 f.
   Conduct of Life, 222, 249
   'Culture,' 222, 226
   'Divinity School Address,' xxviii, 253, 256
   'Friendship,' 252
   'Fugitive Slave Law,' 229
   Journals, The. See Introduction and Notes, *passim*
   Letters and Social Aims, 245
   'Life and Letters in New England,' 253
   'Lord's Supper, The,' xxxiv, 219, 223
   'May Day,' 257
   'Method of Nature, The,' 253
   Natural History of the Intellect, 251
   'Nature,' 252
   Nature, xxv, 220 f.
   'Over-Soul, The,' 226, 239
   'Politics,' 229
   'Preacher, The,' 220, 254
   'Progress of Culture,' 252
   'Right Hand of Fellowship' (*Uncollected Writings*), vi
   'Self-Reliance,' 236
   Society and Solitude, 222, 229
   'Sovereignty of Ethics,' 237
   'Spiritual Laws,' 251
   'Works and Days,' 222
Emerson, William (R. W. E.'s father), xii, 236, 246
Emerson, William (R. W. E.'s brother), xiii, xxxvii, xxxix
England, 77, 128 f., 209
Episcopalians, 146
Eternity, 8, 10, 17, 35, 239
Evil, 8, 76, 103, 106, 126, 140, 175, 221, 256, 258 f.

Faith, xiii, xxvii, 38, 73, 84, 157, 160, 175, 237, 250
Fast-Day, xxx, 216, 228 f.
Fénelon, xxxviii, 107, 133, 249
Finney, C. G., xxxiv

Fontenelle, Bernard, 252
Fox, George, xx, xxxviii, 134, 186, 249, 255
Franklin, 110, 208
Freedom, xxiii, xl, 4 f., 85, 87, 101, 164, 169, 215, 236, 244
Friends, 19, 58, 63, 98, 144, 154 ff., 192
Funerals, xvi

Geology, 112
Geulincx, 240
God, xiv, xxiii, xxv f., xxxv, 2 ff., 4, 21, 40, 44, 72, 83 ff., 92, 101 f., 114, 116, 120, 131 f., 136, 148, 151 ff., 155, 162, 170, 174 ff., 186, 188 f., 200, 203 f., 220 f., 225, 231, 237 f., 240, 243, 247 ff., 252 f.
   Benevolence, 31, 35, 43 f., 64 f., 94, 159; Grace, 27, 253; Holy Spirit, xx, xxiv, xxvi, xxvii, 136; Omnipotence, 87; Omnipresence, xxviii, xxxix, 211; Providence, 9, 23, 33, 41, 61, 68, 77, 121, 124, 129, 139, 174, 180, 197, 228; Trinity, 84, 148, 233
Goethe, xii, 245, 249
Gospel, Christian, xxvi, xxxv, 11, 161, 223, 234, 259
Government (*see* State)
Greenwood, F. W. P., xxxvii, 246 f.
Grotius, 208
Guilt, 84, 142

Half-Way Covenant, 224
Happiness, 4, 7, 30, 35, 85
Harmony, 6, 10
Harvard College, xi, 228, 261
Harvard Divinity School, xi, xiii, xv, 218
Hedge, F. H., 246
Hero, Heroism, 152, 197
History, 55, 112, 209
Hodgin, E. S., vi
Holmes, O. W., 218
Home, family, 2, 13 ff., 191, 216 ff.
Honor, 155 ff.
Hopkins, Samuel, 241
Horton, E. A., xxxvi
Hume, David, xx, xxviii, 240
Huntington, F. D., 246
Hymns, xxvii, xxxi, 145 ff., 246 f.

Idolatry, 152

INDEX

Immortality, 9, 85, 105, 138, 149, 163, 216, 219, 238, 243 ff., 251

James, 124
Jefferson, 208, 229
Jesus, xx, xxxv, xxxviii, 14, 29, 32, 56 f., 69, 90 ff., 100, 106, 114 f., 124, 140, 148, 156, 162, 169, 177 f., 189, 193 ff., 199, 208, 223, 233 ff., 244
Judaism, Judea, xxxv, 22, 55 f., 90, 132, 162, 193

La Grange, 176
Law, moral, moral sentiment, xxiv, 3, 10, 35, 93, 118, 122 f., 194, 252
Law, natural, 116, 209
Leighton, Archbishop, 133
Le Saurin, Jacques, 253
Liberty (*see* Freedom)
Lord's Supper, vi, xvi, xxxiv ff., 31 f., 54 ff., 73, 219 f., 223 f., 252, 255
Love, 5, 16 f., 19, 32, 50, 69, 88, 94, 115, 130 f., 136, 142, 149, 152 ff., 161, 191, 194, 212, 244, 250
Lowell, xxxiv
Luther, Martin, xxxviii, 52, 117, 177, 208, 249
Lyceum, xxxvi

Malebranche, 240
Man (*see* Human Nature, Soul)
Man, natural (*see also* Human nature), 113, 239
Man, Spiritual (*see also* Human Nature, Soul), 113, 239
Marriage, xvi, 31
Mather, Cotton, xiv
Mather, Increase, xiv
Mayhew, Jonathan, xxx
Methodists, 146
Milton, 236, 246, 249
Ministry, Christian, xv, xxi, xxxii f., 22 ff., 31 ff., 67 ff., 76, 217 ff., 226 f., 238, 243
Miracles, xxvii, 56, 95 f., 120 ff., 160, 203 ff., 234, 239 f.
Moral Sentiment (*see* Law, moral)
Motives, 1, 19, 26, 36, 59, 132, 162, 184 f., 242, 245
Music, 145 ff.
Mysticism, xxv f.

Napoleon, 111, 154, 249
Nature (the world), xxviii, 2, 33, 39 ff., 43, 107, 112, 116, 121, 170 f., 175, 207 ff., 216, 221 f., 240, 252
Nature, human (*see also* Man, Soul), xxvi, 2, 8, 35, 45, 64, 100, 105, 113 ff., 138, 152, 161, 166 ff., 174, 180 ff., 189, 196, 200, 203 ff., 221 f., 230 f., 235 ff., 243 f., 252 f., 257
New England, xxx f., xl, 38, 43, 223 f., 246
Newspapers, 78 f.
Newton, 51 f., 110, 117, 152, 173, 175, 208

Over-Soul, xxiv, 237

Paley, W., 220, 249
Parker, Theodore, v
Parkman, Francis, 34, 262
Party, Parties, 78, 82 ff., 86, 229, 231 ff.
Past, The, xxvii, xxxiv f., 8, 216
Patriotism, 81, 230
Paul, Saint, xxv, 23, 55, 101, 117, 124, 133, 156, 219
Peace, xxxviii
Penn, George, 134, 249
Perfection, 92, 104, 128, 139, 180, 236
Perry, Bliss, xx
Peter, Saint, xxv, 133
Plato, Platonism, xl, 242, 244
Plutarch, 248
Poetry, 42, 145 f., 221, 246, 249, 251
Politics, xxx, 76, 80, 201, 229
Prayer, xxi, xxxii, xxxiii f., 1 ff., 18, 24 f., 50, 215 ff., 229, 237
Preaching, xix f., xxi, xxxi, xxxix f., 24 f., 28, 68, 218, 221, 227 f., 230, 237
'Preaching Record,' vi, xxxvi f., 247 f., 257, 261 ff.
Priestley, xxxviii
Principles, 14, 48, 51, 88, 99, 105, 110, 135, 161, 184
Protestants, 146, 224
Proverbs, 61 ff., 172, 217, 225

Quakers, 134, 186, 255

Reason, xxv, 4, 29, 186, 206 f., 210, 215, 252
Reform, 52, 66, 81, 198
Regeneration, 114, 119

275

INDEX

Religion (*see also* Christianity), xiii, xxiv ff., xxxviii, 15 f., 28, 65, 69, 73, 75, 99, 105, 152, 156, 165, 188 f., 191 ff., 199, 220, 226 f., 251, 255 ff., 259
Resurrection, 52, 125, 140 f., 244
Retribution, 11, 101 f., 244
Revelation, xxvi, xxix, 11, 27, 85, 100, 189, 218, 220, 225, 245
Revere, Paul, xiii
Revivals of religion, xxx, 231 f.
Revolution, 194, 199
Ripley, Samuel, 215, 217
Robbins, Chandler, xxxi, 246, 257
Romantic movement, xii, 221
Rusk, R. L., vi

Sabbath, xxxii, 20, 54, 72, 227
Sacraments (*see also* Baptism, etc.), xxxviii, 31
Salvation, 24, 96, 111, 177 f., 239
Sampson, George, xxii, 248, 255
Schlegel, 248
Schleiermacher, xii
Science, xxviii, 41, 52, 173, 220 ff., 252 f.
Scougal, Henry, 133
Sectarianism, xxi, 230
Self-culture, xxxviii, 99 ff., 235 f.
Self-love, 48, 128, 231, 239
Self-reliance, 105 ff., 236 f., 253
Shakers, 146
Shakespeare, 152, 208, 249
Sin, xx, 1, 6 f., 9, 19, 58, 83 f., 87, 93, 161, 169, 211, 225, 231 f., 238, 243
Slavery, 5, 198, 229, 256
Society, social life, xxx, 5, 46, 54, 60, 63, 75 ff., 117, 127 ff., 164 ff., 191 ff., 227, 255 ff.
Socinus, 177
Socrates, 52, 107, 205, 208, 248
Soul (*see also* Human Nature, Man), xxv, 1, 27, 47, 50, 70, 96, 105, 109 f., 113 ff., 116 f., 130 f., 136, 143, 156 ff., 182, 196 ff., 236, 238, 244, 249
State, The, xxxi, 75 ff., 82, 230, 251
Steele, Anne, 147

Stoddard, Solomon, 223 f.
Stoics, Stoicism, 52, 133, 200
Style, literary, xi, xviii f., xxxi, xxxiii, 29, 91, 147, 218, 246
Sunday Schools, 196, 198, 240
Swedenborg, 186
Sweet, W. W., vi

Tacitus, 209, 217
Taylor, 'Father,' 256
Taylor, Jeremy, xxxviii
Teacher, teaching, xi, xxxix, 91 ff., 192, 196 f., 199, 202, 232 f., 256, 259
Tell, W., 152
Theology, xxiii, xxv f., xxxv, xxxviii, xxxix, 27, 56, 84, 148, 173 f., 199, 230 ff., 238, 251 f.
Time, xxvii, xxxiv, 4, 10, 67, 70, 117, 171, 238 f.
Truth, xix, xxv, xl, 4, 28, 64 f., 70, 72, 87, 91, 93 f., 102, 125, 193 ff., 201, 225 f., 228, 230, 233 f., 239, 243, 257

Unitarianism, xii, xiv, 86 f., 175, 216, 232 f., 241, 255 ff.

Virtue, 4, 6, 13 ff., 17, 80, 83, 87, 205, 217, 231, 243

Walker, James, xxi
War, xxxi, 112, 180, 229
Ware, Henry, Jr., xiii ff., xxi, xxxvi f., 218, 220, 238, 256
Washington, 110, 117, 152
Watts, Isaac, 147
Wesley, 237
Wilberforce, 256
Wordsworth, xii
World, natural (*see also* Nature, Human Nature), 1 f., 112 f., 116; spiritual, 10, 113 f., 116 f.
Worship, 72, 218, 228, 232, 237

Youth, xix, 30, 37, 44, 75, 172, 184, 192, 229, 239